THE DARK SIDE OF THE MARKETPLACE

THE
DARK SIDE
OF THE
MARKETPLACE

The Plight of the American Consumer

Senator Warren G. Magnuson
and Jean Carper

Prentice-Hall, Inc.
Englewood Cliffs, New Jersey

*This book is
dedicated to the
American consumer and to
the millions of ethical
and responsible
American businessmen.*

*The Dark Side of the Marketplace:
The Plight of the American Consumer*
by Senator Warren G. Magnuson and Jean Carper
© 1968 by Warren G. Magnuson and Jean Carper

Library of Congress Catalog Card Number: 68-20369

Printed in the United States of America • *T*

Prentice-Hall International, Inc., London
Prentice-Hall of Australia, Pty. Ltd., Sydney
Prentice-Hall of Canada, Ltd., Toronto
Prentice-Hall of India Private Ltd., New Delhi
Prentice-Hall of Japan, Inc., Tokyo

FOREWORD TO THE
CONSUMERS UNION EDITION

This book is about consumer deception and those who perpetrate it. It is about some laws that aid and abet the deceivers, and about the need for other laws to protect consumers. That is not an original theme. It has been the concern of Consumers Union for about 32 years, and of others during that time, and for centuries before.

About 2,500 years ago, a Scythian philosopher named Anacharsis came up with a sardonic judgment about the marketplace. "The market," he said, "is the place set apart where men may deceive each other." In the relatively simple marketplace of 600 b.c. Scythia, buyers and sellers were on a more or less equal footing; if deception were the order of the day, it could be practiced equally. But in today's complex marketplace, as the authors of this book show, deception is the seller's province. He knows the territory.

In a narrative rich with facts, figures and case histories, the authors delve into such selling frauds as phony special price, bait and switch, referral selling, the free gimmick and the fear-sell. They present in appalling detail the credit and debt collection traps of our time—irrevocable and deceptive contracts, garnishment, confession of judgment, holder in due course and repossession. They explore the uncontrolled sale of hazardous consumer products, medical and health quackery, and such outright corporate cynicism as the cigarette industry's refusal to recognize that it's peddling a hazardous product.

Anacharsis also had something to say about laws: "Written laws are like spiders' webs, and will like them only entangle and hold the poor and weak, while the rich and powerful will easily break through them." Not very much has changed here, as this book makes painfully clear. Citing chapter and verse, Senator Magnuson shows how inadequate laws *are* all too often spider webs for the poor—and not so poor—and he spells out his recommendations for "strong, decisive action" to be undertaken by Congress and by state and local governments.

This book is the work of its authors and not of Consumers Union. It should not be assumed that CU concurs with all their opinions, details, emphases and recommendations. But CU considers *The Dark Side of the Marketplace* an important book, very much in the consumer interest, and we are grateful to the publisher and to the authors for allowing us to make this special low-cost edition available to CONSUMER REPORTS readers.

THE EDITORS OF CONSUMER REPORTS

Mount Vernon, New York
March 1968

CONTENTS

CONTENTS

INTRODUCTION

When this book was begun, I had some realization of how poorly the American consumer is protected and how he is exploited by the unscrupulous and irresponsible few of the business community. But I, probably like most, had not fully felt the depth of the problem: its serious social consequences, its detrimental effect on ethical business, its viciousness among the poor, its threat to human life; in short, its true cancerous qualities in the fiber of American life.

It is my firm conviction that the consumer, too, would be shocked and surprised if he knew how inadequately protected he is, how lax we have been in guaranteeing fair play and justice between buyer and seller.

Our concepts of consumer protection, though rapidly changing, have not yet caught up with the twentieth century. Our laws, our government regulatory agencies, our self-regulation by business itself—in short, our total approach to consumer problems—have not been modernized to cope with the recent explosion in consumer buying and credit and the changing conditions in technology and marketing. Most regrettably, that ruthless medieval philosophy "caveat emptor" is in some instances still too much with us.

As we all know, the law is not a codified rock of ages, immutable and unchangeable. It is a living body of man's thinking, evolving to reflect society and to satisfy the needs of changing social patterns. Some critics of the new "consumer movement," which is taking full shape in the 1960's, object to government proposals for consumer protection because they fear it will destroy the laissez faire relationship between buyer and seller which in their minds has existed virtually unchallenged for centuries. Why, they ask, if we have never needed a consumer movement before, do we need one now, suddenly in the mid-twentieth century? Why, in the 1960's, is there this awakening of consumerism, not only in America but in European and other technically advanced countries, with the common theme, as a British lawyer put it: "The time has come for a breakthrough in the law as it affects the consumer"?

In actuality, the concern for consumer protection, both here and in Europe, is not really new. What we see today is the culmination of an ever-growing momentum of consumer concern, rooted in the Middle Ages, and brought to fruition by merchandising changes wrought by modern technology.

The doctrine caveat emptor originated in the Middle Ages and was predicated on the equality of bargaining positions between buyer and seller, which was quite realistic at that time. First, all goods were displayed (grain, vegetables, cloth) on the open market and could be examined thoroughly for defects. Secondly, a man bargained almost entirely with his neighbors, who cheated him only at the risk of severe social repercussions in the community. A buyer who actually had the poor sense to believe the sales pitch of a stranger was regarded as a fool by his friends.

Nevertheless, even in the Middle Ages, as trade expanded, the courts realized that caveat emptor was inadequate to protect consumers. If an Englishman bought a precious stone from Persia, how did he in fact know it was not misrepresented to him? Thus, even during this time of fierce individualism, judges decreed that a man had recourse in court if he could prove the seller had made a positive promise, a warranty, providing it was not a case where the buyer could clearly see the defect. In the fifteenth century, a judge ruled: "If a man sells me a horse and warrants it has two eyes, and it has not, I shall not have an action for I can know this for myself from the beginning."

In today's complex technology and mass marketing structure, we can hardly make such judgments on the quality of the merchandise or the fairness of the bargain. We deal mostly with strangers. Our entire economic system of distribution has evolved from one of distrust to one of trust, and the basis of consumer protection, as it was in the Middle Ages and should be now, is to protect the buyer in societal circumstances which make him helpless, or put him on an unequal footing with the seller.

As the Middle Ages gave way to the rise of cities, the Florentine banking families, the Industrial Revolution and mass production, consumers became increasingly farther removed from the source of their goods, and ever more at the "mercy of strangers." We have seen pronounced changes in this direction since World War II. The corner grocery store, with free shopping advice from the grocer, has been supplanted by the supermarket with its rows of impersonal foodstuffs, where the package itself must do the selling. The upsurge in production and the explosion of credit within the last twenty years have intertwined to foster unprecedented consumption of automobiles, television sets, washing machines, foodstuffs, clothing, by all economic classes.

We are at a pinnacle of consumer prosperity. And it has been said by economists that the measure of a country and its leaders is not so much how they handle their problems in a crisis, as how they handle problems in time of prosperity. In my opinion, if the historians of the future chose today as judgment day, we would be found somewhat deficient. For although consumer legislation has paralleled changing conditions throughout our country's history, the acceleration in recent years of consumer buying, with its corresponding problems, has left the legal structure to deal with it far behind. Surely many of our laws are still sound, but many others are antiquated, unable to meet the requirements clearly dictated by present-day needs.

As early as the late nineteenth century, the consumer movement began to crystallize, as demonstrated by concerted federal legislation. In 1872 we made it a federal crime to defraud through the use of the mails. The Interstate Commerce Commission which regulates interstate carriers—buses, trucks, railroads, barges—was created in 1887. At the same time came an intensive campaign to clean up our food. Beginning in 1879, more than one hundred bills were introduced in Congress to regulate food and drugs, before the public and Congress were jarred to action by the chilling exposé of unsanitary conditions in Chicago's stockyards by Upton Sinclair's *The Jungle,* published in 1906. That year, Congress passed the first Federal Food and Drugs Act, followed by the Agricultural Meat Inspection Act in 1907. Since that time we have seen the emergence of the major regulatory agencies: the Federal Power Commission, the Federal Communications Commission, the Civil Aeronautics Board, the Securities and Exchange Commission, and the Federal Trade Commission, which is directly charged with preventing deception in the interstate marketplace.

Since I first came to Congress in 1936, I have seen the national concern over consumer protection greatly accelerate. In 1938, we extended the jurisdiction of the Federal Trade Commission to empower it specifically to prevent consumer deception. That same year we passed the Food, Drug and Cosmetic Act. After a period of dormancy during World War II, consumer protection efforts were renewed. In 1953, we passed the Flammable Fabrics Act, outlawing explosively flammable fabrics used in wearing apparel. Soon afterward came legislation requiring that refrigerator doors be designed to be opened from the inside, preventing children's entrapment. With the Kefauver-Harris Drug Amendments, we had in 1962 significant reforms in the labeling of prescription drugs and the testing of new drugs. About that same time Senator Paul Douglas introduced the first consumer credit reform law, calling for "truth in lending," a disclosure of finance rates in percentages. That this bill did not pass the

Senate until 1967—and then unanimously—dramatically shows the rapidly changing mood of Congress and the American people in favor of a sound legislative basis for consumer protection.

The sixties have rightly been called the Decade of the Consumer; not since the 1930's have we seen such movement for an end to social injustices. As President Lyndon B. Johnson, who has been a powerful supporter of progressive consumer legislation, said in his 1967 consumer message to Congress in which he called for a number of consumer protection measures: "The Government must work to make the consumer choice fully effective. The consumer must be protected against unsafe products, against misleading information, and against the deceitful practices of a few businessmen that can undermine the confidence in the vast majority of diligent and reputable firms."

Although the Senate Commerce Committee, of which I serve as chairman, has traditionally been concerned with only such matters as the preservation of a balanced and efficient transportation system, the channeling of the media of communications for the public good and the monitoring of the soundness of our international trade policies, we have recently expanded our scope of interest to include consumer problems. During 1965, we reported out the Cigarette Labeling Act; held hearings on tire safety and marketing, and packaging and labeling practices; and initiated investigations into natural gas pipeline safety, frauds on the poor and fraudulent mail-order advertising.

In 1966, the Committee reported and Congress passed two landmark bills setting minimum safety standards for tires and automobiles. The Fair Packaging and Labeling Act and the Child Protection Act were reported and passed that same year. In 1967, the committee sent to the Senate and the Senate passed a bold, workable natural gas pipeline safety act. We are now studying measures to curtail fraudulent door-to-door salesmen, strengthen the cigarette labeling law, effect reforms in automobile insurance and set minimum safe standards for the emission of radiation from electrical appliances, diagnostic equipment and other devices.

This book, however, does not chronicle what has been done, or is being done, nor does it restrict itself to problems in which the Senate Commerce Committee has been directly concerned. It rather explores what still must be done and can be done in this enlightened age of consumer protection. It represents what I believe to be our most pressing consumer problems for the future—problems which have not before been surveyed comprehensively in a serious light, or received wide public attention.

It will not be surprising to my friends and colleagues to note that the book is decisively split into two areas: protection of the consumer's economic welfare and protection of his health and safety. The economic issues of consumer protection, which have concerned me during the last few years, are so outrageous and explosive that they can be ignored only with serious threat to the fiber of society; they must be forcefully brought to public attention. The preservation of life through an ever-growing awareness of the hazards and their correction by law has been my most single-minded pursuit during my career in Congress. To have omitted either of these concerns would have done an injustice to the purpose of this book.

There are many people who have contributed substantially to the making of this book with their ideas, information and critical reading of the manuscript. I would like to acknowledge especially the following, without whom this book could probably not have been written. Commissioner Mary Gardiner Jones and Commissioner Philip Elman of the Federal Trade Commission; Gale P. Gotschall, assistant general counsel of the FTC; Charles A. Sweeny, and his staff, of the FTC's Bureau of Deceptive Practices; Mrs. Esther Peterson, assistant secretary for Labor Standards, U. S. Department of Labor; David Swankin, director of the Bureau of Labor Standards, U. S. Department of Labor; Miss Betty Furness, special assistant to the President for consumer affairs and her staff; Barnett Levy, director of the New York Bureau of Consumer Frauds and Protection; Philip J. Rock, director of the Illinois Division of Consumer Fraud; Donald Navoni, chief of the Consumer Protection and Anti-Trust Division of the attorney general's office in the state of Washington; Thomas Lynch, attorney general of California; the staff of the Ohio Consumer Frauds and Crime Section, attorney general's office; the Neighborhood Legal Services offices throughout the country; the Consumers' Education and Protective Association of Philadelphia; Dr. David Caplovitz, associate professor of sociology at Columbia University; Congresswoman Leonor Sullivan and her Consumer Affairs Subcommittee of the House Banking and Currency Committee; Thomas C. Roberts, vice-president, Association of Better Business Bureaus International; the Better Business Bureaus throughout the country; Senator Harrison Williams, Jr., and his subcommittee on Consumer Interests of the Elderly of the Senate's Special Committee on Aging; William S. White, legislative assistant, Bureau of Disease Prevention and Environmental Control, U. S. Public Health Service; the staff of the Bureau of Medicine, Food and Drug Administration; Irene Bartlett, program associate (New or Unproven Methods) of the American Cancer Society; Jerry Walsh, special educational consultant to the Arthritis and Rheumatism Foundation; Henry B. Montague, chief postal inspector, Post Office Department; Charles Miller, director of Fraud and Mailability Division, Post Office Department; Morris Kaplan, technical director, Consumers Union; the staff of the Senate Commerce Committee; and my wife, Jermaine.

Obviously, these people are not responsible for the ideas, conclusions and recommendations put forth in this book, and in some cases may not even agree. However, I am certain that we all share the common conviction that in this mid-twentieth century it is no longer a question of *whether* the consumer will be protected, but rather a question of *how*.

PART ONE

CHAPTER ONE

CAVEAT EMPTOR

One evening two men in a Cadillac paid a call on an elderly couple in a small town in Arkansas. One of the men, a Mr. G., president of the Superior Improvement Company in Little Rock, presented himself to the couple as an important executive affiliated with Alcoa Aluminum Company. He told the couple that after a careful examination of their house he had chosen it to be a model home as part of a new advertising campaign to sell aluminum siding. Photographs, he said, would be taken of the house "before" and "after" the siding was applied and would be featured in beautiful brochures. Salesmen would bring prospective customers to view the house, and for every sale made as a result, Mr. G. promised to give the couple a commission of $100. When urged to sign an agreement, the couple protested that their house was old and they were thinking of using their savings to rebuild. But the promises of Mr. G. were irresistible. He asserted he was giving them the siding at $1,000 below cost, cheaper than they could get it anywhere, and that with the commissions their house would be transformed into a showplace of beauty for virtually nothing. "Well, then, he said one thing that kind of struck me," the homeowner later recalled. "He said to say a little prayer and pray to the Lord and let Him guide us as to whether to sign the contract." Touched by this display of humility, the man and woman signed a contract for $1,480 and gave Mr. G. a down-payment check for $200.

By the next morning, the couple was no longer so spellbound by Mr. G.'s promises. Skeptical, they checked around and discovered they could buy aluminum siding for much less than Mr. G.'s "bargain factory prices." The homeowner, realizing he had been fleeced, tried to stop payment on the check, but was told that one of Mr. G.'s representatives had been there that morning as the bank opened and cashed the check. Repeated attempts to reach Mr. G. by phone at his Little Rock office were futile. He was always "out," and, said the homeowner, "His secretary kind of laughed like it was a big joke." Finally, in desperation and worry over his wife's ill health, which had been aggravated by the transaction, the man borrowed money from a bank and paid off the bill in full. He was informed by a lawyer that if he refused to make payments, the finance company Mr. G. had sold the contract to could sue him—and collect. The workmen had already tacked up the siding, such as it was. And the contract he had signed was legally binding, regardless of the verbal misrepresentations.

Hundreds of persons in rural Arkansas, Tennessee and Kentucky, since 1960, have been seduced by Mr. G.'s prayers and phony promises into paying exorbitant prices for shoddy workmanship and poor quality materials. Mr. G. claimed his aluminum was manufactured by Alcoa, Kaiser or Reynolds Aluminum Co.; it was in truth an off-brand, most of it shipped from Illinois. He told customers that it would "never chip, crack, fade or soak up water, would never need paint and had a lifetime guarantee." To many a homeowner's dismay, the siding was not applied by "factory-trained personnel" as promised, but sometimes by local teenagers. It fell off; the caulking was not done properly; the upper layer of finish could be rubbed off with the sweep of a hand. Some homes were left unfinished, aluminum and trash piled high in the yard. One man's house was such a shambles within a year, pockmarked by the fallen siding, that he needed a completely new siding job. The only thing he had bought from Mr. G. was a $2,400 debt.

Mr. G. and his salesmen preyed shamelessly on the illiterate, the poor, the old and the guileless. One man said Mr. G.'s salesmen kept him up most of the night begging him to sign a note; weary and fatigued, he finally did. An elderly Negro was coerced into putting his X mark on a contract. Many were induced to part with their pensions and social security checks. Others said they were tricked into signing mortgages on their homes, and one couple swore their names were forged to a promissory note. In this brutal marketplace, there was no compunction about tacking aluminum siding on a shack in the fork of a dust-covered road and proclaiming it a "showplace."

Many people understood that because of the $100 bonus, they would have to pay little or nothing for the siding. Instead, once their names were on the contract, few homeowners ever saw Mr. G. or any of his salesmen again. No one brought prospective customers to view the renovated house as the salesmen had promised. Some people waited and waited, actually stayed home for days on end, fearing to leave the house, waiting for the customers that never came, until their hope turned to anguish.

Many were left with disastrous debts. A young schoolteacher signed a contract with a total price of $3,650. By the time monthly payments were figured out—84 of them at $73.45 each—he discovered he had agreed to pay $6,132 over a period of seven years. Horrified, he borrowed money from his credit union and managed to persuade the finance company to let him pay off the debt; the company insisted, however, that he pay them more than $1,000 interest for use of the money for "less than a month."

Another couple signed a contract with Mr. G. for what they thought was about $2,000 and a mortgage on their house. Said a government lawyer: "When they sat down that night and in their sober judgment figured out what that was going to cost them over a period of 84 months—84 payments—they were not going to pay $2,000; it would be some $4,000 to $4,400. That fellow attempted to commit suicide." Another pensioned purchaser came home and found his elderly wife unconscious on the bed. She recovered but confessed she had been so worried over the transaction with Mr. G. and the prospect of losing their home that she drank Lysol.

Early in 1964, the Federal Trade Commission issued a complaint against Mr. G. and his company, charging him with a dozen "unfair and deceptive practices." After hearings, he was ordered by the FTC to stop using such sales practices in interstate commerce. Mr. G. chose to take his case through the courts, and finally in early 1967, when the Supreme Court refused to hear his case, he was forced to comply with the FTC ruling. (It is interesting to note that the primary basis for Mr. G.'s defense was not innocence of deceptive selling, for he admitted that he had promised bonuses to prospective buyers. His main contention was that he was not engaging in interstate commerce and that, therefore, the FTC had no jurisdiction over his actions. The FTC can intervene only when it can be proved that a misdoer is operating across state lines.)

It might appear that Mr. G. will be forced by the FTC to stop using his lucrative, deceptive sales pitches (his annual volume of business was estimated at $400,000). On the contrary, Mr. G. shows every intention of carrying on. He has mapped out for the FTC his blueprint for future business: he will not advertise in interstate newspapers or other media, will not use the mails to send out brochures and will not make sales to residents in other states. In other words, he pledges not to work his deceptive arts on anyone, except, of course, the unlucky prospects he may find within the borders of Arkansas.

At this writing, Mr. G. is still in business, his Superior Improvement Company still in existence. If complaints received by the Better Business Bureau of Little Rock are accurate, his salesmen are still active in Arkansas, using misrepresentations and "questionable advertising and selling practices" to unload shoddy jobs and merchandise at unconscionable prices. Who is to stop him?

Although the Federal Trade Commission may be reluctant

to admit it for fear of seeming to condone deceptive practices, the sorry truth in this matter is that as long as Mr. G.'s corporation scrupulously avoids interstate commerce, it can operate with impunity, free from FTC jurisdiction or intervention, no matter how blatantly dishonest the sales practices or how appalling to human sensibilities the amount of human misery left in their wake.

It is certain that the authorities of Arkansas, when informed of this company's intention to hide behind state lines out of the reach of the FTC will *want* to take measures to protect the residents of Arkansas. But the question is: will they be able to? Do they have the authority under existing state law? Although it is impossible to predict the outcome of any legal action—and some states have achieved surprising victories with the imaginative use of seemingly inapplicable laws—legal authorities advise me that Arkansas probably does not have the legal machinery necessary to fight companies like Mr. G.'s. Arkansas does not have a comprehensive law covering deceptive selling. It has only a variety of laws forbidding the use of certain deceptive practices to sell specific products, but aluminum siding is not among them. It is true that Arkansas, like other states, has criminal fraud and false pretenses statutes, resulting in fines or imprisonment for those adjudged guilty. But these statutes are a poor vehicle for preventing deceptive selling. Indictments under the statutes are exceedingly rare and convictions even rarer. As far as we know, neither federal, nor state, nor any other known authority can under present law take action to protect the citizens of Arkansas against the gouging of companies like Mr. G.'s.

Although the case of Mr. G. is one of the most dramatic on record of how deceptive sellers can operate outside the reach of the law, it would be a mistake to believe that Arkansas is like the old Oklahoma Strip of the 1880's: the only place where robbers could operate without interference from the law. On the contrary, although Arkansas is uncommonly hampered by weak consumer protection laws, it is hardly unique. Consumer deception flourishes nearly everywhere in the country, quite often unimpeded—and sometimes even abetted—by the law. As Helen Nelson, former consumer counsel for the governor of California, has said: "More money is being taken from Americans at penpoint than by gunpoint and the pen often makes it legal."

Deceptive selling by the unscrupulous few in the business underworld is, in fact, our most serious form of theft. It cheats Americans of several billion dollars yearly, more than is lost through robbery, burglary, larceny, auto theft, embezzlement and forgery combined. Unlike the con men of yesterday who were often so heavy-handed that they offended the law, today's modern bandits of the marketplace are the masters of the light touch. With their insidious misrepresentations, silver-tongued lies, half-truths and exaggerated promises, these men can reach even deeper into our pockets without producing a rustle to disturb the law, or often the victim himself. From coast to coast we are exposed to their Pandora's box of selling tricks—some old, but handily adapted to modern circumstances, and some new, carefully devised to outwit the law.

Although these schemes are staggering in scope and diverse in their nature (the Better Business Bureau has identified eight hundred different varieties), they invariably have several things in common: they are lucrative, they are subtle and their purveyors rarely come in conflict with the law. According to a nationwide survey for the President's Commission on Law Enforcement and Administration of Justice in 1966, nine out of every ten victims of consumer fraud do not even bother to report it to the police. Fifty percent of the victimized felt they had no right or duty to complain; forty percent believed the authorities could not be effective or would not want to be bothered; ten percent were confused about where to report.

It is startling to consider that the vast majority of Americans victimized by consumer fraud feel that the law can or will do nothing to help them; but it is even more startling to realize that in many instances those victims are absolutely correct. Our legal remedies against consumer deception and fraud, some of which were adequate fifty, even twenty, years ago, are now so outdated as to leave the consumer nearly helpless. Under our present laws, with rare exceptions, we neither give relief to the victimized consumer nor effectively halt the swindlers.

The scheme so successfully used by Mr. G. is but one of five major schemes on which today's pyramid of deceptive selling rests. Although Mr. G. combined several techniques, his primary deception consisted of convincing homeowners that by making their home a "model," he was giving them "a special low price." (The phony "special price" is also used to sell a variety of items, including encyclopedias, automobiles, carpeting, roofing and jewelry.) According to the Federal Trade Commission, the four other schemes that are currently most responsible for fleecing American consumers are *bait and switch advertising*, including "lo-balling," *chain-referral selling*, the *free gimmick* and the *fear-sell*.

Of these, the most troublesome to detect and curtail is bait and switch advertising, in which the merchant advertises goods *which he has no intention of selling* in order to switch the prospective buyer to another item, invariably higher priced and with a greater margin of profit. Not only is bait advertising perfectly legal in most states, but it is so subtle that most victims are never aware that they have been deceived. We all see bait advertising continually, but probably few of us are aware of its insidious calculated nature.

Typically, this is the way the scheme works. A housewife in Alexandria, Virginia, recently noticed this advertisement in the classified section of a newspaper:

> SEW MACH.—1965 Singer
> Touch and Sew ***
> Reposs. Balance. $86.40
> New Mach. Guar. Dealer,
> Credit Dept. ***

When the salesman arrived at her home, following her telephone call to the company, she was appalled by the machine he carried. He set it down on the table and said: "Well, this is the machine." It was not the new one described in the ad. Rather, as the woman put it, it was "an old beaten-up Singer about 25 or 30 years old. . . . I'd seen machines in better shape at rummage sales." It was battered, scratched, and was a straight-stitch machine with no attachment. "I wouldn't have given more than $5 or $6 for it," she said. Noting her disappointment and admitting his "mistake," the salesman saved the day. He rushed to his car and brought in two sparkling, new, off-brand sewing machines priced at $289 and $365. The housewife chose the one for $289 and was given a discount because it was the "salesman's first day."

There were several glaring misrepresentations, designed to lure prospective customers, in this advertisement. The words "Reposs." (ostensibly standing for repossession) and "Balance" led the readers to believe the machines had been partially paid for by a previous purchaser and thus were being offered for a song. The signature "Credit Dept." created the same impression. In truth, the use of the Singer name was only a lure to support a full-time business of selling off-brand machines. This was proved by the fact that the dealer sold only two or three Singers a month, but spent $400 per month advertising them. Almost the total volume of his business was in the less well-known brand, the more expensive model to which customers were "switched."

Sometimes the salesman actually produced the advertised recent-model Singer, but then actively disparaged the "bait" by finding fault with it: "This machine is delicate and not functioning as it should." "We get a lot of complaints on these Singers." In most other instances, as in the case of the Alexandria housewife, the bait was so offensive that it had "built-in dissuaders," and prospects rejected it on sight. The way was then cleared for the salesman's pitch on the more profitable merchandise. In describing the subtlety of the approach, an FTC lawyer noted: "The prospective purchaser is led on without suspecting the insincerity of the salesman's presentation, and the switch is made to the higher-priced machine of a different make as though the transition were the suggestion of the prospect and not the salesman."

This unfair and deceptive advertising of a product without intent to sell goes on incessantly, with all kinds of merchandise: vacuum cleaners, television sets, carpeting, automobiles, radios, washing machines, furniture. Nor is it confined to door-to-door selling. For some stores, "bait and switch" advertising is the mainstay of their business. An appliance store advertises, for example, a 17-inch-screen TV for $99, but woe to the salesman who actually sells it. Said one store manager, referring to an advertised GE portable, "Any guy who lets that set go out the door goes with it." This merchandise is, in sales lingo, "nailed to the floor," and it is the salesman's job to knock it, to disparage it in any way and to switch the customer to a more expensive model.

In an exclusive series of articles for *Home Furnishings Daily,* an anonymous salesman confessed that his store in New York City periodically featured phony special items in the newspaper, "to pull the shoppers in." He described the sale items: "First special in the ad is a 21-inch console television for $66. This always is a floor sample of ancient vintage and requires an aerial antenna of greater power than we have in the store to bring in a picture. Second special in the ad is a 10-cubic-foot refrigerator for $199. It is a make produced by a manufacturer swallowed up several mergers back. The color of the box might be described as an off-white with a slight tendency toward yellow. The guarantee on the unit is for six months. Third bargain special is a famous-make 9-pound washer for $99. We have a beautiful wringer-type washer to show those attracted by this item, but strangely enough most of those attracted somehow assumed we were referring to a fully automatic washer in the ad. Completing our quartet is a 36-inch range for $65. There is really nothing striking about this stove unless it be the fact that it is two-tone in color with the sides being black. It has no oven heat control and a speck of rust has begun to appear in the chips in the enamel on top. After a customer has viewed any of the above mentioned specials, it is quite natural that he will ask to see something a bit better. With the step-up, comes my chance to make a sale at a good price."

A variation of bait advertising is lo-balling, and it is so new that the FTC used the term for the first time in 1967 in a case involving automobile transmissions. In lo-balling, the company advertises or promises a service at an outrageously low price and actually performs the work at the advertised price, but only as an enticement to get possession of the automobile (lo-balling to date has been almost exclusively associated with automobiles) so the company can gouge the owner for additional unneeded repairs.

The lucrative routine goes this way, as illustrated by the experience of a man in Washington, D. C. He responded to an advertisement promising to reseal his car's transmission for labor charges of $22 plus an extra charge for needed parts. He was promised one-day service. When he left the car, it was functioning properly except for an oil leakage, which was to be corrected by resealing the transmission.

"About 4:15 the same day, I went back and they had a transmission lying on a work bench, and they said: 'This is your transmission and here are some parts of metal that were found in it and the pump is completely shot and needs replacing.' So I talked to the manager and said, 'What will that cost?' He said, 'Well, it would cost about another $42,' which raised the cost of the job to about $76.

"So I told him to go ahead with it, take the things that were torn down if they needed a new pump, to put it in. He said it would be ready the next afternoon.

"Well, I called the next morning to find out if the car would be ready and he examined it further and said: 'All the bushings are shot and need replacing.' I said, 'What is that going to cost?' He said, 'Well, the total job is now $107.'"

Through this technique, lo-ballers have been known to run the price on transmission repairs up to $400 and $500.

Some of the three hundred franchises of the Aamco Transmission Company, which sponsors television commercials starring actress Zsa Zsa Gabor and does a 25-million-dollar business in forty states, have been accused of lo-balling.

In Columbia, South Carolina, for example, three officers and employees of the local Aamco franchise were charged with conspiring to obtain money under false pretenses after a carefully marked 1959 automobile was left with them by state investigators for repairs. The transmission had previously been rebuilt, the parts marked by a competent mechanic, and was in good working order. Only the governor was defective. Aamco employees, however, tore down the transmission, declared it "burned up" and rebuilt it at a charge of $189.17. Subsequent examination of the transmission by a mechanic hired by the state revealed that some of the "new" parts listed on the bill were in fact the old parts which had been marked. Only two of the old marked parts reportedly had been replaced: the defective governor and a front seal valued at $2.25.

The attorney general of Minnesota, in October 1967, obtained an injunction prohibiting Aamco dealers in the state from continuing to use lo-balling and other misleading practices which deceive customers.

There are fads in frauds, as in other areas of life. One of the most vicious and fastest-growing is chain-referral selling. Less than ten years ago, it was of minor concern, but as United States postal officials observe, it has "snowballed overnight." It now constitutes a major problem, so much so that the U. S. Postal Inspection Service has established a special project to help combat it and has initiated 234 investigations, resulting in 34 convictions as of June 1967.

The gist of the swindle is that customers are led to believe that by referring the names of acquaintances as prospective customers, they will have to pay nothing for a piece of merchandise, and very often will make money. For each friend who is sold, or who agrees to participate in the "advertising campaign," as it is invariably called, the victim is promised a commission. Salesmen frequently erase customers' doubts by telling them that 80 percent of those referred actually "participate" as proved by past experience. In truth, postal inspectors, by painstakingly searching through company records, have discovered that only about 5 percent of the referred actually sign up. And of course once they have sold the original customer, some companies don't bother to follow up the leads supplied, or to remit the commission if a referred friend does buy. This deceit is all the more cruel for it is being practiced on elderly people who find the lure of making a few pennies to augment their meager income irresistible.

One could produce hundreds of cases of companies perpetrating this fraud, but an especially reprehensible example was recently seen in Oklahoma City. Of this firm's activities, an investigating postal inspector, usually unemotionally objective in his reports, was moved to remark: "The viciousness of referral selling has probably never been more dramatically portrayed." He went on to write in a final report: "The operators through their well-schooled, high-pressure salesmen imported from faraway points, induced more than 1,000 financially distressed persons in Oklahoma to sign purchase contracts and promissory notes for the purchase of major household appliances, including food freezers, refrigerators, kitchen cooking ranges, stereos, television receivers and washing machines. Each item was sold at the grossly inflated price of $660.96 on a three-year payment contract, despite the fact that identical items could at that time have been bought in numerous retail stores in Oklahoma for less than $300 each, and some for less than $250."

Particularly saddening was the experience of one man who had recently lost his left hand in an accident and could no longer work at the trade he had practiced for years. "He was burdened by medical bills, and had just taken a job at Goodwill Industries for $1 an hour," wrote the inspector, "when he received a neatly printed note in facsimile script signed by an acquaintance. It said:

Hi,

In a few days, at our request,
a friend of ours will call you for
an appointment to explain the details
of a *fabulous profit sharing program.*
You will be paid $500 for the few minutes
you devote to looking into this plan.
Since you are not obligated, hear this
out and make your own decision.

Sincerely,

"After receiving the note, he got a telephone call from the company setting up an appointment for the 'friend' to call on him and his wife. With a printed chart, the salesman showed how he could make as much as $900 in three months' time, by referring names of his acquaintances to the company and signing little introductory notes the company would obligingly mail to persons whose names he furnished.

"The victim explained his dire financial circumstances, that he couldn't afford to pay for anything. The salesman assured him it was an 'advertising program' and was a means to pay all his medical bills. He was then shown the company's 'Advertising Commission Warranty.' The victim said he had no need for the appliances 'advertised' by the company, but the salesman said he had to sign up for one appliance in order to enter the program. The salesman was so convincing that the man believed the program would relieve his financial distress and he signed the papers to enter the program. The next day a stereophonic record player was delivered to his home and about a week later he received notice from a finance company that they had purchased his installment contract and that his monthly payments should be made promptly each month to them for the next three years."

This poor man sent twenty-six names to the company, but never received a single dollar in return. He is now burdened with an unwanted stereo and finance payments that put him more deeply and hopelessly in debt.

The company, operated by four persons, three from one family, cost the public an estimated $500,000 loss although it operated less than one year. Toward the end of the company's short life, its two sales offices in Oklahoma City and Tulsa were stuffed with thousands of unopened referral forms mailed in by numerous victims.

An interesting postscript to the case is that the officers of the company were arrested for mail fraud, but only the sales manager was found guilty. The other three, including the president and the vice-president, were declared innocent in a retrial in April 1967. This points up how difficult it is to get a criminal conviction for consumer fraud and thus how inappropriate our traditional criminal remedies are in stopping consumer deception. For it must be proved under the criminal fraud statutes that the scheme not only deceived consumers but that the seller also consciously and deliberately set out to deceive. No matter how distasteful the scheme nor how many hundreds of consumers were cheated, if the jury doubts that the perpetrators sincerely *intended* to defraud, then they must find the defendants not guilty. The defendants in this case claimed that, although they may have been misguided, they actually believed that the scheme would work and carried it out in all good faith.

In granting a new trial on appeal (the verdict was guilty in the first trial), the appellate judge outlined the criteria by which the jury must come to a verdict by quoting a previous decision from the 10th circuit:

"It matters not how visionary you may find the enterprise to be, or how unreasonable the prospects of success . . . if the defendants actually believed in them. Promises made in good faith, whether they be glittering or attractive or not, are not criminal. If you believe . . . that the representations made by the defendants . . . although glittering, attractive, persuasive and alluring, were made in good faith and not as a part of a deliberate plan to scheme or defraud or to obtain money by false pretenses, then it is your duty to find the defendants not guilty. . . ."

Being convicted of a criminal act is surely a grave matter, and I certainly would not suggest that we change the criteria for determining such convictions. No man should be branded a criminal and fined or imprisoned who has not been proved guilty of bad faith or intent to commit a wrongdoing. But the real question in protecting consumers is not whether a person who carried on such a scheme *intended* to defraud and therefore is a criminal. The pertinent question is: should the law allow a vast number of the public to be seduced into misery—have their money stolen and their lives demeaned— by the actions of *any* soul—guided or misguided, bad-intentioned or good-intentioned? Whether such a person *intended* to deceive is quite irrelevant, if in fact he *did* deceive and is allowed to continue to deceive. In some instances of consumer fraud, criminal prosecutions are warranted. But by depending excessively on laws that punish the seller rather than stop the practice, we have yet to catch up with the realities of consumer protection.

Another pernicious type of selling which is sweeping the country is the "free gimmick," invariably accompanied by innumerable misrepresentations. It is doubtful that any American of any economic class is untouched by this scheme. A lawyer in New York whose wife was tricked into subscribing to three children's magazines under the impression that it was a "service" from the Board of Education recently wrote: "If wives of persons who are supposedly above average in education, sophistication, etc., and especially the wife of an attorney, can be so easily taken in, you can imagine what this person (a door-to-door saleswoman) must be able to do with less sophisticated persons."

The sales pitches are familiar: "This lovely *x*-cubic-foot freezer is yours absolutely free if you subscribe to our food-freezer plan." The food is usually low quality, overpriced, and the freezer is hardly free. The cost of the food more than covers the retail price of the freezer.

"Congratulations! You have just won second prize in our drawing for a vacuum cleaner, which entitles you to $150 off

the purchase price." It turns out that after the $150 is sub-
tracted from the phony $289 "regular" price, the cost is $139
which is still overpriced. The same giveaway principle is
widely used in peddling sewing machines: "You have *won* a
free sewing machine; the only charge to you is the price of
the cabinet." The $59 "cabinet price," in truth, covers the
cost of the machine and gives the seller his usual profit.

The variety is endless: "Your telephone number has been
chosen for this free gift. . . ." "We want to give you five
dancing lessons absolutely free if you can answer this question: Adam and Eve had two sons. One was Cain and the
other was ——?" (One perverse man answered Aaron, but
after the telephone solicitor recovered, she allowed that his
answer was close enough—they both started with A.)

Unfortunately, another area in which the giveaway is becoming increasingly prevalent is in "educational materials,"
encyclopedias, magazines and other books. In 1966, magazine subscription rose to the top of the Better Business
Bureau's complaints list. That year the BBB processed 162,537
"instances of services" concerning magazines.

A magazine salesman of fifteen years' experience, who
finally quit the business, came to my office last spring, anx-
ious to make known the deplorable tactics being used in some
magazine selling. He told how the sympathy "college kid
gag" had given way to the something-for-nothing pitch. "Pretending you're a college kid trying to win points for a scholar-
ship is still used in some places," he said, "but the biggest
thing these days is the free-postage pitch. We tell people
they get the magazine free if they will only pay the 42 cents
a week postage. And they really believe it! I know some
salesmen making $20,000 a year this way. Using this pitch
myself I have sold $99 worth of magazines to people who are
blind, who don't have shoes for their kids or a stitch of carpet
on the floor. It's a rotten business, and I'm sorry I stayed in
it as long as I did."

Certainly not all magazines are sold this way, and it is
unfortunate that a handful of offenders are marring the repu-

tation of the ethical dealers and publishers. The same can be said for encyclopedias, although it can also be said that many famous-name encyclopedias from supposedly reputable companies are sold by deceptive salesmanship. Consistently, the FTC has warned and brought complaints against companies that misrepresent their sets of encyclopedias as being free, an advertising promotion gift, if the customer will only pay to keep it up to date. In July 1967, my staff and I asked William Hesse, a graduate student at the University of Washington, and one of the Congressional interns in my office, to discover whether a newly established encyclopedia sales office in Washington, D. C. was engaging in deceptive selling by pretending to give away free sets. Hesse answered an ad promising $550 per month guaranteed salary for doing "advertising and promotion," and was put into training. The sales pitch turned out to be laden with falsifications. Hesse was repeatedly warned never to admit he was a salesman, but to say he was "with the Promotional Division of E. E. (Educational Enterprises, Inc.) and only seeking "testimonial advertising" for the "first Major International Reference Library," whose first major sales campaign was to get under way in 1968.

Door opener (to wife only): "Hi there, I have to see your *husband*" (say it like you know him).

Door opener (to husband only): "Hi there, I have to see you for a minute!" (say it like you made a special trip just to see him; give him your name and shake his hand).

"The reason we call in the evening like this is because we have to talk to the man of the house and the wife together. OK? (*Smile*) "I'm not a salesman so please don't be alarmed. I've been asked to interview some of the families in this area. . . . You know what testimonial advertising is, don't you? Well . . . Educational Enterprises has finally gone into Testimonial Advertising. The families that we are interviewing right now, families like yourselves, that are helping us out, we are paying them very handsomely for their help, not in cash but in the form of merchandise."

After showing them a sample of the "beautiful library," he gets to the heart of the lie, as outlined in the long, memorized speech: "That's right, you would receive this beautiful $489 masterpiece, all twenty volumes within the next two weeks, postage prepaid, as an advertising premium in exchange for your promise to write us a testimonial letter and signing the Owner's Register Card which gives us permission to use your name as a registered owner of the National Encyclopedia." Later in the canned pitch comes the catch: "Gee, I almost forgot. There is one thing I have to make crystal clear to you. We give you the Cadillac so to speak, but we have to draw the line somewhere. We don't give you the Gas and Oil. In other words, you get this complete library within two weeks, but we don't keep it up-to-date for you, too."

The salesman makes it clear they wouldn't want to place a set in the home of an "insincere" person who wouldn't "appreciate" it. There are only two things expected to show appreciation, he explains.

". . . the yearbook service that comes out each year, that adds onto your set, that keeps it up-to-date. Well, we don't give these to you or anyone. You can understand this I'm sure." Farther on, "See these coupons here?

"We have at present over 2,000 experts in every field working in our Library Research Department in New York City. Anytime something new comes up and you want to know more about it right now, all you would have to do is clip out one of these research coupons and send in a letter with the coupon to our Research Department in New York."

It turns out that the "yearbooks" are priced at $15 each for ten years. The "research coupons" cost $5 apiece, and the customer must buy ten coupons each year for ten years. All of this adds up to $650, but somehow because of "mass production," the company has been able to cut the cost to $335.50 —just nine cents a day. The salesman gives the customer a calendar bank in which to deposit his daily dime, and attempts to persuade him to pay it all off in two years instead of ten.

The pitch is peppered throughout with insincerities and lies. On the contract there is no mention of a "free" encyclopedia. The salesman is instructed to write "20 volume encyclopedia" and the price. All of the other is verbal misrepresentation, which is difficult to prove in court. Such words are not binding, but the customer's signature on the contract is.

Aside from harm to the customer, it seems to me reprehensible that grown men are hiring young boys and teaching them to lie with such cynicism and contemptuousness. For many of these young men it is their first introduction to the world of business. The better-educated boys who already have a career planned may come away with a bad taste for business in general. (There were fifteen boys in Hesse's class and how many stayed with it, we don't know. Hesse left after three days and reported several boys had already confessed to him that they didn't "have the stomach for it.")

Other boys may find their lies so successful they make such selling a way of life. The reformed magazine salesman who came to my office said his career started when he took a temporary selling job, pretending he was working his way through college. He intended to stay only three months, but found it so lucrative, he stayed fifteen years. He admitted his conscience bothered him in the beginning, but "I got so wound up in making that sale, I got so I didn't notice it."

Perhaps no sales pitch has been around longer than the "fear-sell." Even the rulers of ancient countries were intimidated into buying amulets lest their souls be damned or they suffer a dreadful accident. In today's sophisticated marketplace, peddlers still make fortunes preying on people's fears. One woman wrote me she had four perfectly healthy maple trees felled by a wandering "tree surgeon," who told her they were rotten and could come crashing down on her house. Gangs of salesmen, according to the National Fire Protection Association, are scouring the country, displaying gruesome photographs of families burned to death in home fires. Their object is to sell home fire-alarm systems which are invariably outrageously priced and sometimes worthless.

Every spring, as regularly as the rain, reports the BBB, the phony chimney repairmen show up. They knock off a few bricks and claim the chimney is about to topple, or claim it is clogged and that the whole family is in imminent danger of dying from carbon monoxide poisoning. Some termite inspectors carry bugs which they plant in the wood, and then inform the alarmed homeowner that unless the "termites" are exterminated, the house will quickly deteriorate. Often the salesmen pose as government inspectors. That they extort millions of dollars from frightened Americans is well-documented.

A classic case is that of the Holland Furnace Company, which for thirty years conducted what Consumers Union branded "one of the most pernicious sales rackets in the country." Holland Furnace, based in Holland, Michigan, with 500 offices throughout the country and 5,000 employees, was the leading furnace-replacement firm in the nation. Through its "tear down and scare tactics" it victimized hundreds of thousands of Americans. Misrepresenting themselves as "furnace engineers" and "safety inspectors," the salesmen frequently dismantled a furnace, condemned it as hazardous and refused to reassemble it, stating they didn't want to be "accessories to murder." The salesmen were merciless. In New England, branch salesmen from one office sold an elderly infirm woman nine new furnaces in six years, for a total take of $18,000.

One woman in San Francisco became suspicious after a Holland Furnace salesman condemned her furnace. She called the Better Business Bureau, which dispatched both an inspector from the local Pacific Gas and Electric Company and a Better Business Bureau representative with a tape recorder. The gas inspector pronounced the furnace perfectly safe and in good repair. When the salesman returned to clinch the sale, he unknowingly delivered his pitch both to the woman and into a hidden tape recorder. It went this way:

". . . the flue pipe instead of taking all of the smoke and fumes up the flue, a good percentage of them are going up in the house. . . . See where she's burnt out over there . . . that's going right up into your house. . . . The warm air plenum is above here, which means that the smoke and fumes go up in here, and then that fan turns on back there. . . . I'm not saying this to scare you, I'm just saying it to impress you. . . . This is worse than the raw gas, because the raw gas you can smell. This is carbon monoxide. . . . This is no different than if you took the exhaust pipe from your automobile and ran it in here. . . . I would actually be doing you a favor . . . by shutting your furnace off. . . . I'm not doing that to sell you a furnace, I'm just trying to be honest with you. . . . It's not healthy. I would replace it and I would do it now. . . . It's leaking. . . . We can allow you $28.50 as junk for that old furnace."

The amazing thing about this fraud, besides the boldness of the company and the size of its loot, is its longevity, which once again painfully illustrates the inefficacy of our present laws to bring deceptive practices to a quick halt. Although victims began complaining about Holland Furnace in the 1930's and the FTC soon after began collecting proof, which is now voluminous, it was not until January 1965 that the company finally was forced to close its doors. The ex-president of the company was sentenced to six months in prison (the first time an official of a major corporation has been held criminally responsible for the misrepresentations of its salesmen), and the corporation was fined $100,000 for violation of a court injunction issued in 1959. The fine reportedly was sufficient to cause bankruptcy. In the meantime, Holland Furnace at the height of its business cost the American public 30 million dollars a year.

If one were writing a textbook on deceptive selling, these five schemes—phony special price, bait and switch, referral selling, the free gimmick and the fear-sell—could be described as the basics of the course. For with a little ingenuity they can be, and are being, applied to the shady salesmanship of any product imaginable, from pots and pans to real estate. The five schemes are used alone or in endless combination with one another and with dozens of other misrepresentations, such as "I'm from the school board to test your child's musical talent"; "Of course you can cancel the contract if you change your mind"; "I'm a veteran just back from Vietnam"; "Our carpeting is cheaper because it is sold in 'factory units'" (a factory unit turns out to be one-third of a yard). "If you don't want the free magazines yourself, we are authorized to donate them for you to the local school; they say they *need* these magazines." "I see that your vacuum sweeper (sewing machine, automobile, washing machine) is completely shot." "You're only signing a receipt," when, in fact, it is a sales contract or promissory note.

In addition to these five basic schemes there are several hundred others. Among the most prevalent, pernicious and costly are:

Charity swindles for nonexistent churches, hospitals, veterans' organizations and so on. This scheme accounts for a 100 million dollar a year loss to the public.

Business opportunity rackets. A person seeking extra income is induced to buy an expensive vending machine with the promise that he can install the machine in a local place of business and collect the proceeds; or a piece of equipment such as a floor polisher with the promise that floor-polishing jobs will be referred to him by the seller. Victims invariably discover that no place of business will take the vending machine and that no jobs are forthcoming.

Unsolicited merchandise through the mail. A package containing vitamin capsules, stamps for albums, ties, books, arrives, and unless the receiver returns it or pays for it, he is bombarded with dunning letters, the last one threatening a law suit. Some swindlers scan the obituary columns of newspapers and address merchandise to the deceased. His survivors, thinking he ordered the goods, pay for it.

Phony home improvements. These swindlers are often fly-by-nights who insist on cash immediately, and for good reason. Their lightning rod "cables" turn out to be silver-painted rope; they resurface driveways by covering them with motor oil; they neglect to mention that when they "paint" a house, they don't use waterproof paint, and with the first rain the paint washes off. For more than thirty years one Irish family known as the "Terrible Williamsons" has worked the country performing phony home-repair jobs. It is said that the clan on the road now numbers at least one hundred.

Substandard correspondence and vocational schools. Undoubtedly this is one of the most disheartening rackets of all, for it preys on the aspirations of the elderly and undereducated who are falsely led to believe they can raise their station in life by subscribing to one of these costly substandard courses. The courses purport to teach such occupational skills as motel management, insurance claim adjusting, data processing, telegraphy, how to pass a civil service examination and how to operate a bulldozer (without ever seeing one). After spending hundreds, sometimes thousands, of dollars on this shabby education, the "graduate" finds that when he goes out to seek a job, he is totally unqualified and no one will hire him.

Land-fraud sales. Thousands of persons, many seeking retirement homes or investments, have bought lots, sight unseen, on the basis of glowing brochures or color slides that bore no resemblance to the actual land site. Some of the "developments" were never developed at all and turned out to be in the swamps, in the desert, on the tops of mountains, under water and even in the jungles and lava beds of South America.

In late 1966, a company called the Western Growth Capital Corporation, promoting Cohise Country Club Estates in Arizona, came into my state of Washington and persuaded 174 persons, after an elaborate free dinner party and a slide presentation, to invest $350,000 in lots in this development. Contrary to assertions of the "public relations director" who emceed the event, the lots had no gas, electricity, telephone service or paved roads. The only paved road in the development was a county road leading to the company's sales office. The "PGA-approved nine-hole golf course" was so overgrown, said one investigator, "you would lose your ball on the green." The "well-equipped pro shop with the year-round pro" was an empty shack that was boarded up. The "beautiful blue lake" was an enormous dried-up hole of forty acres. After obtaining signatures on sales and promissory notes, the sales crew promptly moved on to Minnesota and then to Pennsylvania.

The corporation quickly sold the contracts to a bank in Arizona. Just recently, the company was declared bankrupt. Thus, the cheated consumer is totally helpless. The bank in Arizona has already sent stern collection letters to the victims in Washington, demanding its money. And the Washington attorney general's office admits, "We are without any recourse even to stop the bank from enforcing the contracts." These people, a few of whom invested their life savings or sold their homes planning to move to the "promised land," must month by month pay for a practically uninhabitable plot of land that they will probably never see.

Why are we unable to control such deceptive practices and to prevent consumer exploitation? Primarily because our present laws are outmoded and inadequate to deal with the modern complexities of consumer fraud. Most of our laws on dishonest selling were designed long ago to catch and punish a few "hardened criminals" and not to cope with the vast web of subtle deceits and credit merchandising abuses that characterizes the businesses of today's "soft-sell" swindlers. Generally, our legal remedies have two defects: (1) they are ineffective in halting deceptive selling, and (2) they make virtually no provisions for redressing the wrong, whether by freeing the cheated consumer of a fraudulently induced debt or by reimbursing him.

The Federal Trade Commission, as the federal agency primarily responsible for stopping deceptive selling on a national scale, has broad powers and has been effective in curtailing unscrupulous sellers in interstate commerce for half a century. Nevertheless, we cannot depend on the FTC alone to halt all deceptive selling nationwide. Even with an addition in personnel it would still be impossible for the FTC to stop all deceptive selling even within its interstate jurisdiction. And the FTC also has certain limitations in its powers to protect consumers.

As we have seen, the FTC cannot stop deceptive selling operations that limit their activities to intrastate commerce, staying within a state's borders, which is where most such selling occurs. Nor can the FTC in some cases move fast enough to halt the swindlers before they have victimized a number of consumers and accumulated a small fortune. Nor can the FTC act on behalf of an individual consumer; it can move only when a substantial number of Americans have been injured (enough to make an FTC action "in the public interest").

Then too, the FTC can only compel the offender to stop working his deceptive arts on future customers; it cannot order him to reimburse those whom he has already cheated or to cancel collection of their debts.

The Post Office Department, as the other federal agency most responsible for halting fraudulent and deceptive schemes, also has been remarkably successful within their jurisdiction. But postal officials, too, are hampered in their efforts to control certain types of deceptive selling by mail. Under present law, they often cannot move fast enough to curtail mail-order schemes and sometimes cannot stop them at all. In testifying to this fact before a subcommittee of the House Committee on Post Office and Civil Service in April 1967, Henry B. Montague, chief postal inspector for the Post Office Department, illustrated the difficulty in halting mail-order land-fraud sales:

"The investigation of the Lake Mead Land & Water Company in Arizona began in 1962. Evidence that the desert property was not in fact 'an enchanted city in the making'; that the 'favorite swimming hole' pictured in the advertising brochure was in truth a cattle-watering pond not even located on the promoter's property; that various springs and wells depicted in the literature were also not located on the property, was not too difficult to ascertain. Proof of intent or personal knowledge on the part of the principal promoter, of course, required considerably more time.

"An indictment was returned in October 1963 and conviction resulted in June 1965. Three thousand home- or investment-seeking persons, many of the elderly class, lost an estimated one million dollars before the enterprise was finally stopped through conviction. The promoter continued to receive payments by mail up to the very end."

Even though a scheme is patently false and postal officials know it, they cannot always stop a perpetrator's inflow of mail containing the lucrative rewards of deceit. Postal authorities must stand helpless, witnessing the bilking of the elderly and the hopeful, until it can be proved that the purveyor of falsity *intended* to defraud, which, as Mr. Montague pointed out, takes much longer than just proving untruth by comparing the brochures or advertisements with the lay of the land. Partially as a result of this time lag while investigators try to fathom the state of a man's mind, the forty-nine land-fraud swindlers finally brought to justice were able to accumulate, through a steady flow of mail payments, more than 50 million dollars from an unsuspecting public before they were convicted and their mail was marked "fraudulent; return to sender."

At the state level, officials who attempt to protect consumers are incredibly handicapped by inadequate laws. Although many states have recently passed effective laws and set up machinery to enforce them, the picture of state consumer legislation is, as a whole, dreary indeed. An informal survey by the FTC in June 1967 showed that only nineteen states could be said to have "good" or "excellent" laws prohibiting deceptive selling practices. At least one-third of the states have pitifully weak laws. Effective consumer legislation is especially lacking in Alabama, Arkansas, Indiana,

Mississippi, New Hampshire, North Carolina, Ohio, Oklahoma, South Carolina, South Dakota, Tennessee, Texas, Virginia, West Virginia and Wyoming.

In a few states legislation is simply nonexistent. Only a handful of states regulate correspondence schools, fraudulent selling of land or unsolicited merchandise sent through the mails. Only twenty states specifically outlaw bait advertising.

Absence of laws, however, is not the only problem in the states. For as the *Columbia Law Review* has noted, "The states have adopted a staggering number of statutes noteworthy for their ad hoc and piecemeal approach to the problems of advertising control and for the very slight degree to which they are enforced." In truth, all but three states—Arkansas, Delaware and New Mexico—have a "Printer's Ink" statute (named for the advertising magazine of the same name) making it a misdemeanor to make an "untrue, deceptive or misleading" statement with the intent to sell a product.

One would think this law so comprehensive that it would virtually wipe out deceptive advertising in the states. Such is not the case, for the law, broad as it is, contains an insurmountable flaw: it is a *criminal* statute, as are many of the other measures adopted by the states to halt deceptive selling. Under the criminal statute, conviction demands proof beyond a reasonable doubt, and carries with it fines, possible jail sentences and the stigma of being branded a criminal.

Since its adoption in 1911, the Printer's Ink statute may have deterred some sellers from deceptive practices, but the number of culprits it has actually brought to justice is infinitesimal. Law enforcement officials overwhelmingly consider the law so unrealistic that they don't attempt to enforce it. A survey by the *Columbia Law Review* in 1956 discovered that during nearly fifty years, only "a handful of prosecutions" had been brought under the Printer's Ink statutes throughout the country. Many attorneys general and county prosecutors freely admitted that they had never tried to enforce it. One reason is that local prosecutors are burdened with trying to halt major felonies such as murder, rape and robbery, and are disinclined to waste their time on such a relatively small "crime" as false advertising or selling. Another reason is that few prosecutors believe they will get a conviction. They have found that juries are hesitant to find a man guilty of a crime for what may merely be "overzealous salesmanship"; consequently, few public officials prosecute.

Two law students at the University of Pennsylvania, investigating the ineffectiveness of consumer legislation, recently found: "Even when a law enforcement official believes that a particular scheme has been made actionable by statute, he often does not prosecute because of a widely held belief that, except in the most egregious circumstances, fraudulent operators should not be treated like criminals. Lawyers, business leaders and prosecutors have stated that 'judges, juries and district attorneys do not like to put businessmen in jail.' One district attorney, when asked by the attorney general to prosecute an alleged fraudulent operator, retorted: 'I can't even get a conviction when they stick a gun in somebody's back; how can I get one when they just talk him out of his money?'"

Trying to completely control consumer fraud by proving criminality is an outmoded concept. But even if the criminal statutes could be enforced (and New York, for example, has achieved rare success in obtaining convictions), it is doubtful that society's purpose is best served by only putting a swindler behind bars. The sentence is usually short (in Pennsylvania one man who made $300,000 selling fake automobile parts was sentenced to a term of one year), after which the wrongdoer is set free to spend his ill-gotten money, and the cheated consumer, who understandably wants no justice so much as his money back, is left to suffer without restitution.

Additionally, the hit-and-miss proposition of locking up criminals who defraud the public is inefficient in halting consumer fraud on a broad scale. Only one operator can be put out of business at a time, after long, costly court proceedings, while thousands of other gypsters—perhaps associated with the same company or swindle—are allowed to flourish. And even after a short prison term, the ex-convict can start up a new racket, using the same fraudulent techniques, and rob Americans of a fortune, while local authorities once again gear up their machinery to start the slow, painful process of gathering evidence against him on the new charge.

The injured consumer can bring suit himself, but few do. They soon discover that lawyer's fees, court costs and time away from employment will cost more than they can possibly recover. A woman in Ohio, who hired an attorney to keep from losing her $15,000-house because of a home-improvement repairs bill of $7,200, had already paid a legal fee of $1,500 and still did not receive her house back. Under strict legal requirements in most states, the complainant must have an exceptionally good case in order to win; many times it is only his word against that of the shady seller.

Invariably, the victim has also unknowingly, by signing the contract, given away a number of rights of defense and agreed that nothing the seller told him, unless specifically stated in the contract, is binding. When a group of lawyers in Pennsylvania were asked in an informal survey what they would do with a client who had been gypped out of several hundred dollars for carpeting in a "bait and switch" scheme, they unanimously agreed: "Send him home."

Clearly, the weak, inappropriate, poorly enforced, hit-and-miss legislation that is the rule throughout the nation is quite undependable in combating the complexities and size of our present-day consumer deception. In this antiquated system of justice, the dishonest steal quietly off to count their loot, while the injured consumer is sacrificed on the altar of legislative short-sightedness.

CHAPTER TWO

SHAME IN THE GHETTOS

When the law lags behind the needs of society, we can expect some ugly consequences. And in the area of consumer protection, the evils of allowing legalized thievery to flourish are nowhere more strikingly evident than among the poor, especially the minority groups in the ghettos. The exploitation of these people by unscrupulous local merchants and fly-by-night operators is one of the silent shames of our country.

From coast to coast, mainly in our urban areas, those who can least afford to pay are paying unconscionable prices for junk, pawned off on them through trickery, deceit and fraud. By signing contracts containing the most inhumane clauses, these poor people legally bind themselves into misery. And when they cannot pay or refuse to pay, they find themselves pushed even further into destitution by a legal system which is incomprehensible to them and which has become perverted from a device for protecting the innocent to a means of abetting the dishonest. Although this is a strong indictment, it is not exaggerated. It is no more than what anyone who has worked in the ghettos or studied these problems will confirm.

In broad perspective, many of the abuses inflicted on the poor, especially in regard to installment contracts, are used to exploit the middle class as well as the poor. But it is in the poverty-stricken areas, where the people are least able to get "good" credit and are the most vulnerable to the persuasions of the prevaricators, that the ugliest manifestations are found.

The plight of the poverty-stricken consumer is all the more poignant when it is realized that his pursuit of goods and credit, which in turn makes him so vulnerable to callous exploitation, is in reality what has been called "compensatory consumption," a desire to infuse his existence with dignity denied him elsewhere by accumulating material goods. An excellent description of the poor's situation is given by FTC Commissioner Mary Gardiner Jones:

"Our poverty-stricken citizens . . . are either on welfare, or hold down the most menial jobs which bring them a pitifully inadequate income and certainly no dignity or sense of pride in themselves or in the job which they are doing. They spend almost 60 percent of their incomes on food and rent alone. They are always in debt, live only on the threshold of a bare subsistence in dismal slums haunted by insecurity and fear and dominated by the constant threat of slipping even further down in the economic and social hierarchy. . . . Yet they are constantly surrounded and reminded of all the material benefits of our great society which are enjoyed by everyone else. . . . Like us they are the recipients of the daily advertising messages of the necessities of life which we should buy, of the constant urgings to buy now and pay later, of the glowing promises of no money down or low weekly payments. The social pressure on them to consume is almost irresistible, not simply because of their actual physical needs for many of these possessions, but also because of their deep psychological needs for self-respect, for dignity, for a feeling of belonging and for approval from their neighbors. . . . The only sense of status which is in any way available to them is through possession of the material accoutrements of our economy . . . an automobile, a sewing machine, a television set or a combination console, radio-phonograph. . . ."

Thus, to satisfy deep human needs, the poor are driven into what David Caplovitz, a sociology professor at Columbia University and author of *The Poor Pay More*, a classic study of the problems of the poor in New York City, has described as a "commercial jungle in which exploitation and fraud are the norm rather than the exception."

It has been well-documented by Professor Caplovitz and others that the poor, who can least afford to have their earning power diminished by high prices, pay dearly for merchandise available much cheaper to the middle class. The poor are at the mercy of high-priced neighborhood stores and door-to-door salesmen. Professor Caplovitz found that in New York City those with family incomes of under $3,500 consistently paid more for appliances than those earning over $3,500. For example, 46 percent of the lower income group paid more than $300 for a table model television; only 37 percent of the higher income group paid such a high price. Similarly, 49 percent of those with the under $3,500 income paid more than $230 for a washing machine; only 35 percent of those earning over $3,500 paid a comparable price.

A comparative shopping study, made by the Mobilization for Youth in New York City, showed that an Admiral 19-inch-screen portable television set cost from $179 to $200 cash on the Lower East Side. An identical set was sold in a major downtown discount house for $139. Three women shoppers in the same survey also demonstrated how costly the color of your skin can be. They each priced the same television set in a Lower East Side store. The quoted price to a young, white law student was $125, to a Puerto Rican housewife, $139 and to a Negro housewife, $200—a racial price differential of 60 percent! Shopping surveys in Boston, Philadelphia, Chicago and San Francisco reveal the same pattern: the poor are paying exorbitant prices, usually 75 to 100 percent more for goods from stores in low-income areas as compared with those in "ethical" stores patronized by the middle class.

With pathetic regularity, the merchandise bought by the poor is shoddy, and they are deceived into buying it. Professor Caplovitz reports the frustration of a middle-aged Negro mother on welfare, who unknowingly responded to a bait ad promising the reupholstery of a couch for $49.95.

"I phoned them and they sent out a salesman. I asked him to show me the material. He pulled out some patterns and looked at them and said, 'These aren't so hot. I really want to give customers something they'll be satisfied with.' Then he flipped to the higher-priced patterns—but I didn't know they were higher priced then. I picked out a pattern and asked him how much. He told me $149. But I only had $49 in cash and wanted to pay only in cash, so I told him that this was too high. He praised the material so much, talking about its quality and durability, that I finally told him that if I could get an account I'd take it. He gave me a contract. I just took a quick look and signed it. They sent for the couch and returned it two weeks later. The work on the seams of the pillows was awful. . . . Six months later, the wire in the springs popped out the side."

Countless poor people are deceived into buying second-hand merchandise, believing it to be new. An elderly lady in Washington, D. C., rather wistfully tells how she was tricked into buying a 19-inch used television for $355 by signing a "receipt." In response to a radio-spot commercial that ironically began: "Empire Furniture and Appliance Company has sold thousands of television sets to people just like you because Empire gives you a TV deal that's unbeatable," the woman called and asked for the company's "free home demonstration—no obligation."

"When the TV was delivered," she said, "I told the driver the set was dirty, but he said it was only dust and can be wiped off. I paid him $25 and he gave me a receipt. . . . He rushed out very fast and I do not have good light in my room. So it was not before daytime next day that I noticed I got an old set and not a new set as ordered. . . . I never knowingly signed a contract and never received a copy of a contract. I only meant to have signed on the clipboard of the delivery man that I received the set. . . . I am not so good in reading and writing and I do not understand words and meanings which are in a sales contract. I would never have signed a contract of any kind without my son or daughter present to read it for me." Yet this poor elderly woman had without her knowledge signed a contract, agreeing to pay $13.75 in twenty-four monthly payments for the old set.

An appliance store in Maryland, according to reports, consistently sells repossessed television sets for as high as $450, after paying only $25 to $50 for them. A prospective customer, enticed by advertising, such as "No-down-payment, have TV in your home *tonight!*" enters the store and is disappointed to find only rows of beat-up old sets. The salesman assures him, however, that the advertised new sets haven't come in yet, but that by signing a contract "ordering" a new set, he can take one of the old sets home to use in the meantime. What the customer actually signs is a conditional sales contract, purchasing the old repossessed set at an exorbitant price. The new sets, of course, never arrive. The contract is sold to a finance company, and according to law, the purchaser must make his payments.

In June 1965, after hearing of some of these shoddy practices, I proposed to the Federal Trade Commission that they establish a special unit to investigate and take action against deceptive schemes being perpetrated on the poor in the District of Columbia. During two years of intensive work, including the opening of a consumer bureau to receive letters and telephone complaints, the FTC antipoverty unit investigated 80 cases and uncovered a variety of abuses. As Charles Sweeny, chief of the FTC's Bureau of Deceptive Practices, reported to me in June 1967: "We are convinced that the types of practices uncovered in D. C. are being used on the poor in every major city in the country."

Washington, D. C., like other major cities, has a "mercantile row" which caters to low-income groups. Here in this area—Seventh Street in the Dictrict of Columbia—one merchant does a thriving business in watches, rings, radios, television sets, eyeglasses and small appliances by selling the prestige of having credit. Salesmen are dispatched onto the sidewalk to detain passersby and entice them into the store by offering them a free gift and a "credit card." One elderly man told how he was approached by a sales clerk who said: "Would you like to come in and get this gift?" He was handed two cards. One read: "FREE GIFT for YOU! No obligation. Don't buy a thing. Don't spend a Minute. Just present this card and Get your FREE GIFT." The other read: "Certifies that Bearer is an AAA–1 Preferred Customer. Instant Credit. No Money Down. Make your own Terms. This card certifies that you have a preferred credit rating and attests to your character excellence."

"Well, you don't know what kind of gift it is until you go inside for curiosity," said the man. So he did and was disappointed to discover he was given only a ball-point pen. But bewildered by the attention and flattered by the offer of credit (he had never been given credit at any store), he did not want to pass it up. He was talked into "opening an account" by signing a conditional sales contract for a watch. His confusion over the purchase (he was "kind of scared because I never had an account before I got this account") is typical of the lack of sophistication of such low-income consumers.

Question by an FTC attorney: Could you tell us, do you remember, Mr. White, when you signed this document?

Answer: Well, I signed it right after I got the account with them, after I realized they wanted me to open an account.

Q: Did they tell you what this document was, Mr. White?

A: You mean before I signed this?

Q: Before you signed it or after you signed it. Were you aware of what you were signing?

A: Well, I knew a little about how to open an account. As far as signing this contract, they told me to sign a contract and I signed. . . .

Q: (Holding the contract): Can you tell me what this is?

A: This is the contract here.

Q: What is the contract for? Do you know what it is for?

A: It is for when you open an account. You have to buy it.

For the privilege of having credit, Mr. White, a Negro earning $60 a week in a government cafeteria, paid $86 for a

cheap watch worth one-tenth that much and paid it off at
$2.50 a week. This store attaches price tags to its merchan-
dise, but what customers don't know is that this amount
hardly represents the item's true value; 90 percent of the
price is markup. The store sells transistor radios for $59.50
which the store buys wholesale at $3.45 each. Toasters are
marked up from $5.49 to $49.50, and sets of aluminum cook-
ware from $6.47 to $69.50—in all cases at least a 1,000 percent markup for the "easy credit."

Another shoddy practice of this Seventh Street merchant,
according to several reports, is to offer free eye examinations, obviously designed to sell extravagantly priced glasses
even to those who don't need them. The store sends out a
mailing, inviting people in for a "free eye examination, no
obligation." A sign in the store also announces: "Have Your
EYES Examined Free; Doctor in the House." Several people
have sworn that after the examination, although they insisted
they didn't want the glasses, the lenses were quickly inserted
into frames and handed to them before they could leave the
store. When they refused to buy them, they were intimidated
into signing sales contracts for the glasses with "You *have*
to buy them; we made them especially to fit *you;* we can't
sell them to anyone else." When one woman so treated complained to a clerk that her vision through one of the lenses was
blurry, the clerk replied: "You'll get used to it." Although a
pair of glasses was advertised at a discount of "from $7.50
complete," glasses often sold for $59.50 and $79.50, more
than twice what other optometrists in Washington charge.

A Negro mother of five children said she was lured into the
store by a direct mailing piece. "My eyes weren't bothering
me," she said, "but I wanted to be on the safe side. . . . I
was given a rain scarf as my free gift, and was introduced to
a man in a white coat who was called Doctor. . . . This man
examined my eyes and told me I needed glasses. He said that
sunlight would cause me to have eye strain and that I needed
sunglasses. Additionally he said I needed glasses for reading.
I had both pairs of glasses made up for me and I signed a

contract to pay for them at $59.50 per pair plus carrying charges of $21.42." The prevailing retail price for such glasses was $32; her glasses were practically zero prescription (Rx .25 cyl, the weakest prescription possible next to plain glass), and an optometrist who retested her vision confirmed that although wearing the glasses would not be harmful, it was quite "dubious" that she needed them at all.

This Negro woman works at a drugstore as a countergirl and is the sole support of herself and five children; she earns $85 every two weeks. Yet $20 monthly, 12 percent of this bare subsistence income, is diverted from the necessities of food and clothing to pay for the unnecessary glasses. Thus— and this is a fact too often ignored—such practices not only exploit poverty, they actually *create* poverty. After witnessing the hardships caused by this one store alone, an investigating attorney for the FTC wrote: "The business methods are so incredible and effect such fraud and deception on that element of the consuming public that he regularly deals with that it is almost impossible to describe them."

Perhaps the most striking revelation to me after reviewing the FTC poverty cases was how skillfully these unscrupulous salesmen prey on the fears and insecurities of the poor, and how susceptible the poor are to such blandishments and threats. Decidedly, those who specialize in selling to the poor are astute students of the psychological and sociological implications of what it means to be impoverished in today's affluent society. These so-called businessmen shamelessly exploit the poor man's desire for credit, his longing for respect, his fear of losing his job, his home—what little security he has built up—and most of all, his fear of being doomed to eternal poverty. In one of the most vicious rackets I'm sure has ever been worked anywhere, a company in the District of Columbia in 1966, under the guise of operating an urban renewal project, frightened countless ghetto residents into signing contracts for aluminum fronts for their houses, at prices as high as $4,000 and $5,000. The salesmen implied that if they did not "urban-renew," they would be "urban-removed."

Many salesmen—both in stores and door-to-door—contemptuously intersperse their sales pitches with "Mister" and insist, "Just call me by my first name." One home-improvement company working the Negro ghettos in Washington, D. C., pointedly used all-white work crews, whom the company representative in the presence of the Negro homeowner always referred to as "boys." In fact, the success of this particular scheme depended almost entirely on the salesman's skill at faking solicitude, insidiously calculated to throw the victim off guard.

It was a referral scheme, and the product was an intercom system, consisting of an AM–FM radio, master panel, six remote speakers, a fire detection and panic alarm system. The company promised to pay $335 for each fifteen names submitted and a $100 prize for each sale made as a result.

Since the financing risk was high—many of the people attracted to the scheme were not working or were on welfare and signed up in the desperate hope of making money—the intercom company sought security for the debt, namely a lien on the purchaser's property. Knowing, however, that the customers would balk at signing away such rights—after all, they didn't think they were buying something; they thought the company was paying them—the salesmen engaged in an ingenious bit of chicanery. After the customer had signed the "participation plan" (conditional sales contract) and the intercom system was installed, a man posing as the company attorney or public relations man casually dropped by the house and made solicitious inquiries about whether the work had been properly done. He carried a checklist, which he meticulously filled in, asking whether the workmen were neat and courteous, whether the customer was genuinely pleased and so on. Almost as an afterthought, he said: "Oh, yes, I nearly forgot. The salesman was in such a hurry that he brought you the wrong form to sign the first time." He wrote VOID in large print across the original contract and asked: "Now please sign these new papers. Just a formality." Disarmed by such unusual deferential treatment, many customers trustingly signed without reading the second document, which apparently was also folded over to conceal its contents. What they unknowingly signed was a promissory note and deed of trust on their house.

It is shameful to see these shabby homes, paint peeling, front porches crumbling, inhabited by the elderly and infirm, and yet replete with an elaborate intercom system that cost more than $1,000 and was worth approximately $200. But worse still is the feeling of desperation that besets these people when they cannot make payments and are threatened with the loss of their homes. A widow in her seventies wrote to the *Washington Star:* "In May, when I sent them $30 (instead of $38.60) so I could buy some food with the $8, the man called saying if I didn't send him the $8 he would take out a lien on my house which I didn't know he had. . . . Please help me. I am an elderly lady, a widow who got fooled."

So many persons in the District of Columbia have been tricked into signing deeds of trust to their homes as security for swindles that the Check and Fraud Squad of the D. C. Police Department has had one investigator exclusively assigned to this problem for two years. The man assigned to that detail, Detective Sergeant Austin A. Moyer, reports that the victims are nearly always Negroes of little education and the racketeers are nearly always those in the home-improvement industry. According to Sergeant Moyer, three unscrupulous home-improvement companies operating in the District illegally obtained a quarter of a million dollars in deeds of trust during the first six months of 1966. In only a few instances was forgery involved. In nearly all cases, however, the homeowner insists he did not knowingly sign a deed of trust, although his valid signature plainly appears on the document. That he was tricked is his word against that of the seller.

Actually, few cases ever come to trial. For once again there is the roadblock of proving criminal fraud, entailing proof positive on five points under the D. C. false pretenses statute.

So difficult are these counts to prove that in only one out of ten mortgage fraud cases is it even possible to obtain an indictment. Thus, nine out of every ten known victims—and countless others who never even come to police attention— are left helpless. If they fail to meet payments on their exorbitant, deceitfully induced debts, the holder of the note can insist on foreclosure, and their house, sometimes even without their knowledge, is put up for public auction.

One cannot long study the rackets aimed at the poor in the District or in any other area of the country without seeing one fact become increasingly clear: deceptive selling generally, and especially in the ghettos, is built solidly on the back of our outmoded law. The success of all manner of schemes and chicanery depends almost entirely on the swindler's assurance of easily collecting the debt through legal channels.

Some local merchants and door-to-door outfits, which use deceptive methods, pretend to make a credit check. In truth, they care little whether the customer can pay. They will burden the poor with unconscionable debts after determining one fact: can they collect legally? Does the person have property which can be legally confiscated and sold in case of default in payments? Does he have a job where his wages can be attached—in the legal term, garnisheed—that is, a certain portion deducted from each paycheck until the debt is paid? It is ironic that many merchants who exploit the poor are no longer interested in peddling merchandise for the profit of a legitimate markup. They use cheap merchandise only as a means of selling enormous credit debts which they can then forcibly extract by using our courts as their collection agencies.

Not surprisingly, the potency of garnishment as a weapon of extortion against the poor has hardly gone unnoticed by the swindlers. So widely is it used that it has given rise to a new phenomenon reported by officials in many cities: "garnishment rings" that operate principally in the ghettos. Examinations of court records in several cities show that certain firms, both dealers and finance companies, dealing exclusively with the poor, account for a suspicious number of garnishments. The merchant in Washington, D. C., selling eyeglasses, for example, filed 411 garnishment cases in court between January 1, 1966, and February 8, 1967. This is compared with only 217 filed by the District's largest department store which does hundreds of times more business.

In Cleveland, Ohio, with the help of a state legislator, local officials and the Ohio Consumer Frauds and Crime Section of the Attorney General's Office, a garnishment racket involving several merchants and finance companies was exposed in early 1967. At least half a dozen appliance stores in Cleveland's East Side Negro section typically operate, report Ohio's consumer fraud officials, by luring desperate people who need instant cash. The stores entice people to sign installment sales contracts by offering them a cash loan on the spot—most often $50, but as little as $25 or as much as $125, which is then added on to the contract in a disguised form. Such a practice—lending money without a license—is illegal in Ohio; it is also in such instances difficult to prove.

Unable to borrow money from legitimate sources, the poor, under the pressure of emergencies, such as medical bills and unpaid debts, find the "instant cash" a powerful inducement to buy merchandise they may not need or want. One man admitted that in December 1966 he bought two television sets, one stereophonic record player, and a tape recorder, *all in one week*, and got $25 from each merchant. He subsequently had three garnishments filed against him. Another man said he was induced to sign his name to a sales contract in return for two fifths of whiskey.

At its worst, the scheme operated this way: a customer purchased a stove at the high price of $239; by the time finance charges, insurance, a "finder's fee" (the stores sometimes send solicitors out door-to-door to find prospects), and a conglomeration of other charges, including the well-disguised cash loan and its interest, were totaled, the price due was $818. The purchaser was given thirty days to make the first payment. If thirty days came and went and the debtor was delinquent, sometimes by only one day, the store insisted on immediate payment of the *entire* balance, which they can legally do under a clause in the contract called the "acceleration clause," reading: "In event of any default, the balance of this obligation shall at once become due and payable at the option of the holder hereof." Obviously, the poor purchaser had no means of raising such a large sum immediately, so the store then repossessed the stove.

Since the merchandise was now used, it brought at public auction perhaps $75, a sum which the store obligingly, as the law required, deducted from the purchaser's debt. Although the hapless owner now had no stove at all, he was still obligated to pay the store the remaining $743, which is known as a "deficiency judgment."

If he balked at paying off $743 for something he no longer possessed, the store had little worry. Their lawyers simply filed a garnishment proceeding in court against his wages; and his employer was required by law to deduct a certain percentage from each paycheck to meet the bad debt and forward it to the store.

Among these many incredible facts of law is another: the cheated Ohio consumer, as is true in some other states, was even deprived of the opportunity of defending himself in court against such exploitation through garnishment. Inserted in fine print into the sales contract he signed was an insidious agreement, legally called a cognovit note, commonly called a "confession of judgment" clause. By signing such a document, the customer waives his right to defend himself in a court of law. He has no chance to confront the creditor with charges of fraud or to show cause in court why his wages should not be garnisheed. The garnishment is slapped on automatically; for by signing the "confession of judgment" contract, the debtor has *pleaded guilty in advance.*

The rights he signs away are awesome, as revealed by the

language in the contracts used by certain stores in Ohio: "We and each of us, jointly and severally, hereby authorize any attorney-at-law in the state of Ohio, at any time after this obligation becomes due, with or without process, to appear for us or either of us in any court of record in the state of Ohio, and confess judgment in favor of the legal holder of this note for the amount then appearing due hereon according to the terms hereof, and court costs, against us or either of us, to release all errors and the right of second trial, and the rights of error or appeal and stay of execution."

Cleveland officials report that partially because of unscrupulous merchants, garnishment has become an overwhelming problem for the city. During the first six months of 1967, Cleveland's Municipal Court alone processed 28,000 garnishments. A few employers, because of the extra accounting work in handling garnishments, charge the garnisheed worker $17.50 to process each garnishment. Some firms automatically fire the garnisheed worker after three garnishments. So critical is the problem among unskilled workers that factories hiring laborers circumvent the law by hiring men on a daily basis, paying them at the end of each shift. Without a regular paycheck, their wages can't be garnisheed.

Unfortunately, exposure of the Cleveland appliance stores that so ruthlessly utilize garnishment did not cause their demise. With the exception of one, they were still operating in August 1967. Said Lewis Earnhart, an investigator in the Ohio Consumer Frauds and Crime Section of the Attorney General's office: "We haven't got the law to stop them."

In Philadelphia, also, we can witness the struggle of the poor against the injustices of the marketplace. Pennsylvania has an unusual situation. It is one of two states that prohibit the garnishment of wages. Instead, creditors here often obtain liens on property, including homes, as security. Pennsylvania, like Ohio, also permits a "confession of judgment" clause in promissory notes. At any time after a payment is missed, the financial institution holding the debtor's note can

automatically notify the sheriff to seize the debtor's property
and put it up for public auction to satisfy the debt. These two
circumstances, along with others, combine to afford the unscrupulous an unbelievably fertile opportunity for fleecing
their fellow citizens in the City of Brotherly Love. It is Cleveland over again, except this time, instead of stealing a man's
future earnings, they steal his home and his furniture.

The following cases came to me through the Consumers
Education and Protective Association (CEPA), a nonprofit
organization in Philadelphia which works mainly among
minority groups to educate consumers, to obtain redress of
wrongs and to achieve reforms in legislation. The group is
supported by such distinguished scholars as Professor Caplovitz, and an attorney who often represents CEPA is John
O. Honnold, Jr., Professor of Law at the University of
Pennsylvania.

In September 1963, a door-to-door salesman persuaded
Mr. and Mrs. John Gallman of Philadelphia, a Negro couple
in their sixties, to have the front of their house painted, tuck-
pointed and stripped, and a new storm door installed. Unknown to the Gallmans, it was a job worth perhaps $200 to
$250 (their house was only fourteen feet wide), but they
agreed to pay the workmen $650. Mr. Gallman cannot read or
write, so he signed the papers with an X. His wife also signed
the contract, noting the price as $650. At the same time,
says Mr. Gallman, the salesman instructed her to sign "something else," which turned out to be a judgment note, putting
up their possessions as security and containing the confession
of judgment provision. Soon afterward, the Gallmans received notice from a local company, the Mid-Penn Discount
Corporation that they owed not $650, but $1,632. That figure,
which apparently included $982 in finance charges—or 150
percent of the actual debt—was filled in on the judgment
note after she signed it, Mrs. Gallman maintains.

The tactics here are common, says Max Weiner, educational director for CEPA. He explains that salesmen trick

people into signing judgment notes for outrageous amounts, sometimes several times what they think they are paying. "On the contract it says, for example, you have bought something for $650. You sign it. At the same time they present you with a blank judgment note, the salesman says, 'Sign this too.' You have just signed a contract for $650, so you assume the note is for the same amount. Sometimes customers are told they are merely signing an 'order' for the merchandise. The salesman takes back the signed note and fills in whatever amount he wants—well, not whatever he wants, for there are laws on the maximum amount of finance charges allowed— but he fills it in for the maximum figure, which in this case was $1,632—without the customer's consent or knowledge."

The Gallmans realized they had been swindled, but they didn't complain; "being quiet people," says Weiner, "they went along making the payments of $33.98 per month, which were to run for 48 months." About two years later, Mr. Gallman suffered an attack of asthma and was out of work. The Gallmans dropped four months behind on their payments. After Gallman recovered, they struggled to make up the payments, and during the next year and a half, they paid faithfully every month and even doubled-up twice on payments, making them only two months delinquent, or $67.96 behind. At this point the finance company had collected 42 of the 48 payments—$1,427.16 of the total $1,632. The Gallmans had only $200 more to go on that ill-gotten, unconscionably high debt, when on May 22, 1967, the finance company decided it was time to close in for the old delinquent payment of $67. (Such timing is not always accidental. Attorneys for the poor across the country report that many companies wait until the debtor has substantially reduced his debt before taking legal action. That way, the company is a double-winner; it has nearly all the money owed on the contract and the man's property as well. It is true that the finance company must return any money from the sale that is in excess of the debt, but the property is hardly ever sold for what it is worth. In numerous cases, the company itself or its dummy bidders arrange to purchase the goods at a disgracefully low price. They, of course, then resell it at a higher price.)

The attorney for the Mid-Penn Discount Corporation demanded a writ of execution on the Gallmans' judgment note, and the sheriff's office, as demanded by law, put the Gallmans' property up for public auction. If the debtor resists, the sheriff's office is required to seize the possessions by force. Thus, on May 22, two sheriff's deputies and eight policemen smashed the glass in the front door and broke into the home of Mr. and Mrs. Gallman with the intent of confiscating the furniture. Mrs. Gallman, described as a "frail, elderly Negro lady," became hysterical and attempted to ward off the men with a barbecue fork. It was later claimed by a deputy sheriff that Mr. Gallman tried to defend his property by unsteadily waving an old, rusty shotgun.

But the law was not to be deterred. Mrs. Gallman, bleeding from a scuffle, was taken to the hospital. Mr. Gallman was overcome by the policemen. And not long afterward, a truck came and emptied the house. All of their furniture, accumulated during thirty-five years of marriage and valued at $2,347 was put on the auction block. It was bought by the vice-president of Mid-Penn Discount Corporation, the finance company that had ordered the auction, for the pathetic sum of $90.

Three months later, Mrs. Gallman was still hobbling around with her foot in a cast; the neighbors and a local dealer had donated some old furniture on which the Gallmans sit, mostly in silence, just waiting. For, although stripped to near-destitution and living off the charity of their friends, these poor people have still not seen an end to the bewildering workings of the law. Both Marie and John Gallman were charged with assaulting a policeman.

Recently Wilson Holmes, Jr., a young Negro in West Philadelphia, seeking extra work to support his family, answered this advertisement in a local newspaper:

More MEN Needed
• Unusual Opportunity •
• Large Part-Time Income •
• Gigantic Full-Time Income •
You may earn as much as
$4–$6 per Hour
with the
Most Revolutionary
New Equipment
No Selling, No Soliciting, No Experience Needed

Applicants should be presently employed, over 21,
have a car and not afraid to work. Small investment . . . all of which can be repaid out of earnings. NO CASH NEEDED. ACT NOW.

The man applied for the job, and was put into three days of
training, learning to use a floor buffing machine. At the end
of the training he was told he "qualified," and that after he
purchased a buffing machine the company would refer jobs
to him, which would easily pay for the machine. He was
taken to a finance company where he "signed some papers,"
including a judgment note for $1,296. He and his wife were
told to stand by the telephone waiting for calls for employment. A week went by and none came. Holmes went back to
the company, only to discover the offices vacant and an "out
of business" sign on the door. Desperate, he went to the
finance company where he begged them to take back the expensive buffing machine and cancel his debt. The company
refused, insisting, he said, "You bought the machine—and
you have to pay for it." Thus, a man already so burdened by
family responsibilities that he in all good faith sought extra
income, was legally bound to pay $1,296 for a buffing ma-
chine which he discovered was sold elsewhere in the city
for $288.75.

When he could not meet payments, the machinery of the
law moved in. The Holmeses received this notice, and a

similar one was tacked up on the outside of their house: "And ye shall receive a sheriff sale: SHERIFF SALE: Friday July 29, 1966, at 10:30 o'clock A.M., E.D.S.T., 5841 Osage Avenue. Household Goods and Contents. Seized and taken in execution as the property of Elizabeth and Wilson Holmes, Jr., and to be sold by William M. Lennox, sheriff."

Ordinarily, the wheels of justice would have moved swiftly and smoothly to rob this man of his property. In this instance, CEPA, as it sometimes can, was able to halt the sale. CEPA rounded up thirty sympathetic neighbors to march in protest in front of the finance company's office. The buffing machine bearing the sign "Worth $288.00, Charged $1,296, SWINDLE" was placed near the curb outside the office. The pickets handed out leaflets to passersby explaining the scheme. It had been merely a racket to sell buffing machines by offering phony employment.

The finance company finally admitted to a delegation from CEPA that Holmes had been swindled. But they disclaimed any responsibility for or knowledge of the swindle. (Under the law, a financial institution is regarded as an innocent "holder in due course"—merely a disinterested party which lends the money, and therefore, except in rare cases, is not responsible to the borrower should the transaction turn out to be shady.) Desiring to end the bad publicity, however, the finance company instructed the sheriff to stop the sale of the Holmes's house, but they refused to cancel his $1,296 debt for the buffing machine. Now Holmes must make regular monthly payments, draining an income he only sought to supplement.

CEPA has been criticized by certain finance companies for bringing pressure through picketing to achieve their ends, instead of going through "proper legal channels." Two automobile companies have been able to obtain court injunctions to stop picketing of their car lots. However, a Philadelphia judge in lifting one of the injunctions said he could see nothing wrong in using "economic pressure" outside the courts.

It is almost a necessity, he indicated, for otherwise the consumer is powerless.

Decidedly, in numerous cases, CEPA's picketing has shamed merchants and finance companies into stopping sheriff's sales. However—and this is a sad commentary on the state of our protective laws—when such extraneous pressure has been unsuccessful or nonexistent, countless persons in Philadelphia have lost their homes after being deceived into enormous debt. One man had his house sold by a bank after he missed only one payment. An elderly couple lost their home in a sheriff's sale after they had been tricked into signing a lien on their house as security for a used automobile purchased by their son. He was charged $3,000 for a three-year-old Chevrolet. Others have been driven onto the street, their homes legally stolen and sold at auction because they were duped into subscribing to a food-freezer plan or buying home fire-alarm systems on a phony referral basis. A CEPA official estimates that in Philadelphia County alone, between 250 and 400 homes are put up for sheriff's sale every month. At least half of the for-sale homes, he says, are to satisfy consumer debts, many of them incurred through swindles.

For anyone who would like a brutal testimonial to the daily realities of the marketplace problems of the poor, I would recommend CEPA's monthly tabloid newspaper, *Consumer Voice*. There is a certain impact and unforgettableness in seeing photographs of the victims and their children carrying signs, "Losing Our Home Due to Misrepresentations," and viewing reproductions of the actual contracts and dunning letters received by the poor. One illustration that stands out as shocking is a collection letter from one of the largest banks in Philadelphia. It was dropped through the mail slot of a couple who had fallen behind in payments of a loan for $225. The man and wife had reduced the debt to $40 when they received the following notice, scrawled in scratchy black capital letters on one of the bank's envelopes:

WE GUESS YOU WANT
THE PIG TREATMENT
AND WE KNOW HOW TO
TREAT PIGS!
WE WILL TELL EVERYBODY
THAT YOU ARE NOT
WORTHY OF TRUST!!

The indignities, terror, violence, despair and helplessness the poor suffer from deception in the marketplace should weigh heavily on the conscience of America. For the cases reported here are not uncommon; such ill-treatment of the poor by unscrupulous merchants follows a similar pattern throughout the country: in Atlanta, in Chicago, in Denver, in Oklahoma City, in Seattle, in San Francisco and even in rural areas.

Running throughout this cacophony of deception is a re-curring, disturbing theme: the complicity of the law, either seeming or real, in supporting fraudulent business practices, while oppressing the poor and the innocent. Such inhumane treatment from the law appears evident from any economic vantage point, but must be strikingly apparent from the viewpoint of the uneducated, unsophisticated poor, who are left in a whirlpool of confusion by credit practices.

Many of the poor don't understand the most elementary facts of economic life: for example, the role of the finance company. They don't realize that their contract has been sold to an impersonal third party, against which they have no legal recourse. In their simplistic thinking, when the product goes bad or they discover they have been cheated, they re-fuse to continue payments, thinking this will achieve results. Instead, such action only brings forth the wrath of that strange institution known as the finance company, with its full backing of the law. Refusal to pay often results in a summons to appear in court to offer defense. Some poor, especially the foreign-born, don't even comprehend the summons because of their inability to decipher the legal language. Others never receive the summons at all because of a corrupt practice known as "sewer service." The summons officer, instead of delivering the summons to a ghetto resident, simply throws it in the sewer, leaves it at an old address or otherwise disposes of it, with the debtor none the wiser. The debtor's absence in court is automatically recorded as default—a confession of guilt. He has forfeited his right to defend himself, and the legal machinery cranks up to enforce payment. Professor Caplovitz found that 97 percent of the court summonses in New York result in default judgment, because of nonappearance.

Unaware of what has happened in court, the debtor is surprised and shocked when the law moves in. A wage earner may get a check with a portion garnisheed; he may be summarily fired, without knowing why; an officer of the law may appear one evening at the door and begin carrying out his furniture. Quite often the law and the merchants or finance companies present an ugly, though perfectly legal, picture of collusion. Routinely in Philadelphia, for example, a deputy sheriff is accompanied by a representative from the finance company when conducting a "Sheriff's Sale" on household goods. It is not difficult to imagine how the arrival of this twosome in a police car must look to Negro ghetto-dwellers already suspicious of the white man and his law.

Entrapped by devious clauses in contracts and duped by the lies of fast-talking salesmen, many of the victimized poor do not have the faintest notion of what has happened to them; they know only that they have been badgered by bill collectors, lost their jobs, seen their furniture or homes swept away, and that the law is somehow implicated. Worst of all, these poor people are nearly helpless to fight back, for they do not know their rights nor how to exercise them.

One of the worst cases of victimization through ignorance is that of a 56-year-old woman several years ago in Los Angeles, who stood silent and helpless while a local radio shop owner methodically took over her property. Mrs. Elsie

Phillips had taken a radio to be repaired, believing it would cost $1, but when she learned the bill was to be $8.90, she dispatched her 20-year-old son to retrieve the radio. Instead, he bought a new radio at payments of $1.25 per week, and Mrs. Phillips signed the sales contract. When payments were not prompt, the dealer obtained a court judgment, ordering return of the radio and $81.50 in court costs and collection fees. It was easy to return the radio, but Mrs. Phillips could not produce $81.50. To satisfy this debt, the dealer then forced sale of her house and lot at public auction. As the only bidder, the radio dealer himself bought the property for $26.50. Mrs. Phillips was allowed to stay on, at $10 a week rent.

A year was required before the deed to the house could be officially turned over to the radio shop owner, and during those twelve months, Mrs. Phillips could have saved her home by paying the $26.50 plus a $25 marshall's fee. But no one had told her, and by the time she found out, the deed had been transferred and there was nothing to do. She simply "sat on the porch of her dingy . . . home," reported *Time* magazine, "and wept."

Faced with similar threats against themselves or their property, most middle-class persons would respond with: "I'll get a lawyer." Persons in poverty, especially minority groups, are so ignorant or leery of the law that they won't seek out legal aid, and sometimes won't even wholeheartedly cooperate when legal redress is offered to them. Neighborhood Legal Services, a nationwide network of offices, funded by the Office of Economic Opportunity, which handles cases for the indigent, reports that their lawyers have great difficulty persuading their clients, mainly members of minority groups, to go to court even when their case is strong. The poor cannot conceive of getting justice from a law which has so viciously exploited them in the past.

In an eloquent statement before the National Conference on Law and Poverty held in Washington, D. C., in June 1965, Nicholas de B. Katzenbach, then Attorney General of the

United States, summarized the feelings of the poor toward the law: "Too often the poor man sees the law only as something which garnishees his salary; which repossesses his refrigerator; which evicts him from his house; which cancels his welfare; which binds him to usury; or which deprives him of his liberty because he cannot afford bail. The adversary system on which our courts are based fails whenever one side goes unrepresented, and judgment is entered by default.

"Small wonder then that the poor man does not always repect law. He has little reason to believe it is his guardian; he has every reason to believe it is an instrument of the Other Society, of the well-off, of the well educated, the well dressed and the well connected. The poor man is cut off from this society and from the protection of its laws. We make him a functional outlaw. . . .

"Seldom in his struggles with a finance company, a merchant, a landlord, or a rigid official, is the poor man even aware that he has rights which perhaps are being violated. If he knows, he may have no way to protect them. And finally, even if he is aware of legal services, he might well be deterred by irrational fear of cost, shame or further exploitation."

Despite fears, many of the poor do receive legal aid through Neighborhood Legal Services or other legal aid channels. Sometimes a lawsuit or other court procedure is necessary to obtain justice. But quite often, when confronted by an attorney, the seller who pawned off shoddy merchandise or drew the victim into a deceitful sale will remedy the wrong with suspicious alacrity.

Michael Frank, an attorney in Southwest Washington, D. C.'s Neighborhood Legal Office, explains: "When I say to such a company's attorney, 'It's illegal,' he gives in immediately. Many companies know they are violating the law, but they do it deliberately because they are sure that few poor people will show up in court to defend themselves, and the company will get a default judgment. If they lose a case, the company won't appeal, because they don't want a precedent against them to be set and to appear on the books. It is little matter to these dishonest firms if they lose one small sale or suit. They are still in business, and they have their healthy margin of profit. We catch them on one; they fleece twenty."

The lawyers in Neighborhood Legal Services and other lawyers working in poverty areas are our brightest hope for bringing justice to the poor and deserve unqualified praise for their successes in protecting the indigent from exploitation. Even so, these lawyers themselves recognize that individual victories in court will not cure the cancer of corrupt selling in the ghettos—that legal reform is also essential. Litigation on behalf of a cheated consumer does obtain individual redress. But for every victim rescued, hundreds of others are left to nurse their wrong in silence, or to release their resentment in other ways—perhaps through violence, perhaps through rioting.

Surely there are centuries-old, deeply ingrained social evils, complex and not clearly defined, behind the current eruption of Negro riots. But one of the evils is generally acknowledged to be the lack of economic equality. We recognize the need to provide Negroes with jobs and equal opportunity to help them climb the economic ladder. But we have given too little attention to how these efforts are counteracted when the Negro's buying power is hideously diminished, when he must pay two or three times as much for goods as the rest of society; when the major part of his earnings is dissipated in credit charges; when he is forced by law to fatten the coffers of the men who have cheated and lied to him; when his own property and person are jeopardized by laws that in the measure of their humanity are as outmoded as the debtors' dungeon.

When business and government—in fact, our whole enlightened society—strain to give equal employment opportunities to the Negro, we should also be far-sighted enough to guarantee that his earnings are not stolen from him through unethical business practices and antiquated laws. If we are not, it should hardly surprise us that his resentment might provide one more bit of fuel for the riot fires. Who can forget the television and magazine news coverage of youngsters in Watts, Detroit, Newark (some but ten years old), smashing windows, carrying off television sets and radios, cursing the men who keep their parents in a perpetual state of intimidation, misery and debt. Memorable are the words of one Watts boy interviewed on television after the rioting. He said:

"Looting and robbing is not the same thing. When you loot a credit store you are just taking back some of the interest they have been charging you for years on them high-priced installment things they sell you on time—$10 down and $2 a week for 900 weeks."

A number of witnesses called before the Governor's Committee investigating the Watts riots did testify that it was not mere coincidence that the prime targets of violence, after the first burst of anger was unleashed, were the establishments of merchants who engaged in sharp selling practices. These witnesses saw a "vengeance pattern" to the destruction of stores in the curfew areas, which they called "a retribution on merchants who were guilty of consumer exploitation. . . ."

During the catastrophic Detroit riots in June 1967, arsonists, according to press reports, systematically burned stores known to engage in sharp selling and credit practices. Thirty-two furniture, appliance and hardware stores, and twenty-three clothing and jewelry stores were destroyed. Reported a columnist for the *Detroit News:* "A Negro woman on relief set fire to a furniture store because she felt she would never be able to pay the bill she owed there. Due to the interest rate, she was being forced to pay $910.12 to satisfy an original debt of $285."

No one would be so myopic as to claim that exploitation by the outlaws of business is the sole cause of racial disturbances. Nor is an opposition to such ruthless exploitation based solely on the possible part it may play in fomenting riots. Simple justice and humanitarianism would demand an end to these practices, even though the consequences were not so evident, nor so serious as riots.

Nevertheless, it seems undeniable that the scandalous

gouging of minority groups by dishonest merchants and salesmen contributes to a potentially explosive situation in every ghetto in America and is one of many discontents leading to riots. This is a fact that has been too little recognized or explored. As Caryl Warner, a Los Angeles attorney who handles cases for the poor victimized by shady selling, said right after the Watts riots: "If that committee [the Governor's Commission to investigate the riots] is interested in finding out some of the real causes of trouble, they can come to this office and read a few of my files. . . . When historians write the story of all this trouble, they're going to wonder how in hell such an incendiary element could have been so complacently accepted and overlooked."

CHAPTER THREE

THE LAW, MORALITY AND BUSINESS

In August 1967, Sidney Margolius, a distinguished writer on consumer affairs for over thirty years, made this observation before the subcommittee on Consumer Affairs of the House Committee on Banking and Currency: "The damage to consumers themselves [from unscrupulous sellers] is greater than many of us may realize. To a large extent—and this may seem a little strong to swallow at first—consumer exploitation has replaced labor exploitation as the real problem of our times."

Commissioner Mary Gardiner Jones of the FTC said recently: "No matter how informed and sophisticated the consumer, deception will take its toll and the very morality of the community is at stake when there is no effective legal action to be taken against such dishonest merchants."

The President's Crime Commission in its 1967 report warned: "Most people pay little heed to crimes of this sort [consumer fraud and deception] when they worry about 'crime in America' because these crimes do not, as a rule, offer an immediate recognizable threat to personal safety. However, it is possible to argue that in one sense these crimes are the most threatening of all . . . because of their corrosive effect on the moral standards by which American business is conducted [and because they] promote cynicism toward society and a disrespect for the law."

These comments illustrate an awakening to the fact that consumer deception is not merely a small hurt suffered by a gullible few and a minor irritant to legitimate business; *it is a significant social problem.* As the Crime Commission pointed out, consumer deception has traditionally been viewed as of little more import than petty thievery. False advertising, a few misrepresentations here and there, a few dollars stolen from the housewife, have been offenses that up until this time society felt it could tolerate, as we tolerate a number of minor social evils, without fearing that our very morality or societal structure is being jeopardized. This is not to say that we have not found such practices objectionable. The Federal Trade Commission and legitimate business, under the leadership of the Better Business Bureaus, have worked for half a century to eliminate false advertising and deceptive practices. We have long recognized that deceptive selling could harm ethical business. But I am not certain that many of us are yet aware of the real hardships such practices inflict on the consumer or their pernicious effect on society as a whole.

Our attitude, though changing, is still very much "caveat emptor." This is borne out by the fact that we have developed few laws on a wide scale to curtail effectively the gypsters' activities or rectify their wrongs. We have vacillated between treating unscrupulous elements of business as harmless delinquents or hardened criminals—neither of which is a realistic approach. Typically, our defense against unethical businessmen has been warnings to the consumer: advice on how to avoid their wily traps, dissect their phony promises, outwit them. Legislators, district attorneys, the community as a whole, were not moved to red-faced outrage by small-scale, seemingly harmless enterprises such as salesmen pilfering a few dollars from housewives and conning rich widows.

While we were enduring without undue discomfort the escapades of a few villains, the complexion of consumer rackets changed. The credit revolution came. With the phenomenal expansion of credit and installment buying, the unscrupulous could now reach deep into the ghettos and the ranks of the uneducated and unsophisticated to extract large sums. A rich new field was to be found in the mass exploitation of great numbers of the lower and middle classes who knew little about the traps of contracts. Sales were easy to obtain through misrepresentations, and because of the exorbitant credit charges, swindlers could make hundreds or thousands of dollars on a single sale. The thieves formed corporations, organized nationwide rings, used all the modern merchandising methods. What they didn't organize, we organized for them. Our courts and our employers became their collection agencies. Our contract laws, with their outmoded provisions developed to fit the economic conditions of another era, became their instruments of extortion. Our prestigious financial institutions became their financiers.

No one can assess the brutalizing effect of such a system. So new is our awareness of the intensity of the problem that we have made little investigation to find out. But we do know that the victimized are telling us in a hundred ways—including picketing and rioting—that the situation has become intolerable. In 1966, Mrs. Esther Peterson, then special assistant to the President for consumer affairs, made a survey of 30,000 representative letters out of nearly half a million she had received. A thousand of the letters—one in thirty—contained language expressing anger and frustration against a system the writers felt was exploiting them. Wrote a man from Dayton, Ohio: "All we need to understand is that we are dealing with organized dishonesty on a huge scale." Said a woman from Los Angeles: "I do not know whether they [an automobile company] plan to come to steal my car, threaten me with bodily harm or whether I will pay the bill out of sheer fright. I am frightened."

Repeatedly, I have heard of victims who, lacking legal redress, reverted to jungle law. A number of those taken in by referral schemes have admitted that, in desperation and anger, they mailed referral letters to friends and acquaintances (some ironically headed "Bonds of Friendship") even *after* they discovered the scheme was a hoax and knew their friends would be swindled too. After the story of Mrs. Phillips, the elderly woman in Los Angeles whose home was sold for $26.50 to her creditor, was publicized in a local paper, four men came to the radio dealer's shop and beat him severely with lead pipes and pistols. In other instances, hysterical victims have tried to shoot the salesman who gypped them, or the collection agent who hounded them. All too often, in despair, the victim turns the gun on himself.

We cannot continue to ignore what, even if no one were protesting, we can see and judge as deplorable offenses to morality. Even one case of injustice is cause of concern to each of us. When such injustice is being practiced on a wide scale, as evidenced by the hundreds of documented cases in the ghettos and thousands among the middle classes, the exploitation transcends individual interest and becomes a problem of urgent, common concern. Responsibility to the injured in society can be denied out of ignorance. But once innocence is dispelled, responsibility is incumbent upon every knowing man, and most certainly upon those in government and business who are in positions of trust and efficacy, and by whose inactions these injustices can continue to exist. As I wrote in the introduction to this book, it can no longer be a question of whether we are going to end this terroristic plundering of the consumer by the outlaws of business, but how we can do it.

Toward this aim our laws must be updated to be truly preventive and not only punitive. Surely in instances where willful intent to defraud is evident, criminal laws should be invoked and such criminal prosecutions will serve as a deterrent to some. However, our primary purpose in consumer protection should be to *prevent* the swindlers from initiating and continuing their lucrative deceptions instead of to concentrate almost entirely, as we have done in the past, on trying to put the wrongdoers behind bars. Also, when a consumer is cheated, we should have some means of redressing the wrong, by restoring his money or freeing him of the debt.

The Federal Government must take responsibility for formulating and enforcing laws that are needed on a national scale. (Essential reforms in credit legislation are extensive and are discussed separately in the following chapter.) But to the states falls the primary task of curtailing consumer deception. The states possess the greatest potential for quickly detecting and halting the unscrupulous. After seventeen months as the President's special assistant for consumer affairs, Mrs. Peterson was convinced: "The letters that pour into us, the requests from agencies, indicate that the place where the real consumer protection is needed, and where the action is needed, is at the state and local level where the people are. One thing has become very clear—consumer representation at the federal level is not enough. The consumer must also receive representation at the state level and also at the local level."

Paul Rand Dixon, chairman of the FTC, has long urged the states "to take business away from us." He has said: "By stopping such practices before they grow into problems of interstate proportions, the need for federal action will be minimized, and the people most directly affected will have a telling voice in deciding what constitutes unfairness and deception. The more effective the states can be in nipping illegal schemes in the bud, the more energy the FTC can devote to dealing quickly and effectively with problems of regional and national significance."

Regrettably, the potential of the states, except in rare instances, is not equaled by enthusiasm, money or needed legislation. As we have seen, the laws of some states are so inadequate that their citizens have virtually no protection at all outside that offered by the Federal Trade Commission. An analogous situation would be if some states had no laws prohibiting murder, rape and robbery, and local officials had to wait until a culprit crossed a state line so they could call in the FBI to apprehend him. Lawlessness would prevail, just as it does now in consumer deception.

This is not a situation in which the Federal Government is alerting states to problems of which they are not already aware. Many state officials, particularly attorneys general who stand "handcuffed" for lack of laws while the gyps run wild, are painfully aware of legislative deficiencies—on both state and federal levels—and soundly support the passage of effective laws. In June 1967, our Consumer Subcommittee of the Senate Commerce Committee queried the attorneys general of the fifty states asking whether they felt that "existing federal and state legislation provides an adequate basis for effective consumer protection programs on the state level." Of the twenty-seven who replied, the vast majority—twenty-three attorneys general—deemed existing legislation inadequate and favored new measures, some urgently. Only Louisiana, Hawaii, Arizona and Vermont did not see the need for more legislation immediately. The last three recently passed comprehensive consumer protection laws.

The ease with which states could assume the legal authority to fight wholesale fraud, if state legislators were so inclined, is phenomenal. The Federal Trade Commission, which is capable of stopping nearly every type of scheme imaginable, operates under a statute singular in its simplicity and brevity. The heart of the statute (Section 45, Title 15 of the U. S. Code) is but nineteen words. It reads: "Unfair methods of competition in commerce, and unfair or deceptive acts or practices in commerce are hereby declared unlawful."

The mark of effectiveness that distinguishes this law from many of the state's criminal statutes is that it is a civil statute aimed solely at stopping deceptive activities without the need to prove the wrongdoer guilty of a crime. Such action is not possible in states which must depend solely on their criminal statutes. Under the FTC law a man cannot be sent to prison; the FTC can simply order him to "cease and desist" from his "unfair, false or misleading" business practices. If he does not do so, he is subject to civil penalties of up to $5,000 per day for each violation.

Proof of *intent* to deceive is not necessary, and this is the core of the law's strength. The FTC law does not demand that anyone divine the state of a man's mind before requiring him to stop making claims that are false on their face. It is sufficient that the claims are false and are likely to mislead prospective purchasers.

In writing the FTC law (it was first passed in 1914 and amended in 1938), Congress was remarkably far-sighted in making it all-inclusive—not only to meet the unfair and deceptive practices of the day but to cope with future problems, those unforeseen schemes that, as Senator Thomas J. Walsh of Montana said when debating the bill, would inevitably arise out of the "ingenuity of the adroit rogue." Rather than enumerate the schemes to be outlawed, Congress wisely made the FTC law flexible enough to outlaw any deceptive practice—past, present or future. Through the law, the FTC has been able to prohibit all of the five deceptive schemes discussed in Chapter One. Referral selling has been halted by the FTC act, although the scheme was unknown until several years after the law was passed.

Congress, a quarter of a century ago, put into nineteen words the power to forestall and halt schemes undreamed of. Unfortunately, many state legislatures have not been so far-sighted as to adopt this FTC statute, giving their state the broad powers enjoyed by the FTC. Only Washington, Hawaii and Vermont have enacted "Little FTC" laws. Several other states, however, including Arizona, California, Connecticut, Delaware, Illinois, Iowa, Maryland, Michigan, Minnesota, Missouri, New Jersey, New Mexico, New York, North Dakota and Texas, have passed general or fairly general deceptive practices statutes which are similar to the FTC law.

Many state legislatures, instead of following the FTC's lead, continue to pass consumer protection laws on a piecemeal "emergency" basis. In Florida a few years ago it was discovered that used television tubes were being palmed off as new; the legislature responded by passing extensive legislation forbidding such deception—down to requiring TV repairmen to note the condition of the tube as "new" or "used" on sales receipts. The law brought TV tubes under control, but left thousands of other products, equally subject to shady selling practices, completely unregulated. Yet in 1967, the Florida legislature defeated a Little FTC law that would have given across-the-board protection.

Louisiana legislators, after a flurry of concern about deceptive selling of fallout shelters, passed a Little FTC law, but the law applies only to fallout shelters. Kentucky's legislature recently passed three separate pieces of legislation, outlawing referral selling, phony "going out of business" sales and the use of the term "wholesale" to mean "discount" prices. It rejected a comprehensive deceptive practices law.

So inactive are most state legislatures in passing consumer protection laws that any positive action is to be commended, and separate laws, such as those forbidding referral selling, serve quick, strong notice to the offenders and leave nothing to interpretation; it would be a public service if every state followed Kentucky's crusading lead and flatly outlawed referral selling. Nevertheless, piecemeal legislation alone does not give states the power to keep a jump ahead of the multiplicity of swindles.

Said Senator Walter F. Mondale, when he was attorney general of Minnesota in 1963: "I think there is one [thing] that is too little understood by our state legislatures, and one which must be understood if the states are going to have effective regulation in this field. Most states attack unfair trade practices by specifically proscribing the then known unfair practices, instead of giving [the enforcement] agency the generalized power to promulgate rules in the fashion that they are permitted to do at the FTC level.

"I'm personally persuaded from our experience in Minnesota that you cannot have effective trade regulation unless you have this power of rule-making to permit you to move flexibly and swiftly to develop a modern definition of unfair trade practices as new techniques arise. Because . . . the scope of possible unfair trade practices is limitless. The ingenuity of those who wish to skirt around a statute [makes] the statutes often relatively useless. And if you enforce them, the person against whom you are enforcing them simply will develop a new technique and little if anything is accomplished."

No one would pretend that passage of a Little FTC law will end all consumer protection problems. Several states and laudably so, have adopted legislation providing powers substantially greater than those afforded the FTC. However, a general deceptive practices statute is as essential in building a state consumer protection program as steel girders are in building a skyscraper. It seems inconceivable that the consumer protection officials of any state, and particularly those in such populous, progressive states as Pennsylvania and Ohio, should have to work under the handicap of no general deceptive practices law. The very minimum of legal protection that citizens are entitled to on a state level is that afforded them in interstate transactions.

The bleak apathy found in most states is even more striking when compared with the spectacular activity in a few states, which confirms what Judge Louis Brandeis once said: "It is one of the happy incidences of the federal system that a single, courageous state may, if its citizens choose, serve as a laboratory; and try novel social and economic experiments without risk to the rest of the country. . . . If we would be guided by the light of reason we must let our minds be bold."

Not only one, but several courageous states have developed bold new approaches to thwarting consumer deception. Their vigorous and imaginative use of legislation shows that when apathy is replaced with concern, the gyps can be halted.

The most significant and promising achievement of the states is the establishment of consumer protection bureaus, usually under the attorney general. The pioneering was done in New York under Attorney General Louis J. Lefkowitz, who set up a consumer fraud and protection bureau in 1957. Since then, twenty-seven other states have established consumer protection units of varying effectiveness and power: Alaska, Arizona, California, Connecticut, Delaware, Florida,

Hawaii, Illinois, Iowa, Kansas, Kentucky, Maryland, Massachusetts, Maine, Michigan, Minnesota, Missouri, New Jersey, New Mexico, North Dakota, Ohio, Pennsylvania, Rhode Island, Texas, Vermont, Washington and Wisconsin. The bureaus provide a *centralized* agency through which consumers' complaints can be funneled. Illinois and New York handle about 150 complaints every day. In 1966, Washington's consumer fraud officials received 5,000 complaints, and California's 10,000. The bureaus which are acknowledged as most outstanding because of their legal authority, experience and initiative are those in California, Illinois, New York and Washington. In these bureaus, the staff follows up on nearly every complaint, sometimes arranging individual adjustments and taking full-scale court action against gypsters if necessary.

Empowering the attorney general or another state official to bring action against deceptive operators is essential in stopping them before they can fleece hundreds and than move on. Prior to the 1961 Consumer Protection Act in Washington, which established a Consumer Protection and Anti-Trust Division under the attorney general, apprehending swindlers was delegated to thirty-nine prosecuting attorneys statewide. This is still the situation in most states. A culprit chased out of one county could set up business in another. A whole ring of swindlers might work in several counties at a time without being detected. To stop a statewide conspiracy, dozens of separate actions under the criminal fraud statutes had to be brought in many counties. Such cases were time-consuming, amazingly costly (according to a local prosecutor, "One criminal action, as it did in our county, can exhaust the entire annual budget of the prosecuting attorney's office") and were not guaranteed to result uniformly in convictions.

Under Washington's centralized division, with its network of warnings and communications throughout the state, mobilization against gyps is swift and complete. The attorney general can bring a single case, sweeping up all of a scheme's promoters at once. In 1964, for example, a multi-state ring of aluminum siding gypsters, chartered in California and head-quartered in Portland, crossed over into Washington and infiltrated twenty-two counties. Within fifteen days, proceedings against the company were brought in Seattle's King-County Superior Court, resulting in a halt of their activities. Moreover, and this is another benefit of one intensive effort, many fraudulently obtained contracts and mortgages were adjusted or canceled, amounting to a recovery of $100,000 for the victims.

Art Hansen, now an assistant attorney general in Washington, recalls that when he was a prosecuting attorney he spent "five frustrating years attempting to bring criminal action against a phony furnace company that was making some very vicious sales in our county, and I was never able to do so." But only two months after passage of the 1961 consumer protection act, the attorney general "obtained a consent decree against the Holland Furnace Co., and stopped the problem completely not only in our county but throughout the state of Washington."

To be effective, the attorney general must have strong powers. The primary weapon against gyps is the authority to obtain a court injunction, forbidding the hucksters to continue their fraudulent enterprise. But an injunction requires a trial, and between the time that the swindler's activities are documented and the trial is over, he can accumulate a small fortune, especially if the court's docket is crowded. Some states wisely empower the attorney general to ask a judge for a temporary injunction. This forbids the company to continue the alleged shady selling, pending the outcome of the injunction trial—if there is one. In many cases, the company, when confronted with the prospect of an injunction trial with the resulting publicity, agrees to stop deceptive selling, and rather than argue the case in court, signs a consent injunction.

In Washington and New York, the attorneys general do not always have to go to court to bring a quick halt to consumer exploitation. In lieu of an injunction proceeding, they obtain an "assurance of discontinuance" which is similar to the FTC's assurance of voluntary compliance. The violators must promise in writing to stop their malpractices, and if they break their promise, their very violation constitutes *prima facie* evidence for an injunction against them. Violation of an injunction carries stiff fines for contempt of court; consequently, unscrupulous firms are highly unlikely to violate injunctions. According to the March 1967 *Harvard Law Review*, there is not a single case on record of a firm continuing shady operations after a state injunction.

One of the eternal and perplexing problems in consumer protection is how to take the rewards out of lying. A great many firms work right up until the time the legal ax is about to fall, then give up, and abscond with their ill-gotten profits. Their pocketbooks are undamaged; they cannot be fined unless they violate the injunction. In truth, what we are saying is "We will let you get away with this once, but if you do it again, we will fine you." Once for some crooks may be enough to last a lifetime. Besides, their profits can be used as capital to set up shop in another state. What we need is a deterrent to entering into consumer fraud in the first place; if we can guarantee that the operators' profits from their incursion into thievery will be taken away, that lying is not lucrative, their incentive will be considerably diminished.

Toward this aim, four states can impose fines (in legal terms, "civil penalties") for misdeeds prior to the time the injunction is final. New Jersey can levy a penalty of $100 for a first violation and $250 for subsequent violations; New Mexico, $500; New York, $500 in cases of false advertising only; and California can fine $2,500 for each violation. This deterrent is formidable, if strongly used, as shown by California's recent landmark consent judgment in a suit against P. F. Collier, Inc., a door-to-door encyclopedia company that has consistently misrepresented its sets as free, if customers pay the cost of "annual revisions." In October 1966, Attorney General Thomas C. Lynch filed suit for an injunction, also asking civil penalties for false advertising practices the company had used for the previous thirteen months in California. In June 1967, the consent injunction was obtained, along with a judgment of $95,000 against P. F. Collier, Inc., for its past trespasses.

Several states can administer the ultimate *coup de grace*, "corporate execution." They can dissolve a corporation engaging in deceptive practices, or as in New Jersey, put it into receivership, sharing the distribution of the assets with consumers the firm has cheated. New York has dissolved approximately one hundred corporations engaged in deceptive selling. Recently, in New York, after the dissolution of a corporation that deceitfully sold transistor radios, victims of the scheme shared $100,000 of the company's assets.

Several states also make vigorous efforts to see that the cheated consumer is compensated. From 1962, when the Illinois bureau was established, until June 1967, it has succeeded through the cancellation of debts and the return of money in saving $1,158,089 for the residents of Cook County (Chicago) alone. New York's bureau in 1966 obtained refunds of $1,064,627 for consumers. Since its creation in 1960, the New Jersey Consumer Protection Bureau has saved consumers an estimated 2 million dollars in refunds and contract adjustments. Many of these refunds are granted through mediation, not litigation, and are small sums of $5 or $10, usually settlements of misunderstanding with local merchants. Individual mediated settlements are vital in maintaining goodwill and offering redress to consumers. But small-scale individual refunds are not a potent weapon in fighting the inveterate gypster with a large-scale operation.

Undoubtedly, the most efficient justice in cases involving sizeable schemes is obtained through what I call the Robin Hood method: a combination penalty-restitution—taking the profits away from the swindlers and returning them to the cheated consumer. To deal with such swindlers, the attorney general should be authorized—and a few are—to ask in conjunction with the injunction, that the culprit's assets be used, and confiscated if necessary, to reimburse the victimized. This

two-pronged justice permits society to penalize, instead of re-
ward, the wrongful seller, and to make amends for the suffering of his victims. It has the added benefit of deterring those
who believe they can circumvent justice by making a fast
killing before the day of reckoning with the court.

Large-scale court-ordered restitution has not been used as
much as one hopes it will be in the future, nor as much as
its benefits warrant. New York, Vermont, New Jersey and
California, as permitted by their laws, do often ask for an
escrow fund to be set aside to reimburse injured consumers,
when obtaining a consent injunction or corporate execution.
Illinois, with an excellent law, has an impressive record in
the wholesale reimbursements of victims.

After a phony home-repair ring swept through Chicago in
1963, Attorney General William G. Clark sought an injunction, listing thirty-three complainants, who had been victimized. He asked that a receiver be appointed by the court to
"take into his possession all the goods and chattels, rights and
credits, moneys and effects, lands and tenements, books, records, documents, papers, choses in action, bills, notes, and
property of every description, derived by means of any practice declared to be illegal and prohibited by the Act to Prevent Consumer Fraud." A total of $17,000 was collected and
apportioned among the thirty-three victims.

The scheme was a particularly reprehensible one. The
racketeers convinced an elderly man, after an "engineer" had
poured water into the cracks of a concrete basement floor,
that water and sewage were collecting under the floor, that
the house was sitting on a cesspool and could collapse at any
time. He signed a contract for $9,000 and gave the men
$4,500 cash. He received $7,500 back from the court. A
couple owning an apartment house were instructed by the
crooked repairmen not to enter the basement for three weeks
or they would be asphyxiated by poisonous chemicals used
to exterminate termites. When the time limit expired, they
found no work had been done. Two chimneys on their building were left so clogged with bricks and mortar that, accord-

ing to a gas company investigator, carbon monoxide was not able to escape, and the couple could have been fatally poisoned. These people had $2,750 of their money returned. Sums ranging between $200 and $600 were granted to the remaining thirty-one.

This fraudulent corporation was dissolved, and to prevent the individuals from starting another corporation under another name, the three men were individually named in the injunction, preventing them personally from engaging in such fraudulent schemes in the state of Illinois.

An additional benefit of the court-ordered restitution is that it is but a pebble in the water. It radiates countless other private lawsuits from victims, using the court's decision as a precedent. Officials in both Illinois and New York say that one of the hopes in obtaining a large restitution is that it will generate citizens to take action on their own.

Consumer protection bureaus have also, through the imaginative and aggressive use of existing laws, obtained and helped to obtain precedent-setting court decisions in support of consumers. In a novel interpretation of a law, the Supreme Court of Washington in 1965 declared referral selling a lottery, and hence illegal under the state's anti-lottery laws. The case, *Sherwood & Roberts-Yakima, Inc., v. Leach,* supported by an *amicus curiae* brief from the attorney general's office, was brought by a man and his wife, who had been swindled by a home fire-alarm scheme in which they were to get commissions by supplying the names of friends. The court held that the whole scheme was permeated with chance, that "the respondents took a chance on whether they could get something for nothing." They had no control over the sales operation after they gave the names, in fact were instructed *not* to contact the referrals before the salesman had made his presentation. Thus, they took a chance that the referrals might not be interested, that the salesman might not adequately make his presentation, that the referral might have already been referred by someone else, that the salesman might not even contact the referral.

Furthermore, the court illustrated that the buyers unknowingly took a chance on the market's becoming saturated, and that the whole scheme was absurd:

"The Lifetone salesman told respondents they could get something for nothing through the referral selling scheme. Respondents are obligated to pay $1,187.28 for equipment costing $225.32. For ease of demonstration, respondents must earn twelve commissions of $100 each in order to get, as promised, something for nothing. This means that twelve respondents' referrals must purchase as respondent did; they, in turn, to get something for nothing must find twelve more people to purchase and so forth, as follows:

	Number of Purchasers
	1
1st round	12
2nd round	144
3rd round	1,728
4th round	20,736
5th round	248,832

Soon the scheme will run itself out; the market will become saturated."

Already, by the fifth round, half of the people in Seattle would have had to buy the alarms; taking the court's figures further, by the sixth round, everyone in the state would have owned an alarm system; by the seventh round, 35,831,808, or the entire population of the Far West; by the eighth round, 429,981,696, or everyone in Europe; and by the ninth round, five billion people, more than all the people on earth.

The court refused to "allow itself to be made the instrument of enforcing obligations alleged to arise out of an agreement or transaction which is illegal." It declared all of the contracts, approximately $130,000 worth, obtained by the illegal referral selling scheme to be void and unenforceable.

In a 1966 decision, New York's Supreme Court (*State by Lefkowitz v. ITM, Inc.*) attacked one of our most widespread, normally untouchable evils: unconscionable sales contracts, under which people are duped into paying 100, 200 or even 1,000 percent more than the merchandise is worth because of enormous credit charges. In the ITM case consumers were sold electric broilers, color television sets and central vacuum cleaners (that reportedly clean the air of bacteria and dust) on a referral basis; they were promised at least $300 for submitting twenty names, and additional commissions for each referral who "enrolled" in the plan. They were told that six to seven persons out of every ten named could be expected to "enroll." Some victims were left with extravagant dreams of making $9,000 to pay off a house mortgage, plus $1,000 profit; "the earnings were unlimited." The story is familiar. Few referral checks came through, and within ten days the company was dunning purchasers for payments, threatening to sue and garnishee their wages, under agreements that some people had signed without realizing they were sales contracts.

Examination of the contracts revealed that some victims were paying $910 for a broiler that usually retailed for $299; others paid $920 for a central vacuum cleaner that usually cost $350; and as high as $1,575 for a color television set ordinarily costing $600. The judge found these prices and the company's sales practices oppressive, unfair and shocking to the conscience. The contracts were declared unconscionable under the state's executive law and the Uniform Commercial Code which states: "If the court as a matter of law finds the contract or any clause of the contract to have been unconscionable at the time it was made the court may refuse to enforce the contract. . . ." The scheme was also defined as a lottery; and the contracts were deemed "utterly void."

The consumer protection bureaus also do a large amount of consumer education—preparing materials for distribution, dispatching speakers, issuing warnings against current frauds. Not only are the bureaus punitive toward unscrupulous businesses, they attempt to be preventive by establishing in cooperation with business, voluntary codes, similar to the

FTC's industry Guides. New York's code of ethics for the hearing-aid industry has been eminently successful, according to the bureau's director, Barnett Levy. After the code was adopted in 1965, the hearing-aid complaints dropped markedly, although only 40 percent of the state's hearing-aid dealers subscribe to the code.

Not an insignificant function of the consumer fraud bureau is that it becomes a repository of leadership for consumer causes—a powerful lobby in state legislatures. Where consumers were totally unorganized before and their voices rarely heard in the legislative chambers, the consumer bureaus have the knowledge and prestige to convince legislators of the need for innovative legislation to protect consumers. Impressive retail installment acts have been passed in several states, including Illinois, Washington and Massachusetts, at the instigation of consumer protection bureaus. Some state bureaus have pushed for the licensing of finance companies, correspondence and vocational schools, home-improvement contractors and television repairmen in efforts to weed out the gypsters by bringing the industry under some state regulation. States without bureaus have also succeeded in passing imaginative consumer legislation. Oregon, for example, is the only state with a law to curb telephone solicitations. It requires that the salesman-caller identify himself in the first fifteen seconds, before he can go into his "contest" or free-prize spiel.

It appears certain that states lagging behind in consumer protection not only fall deeper into the shadow of unfavorable comparison, but actually are caught in a deteriorating situation. For, as the fraudulent operators are driven out of one state, they migrate to another with weaker laws. Philip Rock, director of Illinois's Bureau of Consumer Fraud, reports that crackdowns in his state consistently drive fraudulent operators to neighboring states. He is convinced that "weak state laws are an invitation to fraudulent operators." After an injunction put the phony home-repair gang, referred to earlier, out of business in Chicago, they fled to Missouri.

Rock notified Missouri's attorney general, who chased them on. Rock does not know where they are now, but he believes they are still in business.

It is probable that unless other states adopt strong laws, they will become the country's reservoirs for swindlers. Already this appears to be true. Col. George Mingle, chief of Ohio's Consumer Frauds and Crime Section estimated that in 1966, Ohio consumers lost 300 million dollars through all types of commercial deception. This is one hundred times more than the estimated loss by consumers in Washington State, which has strong consumer protection laws. Washington Attorney General John O'Connell placed the loss in 1966 from consumer deception at 3 million dollars, as compared with 11 million dollars in 1961 when the state passed its Consumer Protection Act. (The yearly cost of operating Washington's Consumer Protection Division is about $80,-000.)

Although Ohio does have a consumer protection bureau, the bureau has no budget, has not officially been established by the state legislature and operates with a small staff of dedicated employees solely at the discretion of the attorney general. Ohio's laws are exceptionally weak. In 1967, a general deceptive practices bill, similar to that of the FTC, was introduced by the Ohio State Bar Association, but died in committee. Although the state is plagued with substandard private business schools, the legislators refused in the same session to license them and bring them under the jurisdiction of the State Board of Education. Despite the scandal in Cleveland over "garnishment rings," the legislature rejected a proposal to bring this evil under some control by licensing finance companies. The legislators did, an Ohio consumer protection official noted wryly, license fertilizer plants.

In fairness, it must be said that many legislators have never considered consumer protection legislation; they are not aware of a problem. In reply to an inquiry about whether Arkansas was considering legislation, an assistant attorney general said: "To my knowledge, the legislature just hasn't thought about it." When I asked a legislator from a Midwestern state, known to have more than its fair share of phony operators, what they were planning to do, he was surprised: "We don't have much of a problem out here; if we do, I've never heard about it."

Consumer problems can be documented, as they were recently in Colorado, by an investigative committee; by even a cursory survey of the Better Business Bureau files; or by a public invitation to consumers to air their grievances. When a magazine article suggested that cheated consumers who lived in states without consumer fraud bureaus register their complaints with the attorney general's office, the response was startling. According to the attorney general's office in Pennsylvania, which at that time did not have a fraud bureau, "literally hundreds of complaints poured in. . . . We had to tell the people that we weren't set up to handle complaints and they'd have to see either a private attorney or obtain a criminal warrant from a magistrate."

Some legislatures take no action because of an unrealistic fear that business interests will object. Experience shows that ethical businesses have been solidly behind the establishment of consumer protection bureaus, and even more so after they have seen their beneficial effects. In Washington the preliminary citizen's committee that studied consumer affairs and recommended strong legislation and establishment of the consumer division in the attorney general's office was composed substantially of reputable businessmen.

Federally, some changes also need to be made. Of urgent concern, I believe, after fifty-four years, is a reevaluation of the adequacy of our federal agency most specifically designated to protect the consumer against deception, the Federal Trade Commission. Although the FTC still provides a sound structure for consumer protection today (it handles about 7,000 complaints yearly), certain deficiencies prevent the FTC from curtailing deception as effectively as it should. The FTC's slow investigative procedures make it no match for the whirlwind gypsters who are in and out of business, sometimes before the FTC can gather information to issue a complaint. Chairman Dixon, concerned over the situation, recently noted that it now takes about one year for "cases to reach the commission level for issuances of a complaint." (In a 1966 home-improvement scheme in Washington, D. C., one company was in and out of business in six months; several victims subsequently lost their homes, and the company stole an estimated $250,000, mostly from the Negro poor.)

Issuance of a complaint is only a beginning for the FTC, an allegation of deception, and does not compel the company to abandon its deceptive practices. Before a formal cease and desist order is issued, the company may, if it wishes, ask for hearings before an FTC hearing examiner, an appeal before the five commissioners and a court review. During the proceedings, the culprit can—and some do—stall for time by exhausting all avenues of appeal, meanwhile milking their lucrative business to its final penny.

In response to a senator's inquiry about the "regulatory lag" during hearings, Chairman Dixon agreed that "if one keeps the case alive going through review to the Supreme Court . . . the promoter can get himself about a four-year period to reap a lot of money." In the case of Mr. G. with his home-improvement operation in Arkansas, the FTC started investigating in 1962, and it was not until 1967, after lengthy FTC hearings and a Supreme Court decision, that he was forced to agree to stop using in interstate commerce the practices proscribed by the FTC.

Chairman Dixon, to help remedy the FTC's powerlessness, has asked, and been supported in his request by President Johnson, for the power to issue *temporary* cease and desist orders—just as some states issue temporary injunctions through the courts. With this authority, the FTC could more quickly cut off a dishonest company's business. After compiling enough evidence to warrant a complaint against a company, the FTC would also be able to compel it to cease using the deceptive practices pending the outcome of formal proceedings, if delay would cause irreparable injury to the public.

Another possibility which has not been discussed, but which in my opinion would be a potent weapon to deter dishonest hucksters from intentionally taking advantage of the regulatory time lag, is granting the FTC the power to ask the courts to impose substantial civil penalties for first violations when it is found that companies willfully (with intent to defraud) commit a deceptive practice. This is similar to the power which permitted California's attorney general to obtain the $95,000 judgment against P. F. Collier, Inc., for deceptive practices committed prior to the final consent injunction decree.

Increasingly, the FTC is and can be, in addition to its investigative duties, a preventive force—an advisor to and co-ordinator for business and state officials. An excellent example is the FTC's Office of Federal-State Cooperation, established in 1965. Through this office, the FTC works with state officials, exchanging information on deceptive practices and companies and helping draft legislation if requested. The purpose is not only to keep tab on swindlers nationwide, but also to stimulate states to handle their own problems before they grow into national scandals.

Our powers to deny crooks the use of the mails also need to be updated and strengthened. Our postal fraud statute, passed in 1872, is a formidable dissuader to the dishonest. But as we have seen, especially in land-fraud sales, postal officials are often unable to cut off a huckster's inflow of money because they cannot prove his intent to defraud. The postal office protects consumers through two statutes. One is a criminal statute which seeks to punish the promoter of a fraudulent scheme, with a penalty of up to five years' imprisonment and a $1,000 fine for each mailing charge. This statute is sweeping. It can ensnare any person who fraudulently uses the mails or commits an act (such as a telephone call) which causes anyone else to use the mails as part of a fraudulent scheme. It is virtually impossible to operate without using or stimulating use of the mails; even causing the mails to be used for payments to a finance company makes the original seller liable.

The second statute is civil, or administrative. Its purpose is to protect the public from being victimized by mail-order hoaxes, and the sole penalty is a cutoff of the defendant's business mail after a hearing before a postal department officer. In both criminal *and* civil proceedings the post office at present must prove that the promoter consciously set out to defraud. One can concur with the necessity of proving intent if a man is to be declared a criminal and sent to jail. But the time-consuming, difficult burden of proving intent under the civil statute provides a lucrative loophole for swindlers who insist their false promises were made in good faith. They can continue to collect their daily parcels of income, even though the land they sold was under water, and the claims they made about their product were flagrantly false. The post office points out that in 737 cases of suspected fraud referred to United States attorneys, 46 percent had to be dropped. Although the schemes were false and misleading, there was not sufficient evidence to prove them fraudulent. An excellent solution—and bills have been introduced in both the House and the Senate to this purpose—is to amend the civil statute, substituting the word "false" for "fraudulent." Then if the post office, after a full hearing, finds that false mail-order claims are being used to obtain money through the mail, it can quickly halt mail remittances to the offender, marking the letters "Return to Sender: Out of Business."

Only that mail which is addressed to the questionable enterprise—and not the promoter's personal mail—would be returned to the sender. As an additional safeguard against interference with legitimate mail delivery, all mail directed to the company's address, which is often a post office box rented for the specific purpose of carrying on a particular scheme, would be held for twenty-four hours. During that time, the promoter could go to the post office, open the mail in the presence of a postal officer and keep that mail not related to the prohibited promotion. This is the same procedure that is in effect under the present civil administrative statute. The objective of the amendment is simply to protect the public from remitting money on the basis of false claims, regardless of a promoter's good or bad intentions. If warranted, postal officials would still be free to prosecute the seller under the criminal statute instead of the civil statute.

Additionally, legislation should be passed to end the nuisance of unsolicited merchandise received through the mail. Under contract law, as interpreted by United States postal authorities, a recipient of unsolicited merchandise can be held liable for payment—if he uses it, gives it way, sells it or otherwise appropriates it. If he lets it sit unopened on the shelf, he has not "entered into a contract by virtue of acceptance," and neither has to return nor pay for it. Many persons, however, do pay for the merchandise, believing they have an obligation to do so. We should make it a federal law that such merchandise is deemed a gift from the sender, freeing the recipient of any obligation whatever in returning or paying for it. (Three states—Illinois, New York and Washington—have already passed such a law.) There is no conceivable reason why a person should be forced to pay for merchandise sent to him without his consent or knowledge.

Undeniably, no group is more concerned about consumer protection than ethical business itself. And rightly so. For no one suffers more from widespread dishonesty in the marketplace than the ethical businessman himself. Not only does shady huckstering destroy confidence in the business community generally, but for every consumer cheated, an ethical businessman is cheated. When a consumer is swayed to make a purchase by false promises or deceit from a fly-by-night or unscrupulous salesman, the legitimate dealer loses a sale. Thus, the businessman, like the consumer, is victimized.

It is indisputable that the operation of fraudulent merchants puts ethical merchants at a disadvantage, often a tempting disadvantage. Seeing competitors take away business and pile up profits through a few misrepresentations is enough to strain the morality of many businessmen. It is not easy to remain virtuous when others around you are robbing you of rightful business, making money at your expense—and getting away with it. The most common excuse for using misleading advertising and sharp selling practices is "Everyone's doing it." The New York appliance store salesman who wrote his "confessions" for *Home Furnishings Daily*, as reported in Chapter One, excused himself by saying his tactics were "forced on him by cut-throat competition." The magazine salesman who came to my office complained: "It used to be a more honest business, but now the competition for mass circulation among the top magazines is so great that if you stay honest, you just won't stay in business long."

In May 1967, an attorney arguing before the Federal Trade Commission for a transmission repair company, suspected of using lo-balling, made the argument that, although he did not admit his client was guilty, if he was prohibited from using lo-balling, the FTC would have to take similar action against nearly every transmission company in the city of Washington, D. C., for they were all using the same tactics of which his client was accused. The implication was that the competition was too stiff to do otherwise than deceive customers. In other words, as one automobile salesman put it bluntly: "Join the crooks or get out of business." There is no evidence, of course, that ethical businessmen are defecting in droves, and self-policing by business itself is to be commended for keeping most selling on a high level. However, my point is that deceptive selling feeds on itself, produces unnecessary hardships on ethical businessmen and can, if not halted, lead to a general lowering of standards in the marketplace.

The responsibility of the business community in fighting gyps is an overwhelming one. And it is a responsibility that ethical business has assumed in the past, and is increasingly assuming. One finds ample evidence of the initiative of ethical business in attempting to regulate its undesirable elements. During a campaign in New York in 1967 to clean up home-improvement rackets, NERSICA, Inc., a trade association of home-improvement contractors, endorsed legislation to license such contractors. Better Business Bureaus throughout the country have stepped up their consumer educational campaigns and their preventive efforts of encouraging people to inquire of the BBB *before* they buy. After a recent exposé of shady magazine subscription salesmen in Florida, the BBB of South Florida set up monthly meetings with the seven magazine subscription agencies in the area, which resulted in higher standards and the near elimination of complaints against such salesmen. National magazine publishers recently asked the FTC to establish a set of trade rules to guide ethical conduct. The BBB of Delaware last year, after tape-recording the phony pitches of bait and switch carpet salesmen, used the recordings to convince local newspapers not to accept bait advertisements. Reportedly, such local advertising has virtually disappeared.

Despite these intensive efforts, the potential of legitimate business for reducing consumer deception has certainly not been exhausted. It is especially critical that business follow not only its long-time policy of policing its own members, but that responsible businessmen adopt a policy of *noncooperation* with the unscrupulous.

It is undeniable, for example, that few swindlers could operate without the cooperation of financial institutions. A few of the fraudulent hucksters do set up their own finance companies, or deliberately choose known disreputable financial institutions that will buy their notes and contracts with no questions asked. But it is disturbing, even shocking, to learn that some of our most prestigious moneylending institutions are supplying the monetary lifelines to fly-by-night outfits and disreputable companies. Some of the contracts in a central vacuum cleaning referral scheme, which cheated 435 people in the New York area out of about $400,000 were held by the Chase Manhattan Bank of New York City. The First Pennsylvania Banking and Trust Co. in Philadelphia reportedly bought at least $70,000 worth of contracts on a referral scheme that swept the ghettos selling fire-alarm systems. In Yakima, Washington, after the fire-alarm scheme was declared illegal under the lottery laws, the largest finance company in the city, Sherwood & Roberts, was left holding much of the paper. It lost about $80,000 when the contracts were declared unenforceable.

It is true that in few instances do financial institutions have a legal obligation to check the background and reputation of the sales companies with which they do business. Under "the holder in due course" doctrine, the bank or finance company can collect and, except in rare instances, is immune from legal responsibility to the purchaser. Some finance companies state this in a letter to their customers:

"The Consumer Finance Companies, Inc., cannot accept any responsibility for your purchase; and offers no guarantee that the representations made to you by the seller of the purchased item is correct. WE ARE A FINANCING INSTITUTION ONLY. Our only commodity is money."

Even though financial institutions are legally unaccountable if they purchase contracts obtained through deception, it seems to me they have a moral responsibility—a responsibility to the consumer, the community and other ethical businessmen—to investigate their clients. A reputable bank or a finance company has much better resources than the consumer for investigating the business methods and reputation of a company before buying up hundreds of contracts which may have been obtained through deception. It also has the sophistication to exercise scrutiny and caution. In handing down the decision in New York canceling the unconscionable contracts, the judge observed that the bank that bought them should have become suspicious when it saw that a broiler was being sold for $900 and a television set for $1,500.

All lenders approved by the Federal Housing Administration to grant home-improvement loans have a list of disreputable firms—firms which have failed to perform satisfactorily FHA-insured home-improvement jobs—called a

"Precautionary Measures List." The list, which is kept up to date (names are continually added, and deleted if the contractor reforms), has at present more than 7,000 names of companies for which the FHA refuses to insure loans, on the theory that it has a responsibility to the public not to be a party to deceit. Thus, every lender handing out FHA-insured home-improvement loans knows which home-improvement companies have acted in an unreliable manner and has a guideline for its judgments in this area.

What are we to think, then, when some lending institutions continue to buy paper from unscrupulous firms on the list? Not long ago, a home-improvement company selling home fronts in the District of Columbia was put on the FHA "Precautionary Measures List" for unconscionable practices, including shoddy workmanship, exorbitant prices and trickery in obtaining deeds of trust on homes. It is known that at least one bank, unable to grant FHA-insured loans for this company, nevertheless continued to buy its contracts and notes, signed by people who did not have the protection of FHA.

Innocence under "holder in due course," it appears to me, is shattered when lenders knowingly expose consumers to firms which are known by the government to be unscrupulous. All consumers, when possible, should at least be afforded the protection of the FHA's intelligence. When a firm shows up on the "Precautionary Measures List," the lending institution should at least make a thorough investigation of the company's practices before continuing to do business with it.

Many concerned banks and finance companies do carefully investigate and shun questionable business offers. Philip J. Rock of Illinois's Bureau of Consumer Fraud reports that the large reputable moneylenders in Chicago are rarely involved in fraudulent schemes. Most Cleveland lenders have agreed to cut off local financing to fly-by-night home-improvement firms, and reportedly these firms no longer find Cleveland a fertile area for fleecing. In Seattle, too, the attorney general's office reports that local banks are withdrawing their support of questionable companies, and investigating thoroughly before buying contracts from salesmen they don't know. There will always be those disreputable finance companies that will collaborate with the gypsters; but the reputations of our banks are too valuable and their responsibility too grave to be involved in shady dealings and consumer exploitation—legal or not.

CHAPTER FOUR

CLOSING THE DEBTORS' PRISONS

A century and a half ago—during the late 1820's and early 1830's—prisons up and down the Atlantic Coast were filled with tens of thousands of persons, jailed for failing to pay their debts. Shocking as it seems today, many were jailed for debts of less than one dollar and some for as little as one cent. So ill-treated were these prisoners that many were left to rot in dungeons without food or clothing. Hundreds died of starvation and illness. With the coming of Jacksonian Democracy in the 1830's and 1840's, the debtors' prisons were abolished. Men can no longer be incarcerated for inability to pay debts, and we look with horror on such a cruel system of debt collection. We pride ourselves on having developed humane, socially acceptable methods of enforcing debt payment. Yet, what is humane and enlightened in one era may appear inhumane in the next. Although we have closed the debtors' prisons, in some ways today's consumers are imprisoned by legal methods of debt collection that in our modern context of social values are as destructive and vicious as the debtors' dungeons.

Americans now work millions of man-hours to pay for outrageously priced merchandise and enormous credit debts that they were deceived into buying, and in some cases do not even possess, as in the case with the repossessed stoves in Cleveland. Mr. Gallman in Philadelphia, whose furniture was confiscated, labored 1,120 hours at $1.25 per hour—or a total of twenty-eight weeks—to pay for an overcharge of $1,400, including $1,000 finance charges forced on him by trickery. Such a travesty—in effect working in slavery without receiving any benefit from his earnings—would never be allowed under our labor laws. As writer Sidney Margolius noted: "We would not permit the things to be done to people as workers that we allow to be done to them as consumers."

One of the purposes of abolishing the debtors' prisons was to allow men to work to earn money to pay off their debts. Yet, thousands of people are fired after garnishment proceedings are instituted because employers do not want to bear the bookkeeping costs of processing garnishments. It appears that under our modern system we have in many cases substituted joblessness for imprisonment.

Countless persons have lost their homes and all of their possessions for minor debts. We would be outraged about imprisoning a man for a petty debt. Still, we allow his home and furniture to be sold to satisfy debts of as little as $25. We would not let a man be imprisoned without a trial. Yet consumers are deprived of millions of dollars' worth of their property at the whim of the creditor without any judicial proceedings whatever.

Clearly, our system of debt enforcement, especially our contract laws, was never meant to deal with the kind of widespread consumer credit that has burgeoned in the last quarter of a century. As Barbara Curran points out in her comprehensive study *Trends in Consumer Credit Legislation,* laws governing credit grew "like topsy," in fragmented, snail's pace fashion. "It is not surprising," she writes, "that developments in the law have failed to keep pace with the mushroom-like growth and expansion of consumer credit itself. Nor is it surprising to find that efforts aimed at dealing with specific problems which have arisen at various stages and in particular phases of development of consumer credit have been ad hoc in nature."

Nor is it surprising that changing times have left our credit laws skewed far toward the benefit of the seller. Mostly responsible for the modern-day imbalance in the legal rights of the buyer and seller is the historical basis of contract law. Our whole legal doctrine which governs contracts is based on a presumption that both parties are of equal ability to realize the consequences of the transaction and fulfill them. At a time when the credit-buying system was highly sophisticated and those trading with each other were usually businessmen and usually on an equal footing with each other, it was reasonable to expect credit buyers to exercise match-wits caution. Rare was the man forty years ago who completed a big transaction without days to study the papers, usually with the help of an attorney. Today, millions sign installment contracts of tremendous legal consequences, often without reading or understanding them, after only ten minutes thought. It is ludicrous to suppose that a buyer with no knowledge of the law is on a par with a dealer whose sophisticated lawyers have meticulously worded the contract to the undisputed advantage of the seller. Yet the law continues to operate as if the credit revolution wrought no changes at all in the buyer-seller relationship, as if that one-time equality still exists.

Our credit laws have become obsolete to deal with the current situation, and it is apparent that we need a comprehensive reappraisal of our whole system of debt collection, including contracts, with a view toward reestablishing a balance in the bargaining power between buyer and seller. No one would want to establish a system in which a man could avoid his rightful debts. Society must retain reasonable and enforceable threats against the man who would falsely incur debts, and willfully or irresponsibly refuse to pay them. Surely the soundness of our vast credit-buying system demands assurances that consumers can be forced to pay, for no society can long tolerate economic lawlessness. But the soundness of any system does not demand, nor can it long tolerate, the enforcement of injustices against its citizens. Allowing such a system to persist can only lead to a crumbling of confidence in society and the law.

To assure justice many of our contract clauses and debt-collection practices that allow consumer exploitation must be abolished or reformed. The problem of such reform is indeed complex. One cannot risk weakening creditor remedies to the point of ineffectiveness. Yet, we are not absolutely certain how important creditor remedies are in the total credit picture. Deprived of easy credit collection, would some sellers clamp down on the extension of credit to the detriment of the economy and to the detriment of some consumers who seemingly need credit to maintain a decent existence? There is no evidence that this would happen, although certain sellers, wanting to maintain the status quo, speculate that it would.

It seems to me that it would more likely create a renewed responsibility in the extension of credit which would be beneficial rather than harmful. Let us all be frank on this point. Although the wise use of credit makes possible a higher standard of living for most of us that would otherwise not be immediately attainable, the misuse of credit plunges many into helpless and needless debts and creates an atmosphere of irresponsibility.

Today's credit debt stands at an astounding 95 billion dollars, excluding mortgage credit. The interest and finance charges on this consumer credit debt is 13 billion dollars, almost as much as the interest payments on the entire 300 billion dollar federal debt. Americans have a remarkable record of repaying debts. Less than one percent of all debts finally are marked off as uncollectable. Nevertheless, a few contract to buy with no intention of repaying. And many merchants sell *knowing* full well the customer cannot repay. The goods are repossessed, wages are garnisheed, bankruptcy is filed. Clive W. Bare, a bankruptcy referee in the eastern district of Tennessee, appraised the situation precisely when he said recently: "Clearly too much credit is being extended today, and too many loans are being made not on the basis of a debtor's character, integrity or ability to pay, but solely because the lender or creditor knows if the debtors do not pay, their wages can be attached."

This is irresponsibility of the most pernicious kind, and if reforming debt-collection measures would have the effect of making creditors scrutinize their debtors more closely, it would be desirable. It is also probable that a clampdown on the easy collection methods that make fraudulent schemes possible would rechannel wages back into legitimate sources, benefiting the ethical businessman and harming only the unscrupulous fast-dealer.

There are some who fear that reforming debt collection would inflict suffering on the poor who would no longer be able to obtain credit for necessities. If this proved to be a problem, it would be far more humane and wiser to develop credit outlets for the poor, such as neighborhood credit unions where interest is low, than to continue to saddle the poor with offensive collection practices which cheat and oppress them by subjecting them to abusive interest and finance charges of 100 percent and more.

Another question without an answer is: What effect will abolishing or revising some debt-collection methods have on the use of others? For debt collection has not one but an arsenal of weapons—garnishment, foreclosure, repossession—which are interdependent in an unknown relationship. It is my guess that creditors will always find an ingenious method of collection, and we must be careful that by abolishing one, we do not give rise to other alternatives, even more destructive. A comprehensive, long-term, scholarly study on the interrelationship of credit remedies would be worthwhile. In the meantime, we can only proceed on existing knowledge with a sense of justice as a guide. It seems to me that reforms must be made in a number of areas before we can say that the debtors' prisons of the mid-twentieth century have truly been closed.

GARNISHMENT

The personal hardships and economic destruction caused by this coercive instrument of debt collection cannot be overestimated. In the nineteenth century, to quote a bankruptcy referee in federal district court in Louisville, the garnishment law "was probably the most progressive law in the country." It was seen as a humane alternative to the debtors' prisons, as well as a boon to the creditor, who could now collect his debts instead of watch the debtor rot away in the debtors' prison without earning a cent. Exemptions were high. For example, in 1910, an enlightened Kentucky legislature allowed garnisheed workers to keep $67.50 per month when the prevailing wage was $75. Thus, only three days' labor went to his creditor. In 1966, although economic conditions had drastically changed, Kentuckians with their wages garnisheed were still allowed the 56-year-old exemption of $16.87 per week; eighteen days' work was going to the creditor, leaving only seven days' pay to support a family at not even subsistence level. In 1967, the exemption was raised to 75 percent, which still pushes those making only $250 a month, or $3,000 yearly, down to $2,250 yearly—well below the recognized poverty level.

Effective July 1, 1967, Tennessee, too, "reformed" its garnishment laws. Previously, the head of a family was allowed $17 per week, plus $2.50 weekly for every dependent child. Thus, a man with four children could keep $27 weekly for living expenses. Under the new law, the exemption for the head of a family is 50 percent, or $20 per week, whichever is greater, subject to a maximum total exemption of $50 per week. The $2.50 per child was not changed. Thus, today in Tennessee, a father of four, earning $60 per week, can bring home $40 of his garnisheed salary, or $2,080 per year, hardly a living wage.

In my own state of Washington, the garnishment law is one of the most harsh in the country. A single person with no dependents is allowed to keep only $25 a week maximum, which on a weekly salary of $100 would be only 25 percent. Those with dependents are allowed an exemption of $35 per week, plus $5 for each dependent, but the maximum allowed is $50 per week. Thus, a man with six children can take home $200 monthly. The folly of this oppressive policy is revealed by the fact that if he were to leave his family, they would receive $325 per month from Aid to Dependent Children, the minimum figure which ADC believes is essential to sustain a family of six.

Moreover, the cruelty of Washington's archaic garnishment law is compounded by the fact that a man does not automatically receive his exemption. One day he may open his pay envelope and find no check at all—merely a notice that his wages have been garnisheed. He then has to go to court and claim his exemptions by affidavit. For this privilege he must pay a $1.50 fee or confess judgment against himself. In other words, he must pay $1.50 for the right to a trial. In ignorance, and sometimes out of poverty, the garnisheed worker does not pay the fee. It is perhaps difficult to believe, but some workers arrive at pay day without a cent. One man in Seattle sent his children to school without lunch on a Friday and went without lunch himself, counting on his paycheck that day. He received instead a notice his wages had been garnisheed. He went to court and was told he could not claim his exemptions until he paid $1.50. Lacking even a nickle, he confessed judgment against himself.

In 1966 in Seattle District Justice Court, there were 15,000 writs of garnishment. Three thousand resulted in confessions of judgment. Neighborhood Legal Services report that a few unscrupulous creditors count on the fact that many of the garnisheed will confess judgment; the collection agency then tacks phony charges onto the debt. One man owed only $560 to a finance company, but he was sued for $680 plus $100 attorney's fees, which were also fraudulent according to provisions in his note. "Some people end up paying debts through garnishment that they don't even owe," says Charles Ehlert, assistant director of Neighborhood Legal Services in Seattle.

Thousands of persons become hopelessly caught in the garnishment trap.

In Cleveland, Ohio, a man and his wife were left with $10 a week with which to buy food after his night watchman's wages of $89.56 per week were garnisheed. In Seattle, a young man bought a motorcycle, and when he found he could not meet payments, repeatedly asked the company to repossess it; they refused, and instead sued him for the purchase price, tying up all of his wages for two pay periods. (He was not aware he could file for exemptions.) Desperate, in May 1967, he went to the seller, but reportedly received no mercy. He went home and took his life. Ironically, the debtor's death made collection of the debt easier. The company no longer had to go through the formality of garnishment proceedings. They merely collected on credit life insurance the young man had bought upon purchasing the motorcycle.

In Chicago, a young auto-worker discovered his entire week's take-home pay of $112.39 had been turned over to the state of Indiana for delinquent taxes, which he reportedly did not know he owed. Requesting and receiving from Ford Motor Company his vacation pay to tide him over, he learned that most of this check had been garnisheed by Indiana. (He had lived in Indiana for a time while working in Illinois and apparently did not realize his income was taxable in Indiana.) The state took $208.84 out of this second check of $363.93. As a result of the garnishment, according to the president of the man's labor union, "Creditors were threatening to repossess his car, he couldn't pay his rent, and he had nothing for his wife and child to live on. He told me he couldn't stand it." Two days later, the young man put a .22 caliber bullet into his brain. It is true, of course, that suicide is not a usual consequence of garnishment. Yet the fact that such an extreme measure results even once or twice should give us all cause to question the severity of garnishment as a remedy.

One of the greatest fears that garnishment holds, and one that is fully exploited by collection agents, is loss of job. Few employers will long tolerate the economic burden imposed on them by processing garnishees. The Boeing Company in Seattle, for example, estimates it is compelled to process 730 writs of garnishment monthly at a cost of $15–20 each, for an out-of-pocket loss of at least $130,000 yearly. A survey in 1964 by Chicago's Cook County Credit Bureau found that

1,100 employers in the area lost 12 million dollars annually on garnishments.

Some companies make it a policy to fire an employee after one garnishment; others allow two or three. And unions seldom dispute such firings, considering them for "just cause." Only two states have any restrictions on such firings. Hawaii forbids them entirely. New York has a partial ban, making the firing of an employee who has only one garnishment during a twelve-month period illegal. Job loss for garnishment is widespread, although at present the statistics are incomplete; one suspects this is because companies are reluctant to admit to policies of firing employees for garnishment. However, a survey in 1965 by the National Industrial Conference Board showed that 43 percent of the employers surveyed had a policy of dismissing employees for repeated garnishments. Secretary of Labor Willard Wirtz testified at the House hearings of the subcommittee on Consumer Affairs that his department, which is doing a study on garnishment at Presidential request, was trying to accumulate figures on unemployment due to garnishment. Data were not complete, but Secretary Wirtz said he believes that from 100,000 to 300,000 workers lose their jobs every year because of garnishment.

Secretary Wirtz noted that in November 1966, members of his department went into the slums to find out more about unemployment—not on a statistical level, but on a human level. "We found," said Wirtz, "that more people explained their unemployment on the basis of garnishment than on their police records—which brought us up short." Indeed, this sorry fact is supported by the experience of welfare workers, who see hundreds added to the public dole, robbed of their jobs by garnishment. According to one study by the Cook County Department of Public Aid in Chicago, about 9 percent of the applicants needed assistance because they had been fired for being garnisheed.

One of the gravest injustices is that many caught between the possibility of losing their job through garnishment and paying off a fraudulent debt choose the latter out of fear.

Mr. W., living in a small town outside Seattle, works at the Boeing Company as a janitor, a job he has had for ten years. He earns $340 a month with which he supports a wife and three children. Almost pathetically concerned about his children's welfare, he has fallen an easy prey to the door-to-door salesman's slick presentations geared to the uneducated. Within recent years he has purchased an encyclopedia at $400; a fire-alarm system for his small house at $800; and in 1966, he signed a contract for $2,671 for aluminum siding, after being promised that he and his family would appear on television as "advertising" and would receive money for the appearance as well as commissions on the resulting sales. When the advertising and commissions did not materialize, Mr. W. was left with payments of $32 per month for 84 months, nearly 10 percent of his salary. When a Neighborhood Legal Services lawyer suggested that Mr. W. stop paying for his shoddy merchandise, sold through trickery, because they might be able to break the contract, Mr. W. refused. He insisted on continuing payments, saying he would rather pay a fraudulent debt than risk being garnisheed and losing his job. The burden finally became unbearable, and Mr. W.'s wages were garnisheed. Boeing, after consultation with his lawyer, allowed Mr. W. to stay on. In May 1967, he filed papers for bankruptcy.

As suggested by Mr. W.'s experience, bankruptcy is an increasingly common method of extricating oneself from the garnishment trap. Ever since the post-World War II credit boom, bankruptcies have been rising steadily at an alarming rate. In fiscal 1967, 208,329 bankruptcy cases were filed in this country, compared with only 10,000 cases in 1946. For the fifteenth consecutive year, bankruptcies rose in number —about 16,000, or 8.3 percent over fiscal 1966. Although bankruptcies in former days were almost entirely confined to businesses, today only 8 percent involve businesses. A startling 92 percent of all bankruptcies are personal—as a result of too much consumer credit.

There is hardly any disagreement at all among authorities

that the main cause of the spiraling bankruptcies is garnishment. Estes Snedecor, a referee in bankruptcy court in Portland, Oregon, remarked at the recent House hearings on consumer credit that it would be a "godsend if something can be done about garnishment." He affirmed that "the underlying causes of personal or consumer bankruptcies are: unemployment, overextension of credit, deficiency claims arising from repossessions of automobiles and appliances sold on contract, excessive interest rates, and unusual medical and hospital bills; but the one overriding cause precipitating consumer bankruptcies is the garnishment or threat of garnishment of wages coupled with an unrealistic wage exemption."

Consistently, the states with the most stringent garnishment laws have correspondingly high bankruptcy rates.

In the two states where garnishment is outlawed—Texas and Pennsylvania—and in states where exemptions are liberal (under some circumstances up to 100 percent), bankruptcy rates are significantly low. Even the stringency of a state's garnishment law determines the number of bankruptcies. The stricter the law, the more often its victims look to bankruptcy as an escape.

In a classic study, "Wage Garnishment in California: A Study and Recommendations," for the *California Law Review* in December 1965, Attorney George Brunn, now a judge, documented this relationship. He compared the garnishment laws of the ten states with the highest bankruptcy rates for 1962 with the ten states having the lowest bankruptcy rates. He found that Texas had only two bankruptcies per 100,000 population; Pennsylvania, four; Florida, North Carolina, South Carolina and South Dakota, which authorize exemptions up to 100 percent if needed to support the debtor's family, had respectively seven, one, three and eleven bankruptcies per 100,000 population. New Jersey allowed 90 percent exemption and had a bankruptcy rate of twelve per 100,000 population; Alaska granted a $350 exemption for married debtors and had a rate of thirteen. In comparison,

Alabama, with only a 75 percent exemption, had 279 bankruptcies per 100,000 population; Oregon, with a $175 exemption, had a rate of 200; Arizona, with a 50 percent exemption, had a bankruptcy rate of 147; California, also with a 50 percent exemption, had a rate of 145.

Moreover, proving that such relationship was not due to chance, Brunn pointed to the experiences of Illinois and Iowa. In 1961, when Illinois liberalized its exemptions, its bankruptcy rate dropped. In three years, it declined 9 percent, while the national average rose 18 percent. Conversely, when Iowa in 1957 abolished its 100 percent exemption in favor of an inadequate $35 per week, plus $3 per dependent, bankruptcies soared at an astonishing rate, quadrupling between 1957 and 1963.

It is thus indisputable that debtors are being driven into bankruptcy under pressure from harsh garnishment laws. Many do not desire bankruptcy, but have little choice. They want to pay their debts and would so so if given time, but garnishment actually prevents them from doing it, both harming themselves and depriving their creditors. Judge Snedecor told of a recent case in Oregon. Three years ago the man had broken his back in an industrial accident, and during his recuperation, he and his family had existed on workmen's compensation. As soon as he learned a new indoor skill and obtained a job, his wages were garnisheed. Unable to maintain his family and meet the obligations of his past misfortunes, he resorted to bankruptcy to obtain a new start on life.

Wrote a man in Wisconsin: "My wages were attached twice in 1959 against debts incurred in a previous marriage. I had remarried and my wife was pregnant and so to protect my job I was forced to file bankruptcy. . . . My total indebtedness amounted to $2,000 and I would have gladly paid it off given a decent chance and with no threat to my job."

When questioned in surveys, as many as 75 percent of the respondents have reported they chose bankruptcy as a less offensive alternative to garnishment. Not only do personal bankruptcies cause hardships on families, they also cost business a loss of more than one billion dollars annually.

Clearly, the purpose of our garnishment law is at odds with its true results. Instead of keeping a man on the job, it more often gets him fired. Instead of allowing a man to pay his debts, it prevents him from doing so. Additionally, garnishment, when used by the unscrupulous, provides police power; in truth, a public subsidization for the collection of wrongful debts. "The county sheriff becomes a backstop for the salesman," as one consumer authority phrased it.

Garnishment could be reformed and suggestions for doing so have been presented in several state legislatures and in Congress. At the very least, proposals to reform garnishment to make it more humane are absolutely essential, but in my opinion they are not enough. On the basis of present evidence, it appears to me that the best reform may well be abolition of this practice altogether. I am convinced that as the evils of garnishment become more widely recognized, Congress will be forced to consider outlawing it just as they outlawed debtors' prisons a century and a half ago. For those who say that such a Congressional move would be government intervention in the buyer-seller relationship, let us remember that garnishment itself is government intercession of the most dubious type—on behalf of the creditor.

An important consideration is: What effect—if any—would abolishing garnishment have on the extension of credit? Some predict that credit would be sharply withdrawn, and it is not difficult to imagine that proposals for abolishing debtors' prisons also brought forth dour predictions that the economy would collapse. That the abolition of garnishment, however, would have any effect on the granting of credit is highly improbable. Evidence indicates that merchants would grant credit as usual and employ other methods of collection, including dunning letters, repossession, liens on property, attachment and execution levies against cars, bank accounts and homes. We have only to look to such states as Pennsylvania and Texas, where garnishment has been outlawed for a century, to observe that they are not suffering from a lack of prosperity. Nor are members of the armed forces or federal government employees unable to obtain credit, although they are immune from garnishment.

If garnishment were a factor in inhibiting credit, one would expect to find that the ratio of consumer credit to retail sales would be high in states with harsh garnishment laws and low in states with liberal provisions or no garnishment at all. Figures from the Associated Credit Bureaus of California for 1963 revealed that about the *same* amount of credit was extended in states, regardless of the severity or leniency of garnishment laws. California and New York, for example, have comparable populations and total personal income. California has exceptionally harsh garnishment provisions (50 percent exemption), and New York has extraordinarily liberal ones (90 percent exemption). Yet, in 1963, 6.6 billion dollars' worth of installment credit was extended in California and 6.1 billion dollars in New York. Installment sales represented 24.6 percent of the total retail sales in California and 25.5 percent in New York.

The percentage of credit given in 1963 in Texas, which outlaws garnishment, was about the same as that in New York, California, Colorado and Alabama (the last two also have severe garnishment provisions). The ratio of installment credit to retail sales in Alabama was 24.4 percent; in Colorado, 25.1 percent; and in Texas, 25.3 percent.

Nor does the per capita income of a state vary in direct proportion to the state's garnishment laws, as, according to Judge Brunn, could be expected if the absence of this threat did, as claimed, damage the economy. The citizens of California and New York have about the same incomes; so do those of Pennsylvania and Ohio (with a harsh garnishment law) and those of Florida and Vermont (also with a stringent law).

After analyzing these and other facts, Judge Brunn concluded in his garnishment study that there is no observable link between the availability of credit and the absence or presence, or stringency or leniency, of garnishment.

Other ways of reforming garnishment have been suggested. One is legally to prohibit employers from firing workers because of garnishment. Aside from the legal entanglements and mechanism needed to enforce such a law, it seems to me unfair for society to pass on to industry the burdensome duty of acting as collection agents for a transaction about which they have no knowledge and over which they have no control. In cases where the debt is phony, we then force business to become an unwilling accomplice to consumer exploitation and fraud, another distasteful task which we have no right to ask. It is true that labor unions could perhaps do more to protect workers against being fired for one or two garnishments, but shifting this societal evil fully onto the shoulders of employers will not end the problem. Garnishment would still be used as a tool for consumer exploitation, and perhaps increasingly so, for the predatory sellers would be even more certain of full collection.

Another reform move is to raise the exemptions to "humane" levels. A working draft of the Uniform Consumer Credit Code, prepared by the National Conference of Commissioners on Uniform State Laws for adoption by all states, recommends an exemption of $100 per week for those with dependents, which would guarantee such debtors at least $5,200 per year free from creditors. Surely a higher exemption provision would be an improvement over the existing situation, but once again it does not prevent exploitation of consumers through garnishment, nor does it prevent a swelling of the ranks of the unemployed. New York's consumers, despite the state's liberal garnishment law, are still being shamelessly exploited by and fired for garnishment. No reform is adequate which allows garnishment-induced job loss. As Judge Brunn has said: ". . . the question remains whether society should consider the threat of loss of employment as a legitimate debt-collecting device. We have given up imprisonment for debt; do we want to tolerate joblessness for debt?"

What about garnishment for taxes, alimony and child support? I believe we will have to make exceptions here with certain safeguards, for these, as distinguished from commercial debts, are debts to society, on which the functioning of the government and children's lives may depend. Additionally, those whose wages are garnisheed for taxes are often in high income brackets, for example, entertainers, whose income may be in the six figures. Nevertheless, reforms would have to be adopted for these garnishees to prevent job loss and inhumane wage attachments. Certainly the government should not be permitted to confiscate all of a man's paycheck, as happened to the auto-worker from Indiana, nor amounts that may cause severe hardships. Vern Countryman, a professor at Harvard Law School, recommends that at least $15,000 of a person's annual income should be immune from garnishment. It has also been suggested that garnishment exemptions be on a sliding scale to income, as income taxes are.

Any garnishment abolition law would also have to include a provision forbidding wage assignments. Most states allow the insertion of a clause in contracts by which the debtor in the event of a default in payments assigns his wages to the creditor. As in garnishment, the creditor can then legally attach the man's paycheck. With the abolition of garnishment it is certain that creditors would increasingly use wage assignment and thus defeat the purpose of ending garnishment.

We should make no mistake about it: eliminating garnishment and wage assignments is not a cure-all, as is evident from the gouging of consumers in Pennsylvania where garnishment does not exist. In the absence of garnishment, foreclosures on homes are more prevalent; repossession is more vicious. Jeopardizing a man's home instead of his job would be no improvement. Thus, the abolition of garnishment alone could be harmful. It must be accompanied by other credit reforms that will prevent even worse debt-collection methods from filling the vacuum left by garnishment.

IRREVOCABLE CONTRACTS

A major trap for the consumer, especially in door-to-door sales, is the irrevocability of the signed contract. Once his signature is applied, the buyer is held responsible for the debt, even though he discovers in the next instant that he was victimized. This situation reflects again how our laws are weighted in favor of the seller. Some conditional sales contracts even specify that the seller can cancel for any reason—if he discovers the customer is a poor credit risk, for example. But the consumer cannot exercise similar rights even though he finds the company to be thoroughly fraudulent.

The malicious grip of unscrupulous door-to-door salesmen could be broken if the buyer, like the seller, were given a reasonable time—at least 24 hours—to reconsider his signed agreement and cancel it if he decided the purchase was unwise or deceptively induced.

In April 1967, I introduced a bill in the Senate calling for a one day "cooling-off" period on door-to-door sales. Great Britain has had such a law since 1964, allowing a seventy-two hour cooling-off period, and Britain's Consumer Council reports that it has been a success, causing no demonstrable harm to salesmen who are open and above-board, and benefiting consumers. Washington, Illinois and Massachusetts have recently legislated cooling-off periods on door-to-door sales. Massachusetts reports that consumer response has been excellent and that some businessmen have even suggested lengthening the period of rescission from one day to three or more days. Many legitimate firms already permit cancellation of a contract within five days at the buyer's request.

Unquestionably, the majority of the country's one and a half million door-to-door salesmen are reputable, but the small percentage that make up the dishonest fringe are a source of major concern. The success of most of the schemes outlined in Chapter One rest squarely on the skills and prevarications of the door-to-door salesman. Bait advertising, referral selling, the "special price," the free gimmick and the fear-sell all sink to their very lowest and most lucrative forms at the hands of swindlers "working a neighborhood."

Moreover, a person in his home is at the decided disadvantage. He has not invited a sales pitch, nor is he prepared for one, as he is when he enters a store or other place of business. The salesman is unwelcome and often lies to cover up his intentions by pretending to be a "fire inspector," "advertising representative" or "market researcher." In a 1965 survey, one-third of all Americans reported they had been approached by salesmen posing as poll-takers. Some victims think they are signing a receipt or delivery slip. One salesman obtained signatures on contracts by saying, "Just sign this so my boss will know I've talked with you." When a group of women in Arlington, Virginia, recently went to court to complain about being duped into taking five-year subscriptions to a number of magazines, the judge said he had not seen a single victim "who knew what she was doing."

An amazing number of people are induced to sign contracts in sheer fatigue. The Consumer Fraud Bureau in California reports that "many home owners purchase encyclopedias, cameras, vacuum cleaners and aluminum siding at 2 A.M., 3 A.M. and 4 A.M., after many hours of high pressure sales techniques. . . . It is an unequal struggle. Worn-out by the salesman (whom they are too embarrassed or polite or afraid to throw out), they wearily sign the contract just to get rid of him. One camera salesman sold a $400 package to a family at 2 A.M. and then proceeded to sell a 70-year-old frail woman visitor another $400 package with the homeowner as co-signer." Another sold aluminum siding to a homeowner at 4 A.M., after he had asked the salesman many times to leave. In all cases, the buyers woke up the next morning and realized the enormity of their mistake. The siding was twice the going price in the community, and "the $400 camera," said a consumer fraud official, "would do everything a $17 instamatic would do, but not quite as well."

All the victims tried to cancel their contracts without success.

Quite frequently, the salesman is hardly out of the house before the buyer realizes he has been victimized. Recently a young woman from Trinidad, new to this country, was persuaded to buy a set of children's encyclopedias for her three-year-old son, which was misrepresented as a "special bargain" for that day only. When her husband found out, he was extremely upset, for they were considerably in debt. In tears, the young wife searched the neighborhood until she found the saleswoman; she begged her to tear up the contract, but the saleswoman refused.

Allowing rescission of a contract would hardly end shady door-to-door selling, for sometimes it is days, weeks, even months, before a buyer realizes he has been cheated. (Some never find out.) But a cooling-off period would put an end to the grim irreversibility of the signed contract and offer some relief from the high pressure and deceitful practices which some salesmen depend on to underwrite their shoddy businesses.

CONFESSION OF JUDGMENT

Many outrageous consumer abuses would be checked in a court of law were it not for "confession of judgment," which is legal in installment credit agreements in all states except nine: California, Connecticut, Maryland, Massachusetts, Minnesota, New Hampshire, New Jersey, New York and North Dakota. By signing an installment contract or promissory note, containing this provision, a purchaser waives virtually all of his rights to due process of law and to a judicial review of whether the debt was just. In effect, he delivers all of his legal rights into the hands of the creditor.

As shown by a typical confession of judgment clause, he agrees to "irrevocably appoint any attorney of any court of record attorney for me . . . to confess judgment in favor of the seller against me." (It is interesting, but perhaps not surprising, that in some cases the attorney who pleads guilty for the debtor is the same attorney who brought suit for the creditor. This conflict of interest is not illegal, although it hardly advances the cause of justice.)

The consumer agrees to "waive issuance of process and service thereof, to waive trial by jury. . . ." Thus, he has no opportunity to meet the creditor in court face to face, or to try to perusade a judge that the debt is unjust. He is not even notified of the judgment against him. Some victims of the appliance store rackets in Cleveland did not find out until they received a paycheck that had been garnisheed. In Philadelphia many people who have signed judgment notes do not know that their house is up for auction until the "sheriff's sale" notice arrives in the mail.

The debtor usually agrees to the added indignity of "reasonable attorney's fees" for his own "representation" in court, as well as that of the creditor. (In Illinois, "reasonable" fees are usually 15 percent of the balance of the debt. A man who owed $3,000 on a car before judgment owed $3,450 afterward, including $450 legal fees.) The attorney does little more than sign his name, sometimes with a rubber stamp.

If there were errors in the original contract or the proceedings, which might be used for his defense, the buyer agrees to "waive and release" those too, "hereby ratifying and confirming all that said attorney may do by virtue thereof." In 1966, Attorney Jerome Schur at the request of Chief Judge John S. Boyle of the Circuit Court of Cook County, did a study of 1,305 cases in the Court's Municipal Division in which creditors obtained judgment under confession of judgment clauses. The study disclosed a number of irregularities in filing the confession of judgment suit: attorneys claimed fees they were not entitled to; some signed with a rubber stamp (showing "the assembly line technique which stresses speed rather than exactness," commented the investigator); some judgment claims were not notarized; some were not even signed, but the blank line was notarized anyway; and in one case a contract was processed that did not even possess a confession of judgment clause.

In four contracts, the number of payments when multiplied by the monthly sum came to more than the total balance. In others it appeared the contract had been tampered with. In 34 cases, the contract was completed in more than one color ink; in four cases it was completed in both print and script; in 26 cases it was filled out in pencil; 29 judgment notes contained blank spaces, which is contrary to Illinois law. Despite these inaccuracies, possible fraud and sloppy attention to the fine points of law, if the court does not detect the error before the judgment is entered, it stands. And, as Mr. Schur points out, the court is so overburdened by the number of judgment suits that meticulous examination is no longer possible.

Immediately, after a customer signs the note or contract, the creditor records the judgment in court, accompanied by an affidavit to its authenticity and a small fee, sometimes $5. The creditor thereafter can ask for an execution on the note, demanding full payment according to the provisions. The court grants the judgment *automatically* without consulting the debtor or hearing any defense he may have to offer. If the workmanship is shoddy, if the company fails to complete the work, if the merchandise falls apart, if it was sold through fraud, the debtor pays regardless. By signing, he has agreed to pay the debt regardless of extenuating circumstances. He has prejudged himself guilty.

Interestingly, the confession of judgment, like garnishment, was once a legal device to benefit the poor. Legally, *cognovit* means: "An acknowledgement or confession by a defendant that the plaintiff's cause, or a part of it, is just, wherefore the defendant, *to save expense,* suffers judgment to be entered without trial."

Today, cognovit in the hands of many credit merchants has become a malicious instrument of extortion, enabling creditors to collect unjust debts and to shift the ordinary costs of doing business to the very people they victimize and to society as a whole through our court system. It is understandable why some financial interests support this distortion of justice, for it relieves them of many responsibilities, hazards and expenses. It obviates the necessity of checking to determine if a man is a good credit risk, for they know, even if their extension of credit is outrageously unsound, he *must* pay without argument. As one finance company in Pennsylvania admitted, "it saves us attorney's fees; there are no complaints to file, no defenses to overcome and no chance that the court might decide the money is not due." The proceeds of a bad debt need not even be shared with a collection agency. Our courts collect the entire debt promptly, efficiently and for free.

The cognovit provision is widely used. According to CEPA's Max Weiner, from 300 to 500 confessions of judgment are recorded every day in Philadelphia's City Hall—nearly 150,000 a year. In the two-week period—from June 20 through July 1, 1966—studied in Cook County, $848,338.44 in debts was legally turned over to creditors through confession of judgment. If this period is average, as the investigators believe it is, *an astounding 22 million dollars' worth of debts is collected yearly in Cook County by confession of judgment,* and 34,000 persons every year are coerced into paying without being allowed a murmur of protest in court against possible injustices of the debts.

That some victims might have just cause for complaining, had they not signed away their rights, was further documented by Mr. Schur's study. Some creditors did not even give their debtors a reasonable opportunity to pay. In twelve cases the creditors executed the confession of judgment *within two months* after the contract was signed. One hapless debtor was struck with a judgment suit seven days after he had signed a contract, *even before the first payment was due.*

So offensive are the abuses of confession of judgment that its use in consumer installment contracts and notes should be outlawed by the states or, if necessary, by Congress. In our judicial system every man has the right to be served in court, to have a trial, to present evidence, to take depositions, to cross-examine witnesses, before he is judged guilty or not guilty. We do not send a man to jail without giving him the right to a trial. We should not deprive him of his home, his wages, his possessions, without the right to trial. Such a systematic deprivation of rights is morally unjustifiable.

It is true, as finance companies point out, that the judgment can be reopened for trial if there is just cause. However, even having the judgment opened is costly, at least $300 in Pennsylvania, a sum that few of the poor can spend to remedy a wrong that should not have been allowed in the first place. Nor is it always possible. A lawyer in Seattle tells me he has attempted several times to get a judgment opened on the basis of false credit charges, but has never succeeded.

Those who would perpetuate the cognovit note predict that without it their businesses will collapse, although nine states are prospering despite its prohibition. It is deeply entrenched; the Illinois legislature, one of the most consumer-conscious in the country, refused in 1967 to outlaw it. Officials in Ohio's attorney general's office report that despite the fact the cognovit note is their biggest problem, they are unable to get a single legislator interested in introducing a bill to outlaw it.

The legitimate merchant with a legitimate claim should not fear to face a debtor in open court. The reputable sellers, however, who investigate their clients, are not the primary users of confession of judgment. In the Cook County study, nearly half of all the suits brought for radios, TV's and hi-fi's came from one store on West Madison Street.

Outlawing confession of judgment will not, we should recognize, accord everyone judicial review of the fairness of a debt. Its abolition will be a monumental victory in freeing the citizens of many states from a legal bondage to unscrupulous sellers. But, as we have seen in New York, which does not allow confession of judgment, 97 percent of all the suits still result in default judgment because the debtor does not come to court to defend himself. Thus, the right to defend oneself can also be defeated through ignorance, sometimes through illegal shenanigans locally in which the court summons is never served. These problems show the need for increased public awareness which will spur a reform of local court procedures and intensive efforts to encourage people, especially the poor, to take advantage of their legal rights. Neighborhood Legal Services, OEO-funded credit unions for the poor and many community groups are vital in guaranteeing these rights. Without education of the poor and the unsophisticated, even the best system of legal protection will flounder.

DECEPTIVE CONTRACT PROVISIONS

Other installment credit practices that should be forbidden by law are the acceleration of payments without cause, balloon payments and add-on purchases. According to some contracts, the creditor can, without giving a reason and in the absence of default payment by the purchaser, arbitrarily accelerate payments, insisting on the total balance immediately. Failure to pay the total sum can result in garnishment of wages, foreclosure on property, repossession of the merchandise and other hardships.

This contract provision produces some especially ugly consequences when used in conjunction with confession of judgment; it puts a consumer at the complete mercy of a creditor's disposition. A person who buys on the installment plan should be assured that both parties are obligated to carry out the bargain in good faith and that the only demands on the buyer are to pay the regular monthly payments, as he is led to believe.

Such a fairness doctrine should also pertain to balloon contracts. Most credit buyers understandably assume that when they are told they owe $77 per month, that is the amount they pay monthly until the debt is satisfied.

Some contracts, however, provide for a frightening final surprise. When the debtor comes to the end of several years of the small monthly payments, he is confronted with one enormous payment of perhaps hundreds or occasionally even thousands of dollars. The payment has suddenly ballooned, thus the term "balloon contract," and unless he can produce the final lump sum, he is put into a squeeze: he faces either the loss of his possessions, sometimes including his house, or refinancing the debt, which means he is paying interest on interest, usually at exorbitant rates.

Some unscrupulous dealers use balloon contracts to deceive purchasers into signing up for merchandise they cannot afford, under the guise that it is "only a few dollars a month." In the District of Columbia one 56-year-old woman bought four air conditioners, worth about $970, for about $2,000. This scheme also involved duping homeowners into signing mortgages. The woman discovered later that unknown to her, in order to pay the debt, she had mortgaged her house for $5,800, on which she agreed to pay 7 percent interest in sixty monthly installments of $33.50, plus a final balloon payment of $5,000. Thus, in five years the woman could have paid off only $2,010, little more than the interest. At that time the creditor could foreclose on the house or refinance the loan.

Under the same financial arrangements, investigators determined that she would not have been able to pay off the debt in her lifetime. Thus, the creditor could have kept her debt-indentured, grinding out interest, and in the end taken the house. Fortunately, this woman arranged a settlement through court.

How people can be milked dry by balloon contracts was further illustrated by the case of another D. C. woman who had her debts consolidated by a company that advertises itself as "private bankers." She signed a balloon note for $3,000, but actually received only $1,500. Unable to pay, she was forced to refinance it with a finance company, this time signing a note for $5,290 and receiving less than $3,000; she understood she was to pay it off at sixty payments of $77; she was not aware of the final balloon payment of $1,800. As security for the loan, she had signed a deed of trust on her home, which she risked losing if she could not make the final payment. As that dread day drew near, a home-improvement salesman who just "happened to be in the neighborhood and noticed that her home needed repairs," dropped in one Sunday afternoon and, learning of her predicament, offered to make certain home improvements and pay off her other debts if she would sign a contract for $3,980. She did. The nature of this unconscionable racket was revealed when it was discovered that the man from the "bank" who gave her the first loan was a brother of the agent of the finance company who consolidated her second loan. And both of these were brothers of the director of the home-improvement company who coincidentally arrived just in time to "rescue" her by luring her deeper into debt.

Although it is possible that for some persons with seasonal occupations and irregular incomes the balloon contract is a convenience and its use may be justified in special instances, it should otherwise be forbidden. For it is misleading, is not executed in good faith, makes the signer vulnerable to unexpected disaster and perpetuates the debt treadmill. Its primary goal is clearly victimization.

One of the most outrageous methods of victimization is through the prorated or add-on contract. To be most lucrative, the scheme is worked this way: when the debt for one piece of merchandise is nearly paid off, the seller induces the customer to make another purchase, which is then added on to the original contract; when the balance is low again, he invites yet another purchase, also adding that to the contract, and so on. If the buyer defaults on a payment, after what can be years, the seller can repossess *all* of the merchandise listed on the contract, for instead of applying the payments to cancel out the debt on any one purchase, he has prorated them among all the purchases, leaving a small balance due on each item of merchandise.

In a famous case, *Williams v. Walker-Thomas Furniture Company* of Washington, D. C., Mrs. Ora Lee Williams beginning in 1957 bought several items from the store on installments. She faithfully made payments. In April 1962, when she had reduced her balance to $164, the store sold her a stereo record player for $514.95. Soon after she was unable to make payments, and the company fell back on a clause in her contract that stated: "All payments now and hereafter made by (purchaser) shall be credited pro rata on all outstanding leases, bills and accounts due the Company by (purchaser) at the time each such payment is made." The company then repossessed everything Mrs. Williams had bought from them since 1957. After $1,400 in payments, she was left with nothing. In a landmark decision, the court declared that the contract could be held unconscionable.

We should go further and declare that add-on contracts are legal only when payments are allocated equitably to assure the buyer that the items are being paid off. One method of accomplishing this would be to require that the payments be proportionate to the purchase price. For example, if a television set cost $200 and a chair cost $100, two-thirds of the monthly payment on the add-on contract would be applied to the television set and one-third to the chair. Items, as they were paid for in full, would no longer be subject to the contract. Surely, a seller should not be allowed to maintain equity in and control over merchandise that has actually been paid for.

REPOSSESSION

Our repossession laws must be amended to provide equal protection to the buyer. A repossession clause in a contract of a company in Washington, D. C., shows the appalling scope of the creditor's rights: ". . . in the event of a breach by the buyer of any provision herein contained, or in the event that the seller shall at any time deem itself or the goods, or any part thereof, for any reason, insecure, or unsafe, then in any such event the entire balance is due and owing under the terms and provisions of this agreement shall, at the option of the seller, be forthwith due and payable, and the seller shall have the right, with or without legal process, to retake the goods, no matter where they may be, and to retain them as its own property without obligation of resale, except as ex-

pressly provided by law, and without any duty to refund any part of the purchase price to the buyer and in such case do hereby waive and relinquish to and forever discharge said seller of and from all damages caused by entry or by such taking or removal of and from all claims by reason of such payments, entry, taking or removal. . . . The seller nevertheless shall have the right of resale for the account of the purchaser. In the event of a resale by the seller of the goods, or any part thereof, after a retaking, the proceeds of the resale shall be applied first to the payment of the expenses of retaking, keeping and reselling the goods, and then to the payment of the balance owing under this agreement; and if a deficiency results after such application, the buyer shall pay such deficiency."

Thus, we see that the seller can take back the merchandise if he believes it to be "insecure or unsafe," even though the purchaser faithfully keeps up payments. " 'Insecure' can mean the buyer is having domestic problems and the seller can repossess," says the former owner of a finance company. In many places the seller can repossess without any warning and by force. According to a judge in Texas, every debt-collection agency hires a crew to go out in the middle of the night and repossess cars off the street by breaking into them. "To repossess merchandise," reports an Ohio official, "creditors kick down doors, break windows and even threaten to take people to jail if they resist. The victims are usually poor and don't know their rights."

We should outlaw arbitrary repossession, permitting repossession *only* when the buyer is in default, and we should forbid sellers from using strong-arm methods, like trespassing, breaking and entering and using force in repossession. Such collection, if buyers will not voluntarily relinquish the merchandise, should be made through the legal process.

Our worst problem with repossession is the deficiency judgment, which is the amount the debtor must pay after he has returned the merchandise, it has been resold and the resale price has been deducted from his original debt. The exploitation carried on in the name of deficiency judgments is notorious. "Extortion pure and simple," is what Lt. Col. Clyde Griffith, a judge advocate at Fort Myer, Virginia, called it before a House Banking and Currency Subcommittee in 1965. He described how soldiers were gouged by deficiency judgments. The soldier buys a used car for $600. Car insurance plus credit life insurance and finance charges raise the total price to $1,200. After paying $200 the soldier decides he cannot continue payments; the company repossesses the car and promptly sells it to a dummy bidder for $200, which is subtracted from the $1,000 debt. The soldier has no car, but still owes $800, much of it for two or three years of credit charges and insurance that he has never even used. The company resells the car at $600 again, packing it with $600 worth of finance charges. Such cars can be sold over and over, producing enormous incomes in credit charges, and are called "Lassies" because they always come home. The same racket was used to exploit the buyers of the stoves in Cleveland through the "garnishment ring." Some of these stoves were sold three and four times, as new, leaving a string of victims, all paying off $800 on the same stove.

Theoretically the repossessed merchandise is sold to help the debtor raise money to pay off his debt. The seller is supposed to try to obtain the highest possible price. In truth, the seller often sells the merchandise dirt-cheap to an accomplice. Under some circumstances public auctions are not required for the sale of repossessed merchandise; the debtor is not told that he himself can redeem the merchandise by purchasing it himself; in some instances the creditor himself can buy the repossessed goods at a *private sale*.

Sometimes the merchandise is quickly repossessed. One man in the District of Columbia had his car repossessed within a week; he was left with an $800 deficiency judgment. In Chicago, a man whose used car was repossessed still had to pay 142 percent of the cash price. Other times the unscrupulous seller waits until the merchandise is nearly paid off before he takes it back. In any event, he ends up with both the merchandise and the full price, and the consumer ends up with nothing, although he has paid hundreds of dollars.

We all know that merchandise, especially a new car, depreciates in value after it is purchased. Within the first week a new car that cost $2,800 may drop in cash value to $2,200. Were a company to repossess this car, it would not bring enough at resale to recoup the loss. Therefore, the deficiency judgment does have a legitimate purpose: it assures the dealer that he will be *fairly* compensated, that he is entitled to the difference between the purchase price and the true market value should the buyer default. This we can agree with. But under present circumstances, some dealers are not being fairly compensated; they are being over-compensated. They are being reimbursed for far more than any true loss; they are in fact piling up enormous, unwarranted profits through deficiency judgments (mostly for unused credit charges) by using merchandise as bait. This situation is grossly unfair and is not in keeping with the intent of deficiency judgments.

First, it seems to me that when a buyer has paid at least one-half of the purchase price on a piece of merchandise, he should be considered its legal owner; and it should not be subject to repossession without a court order. At that time the judge could consider any temporary financial difficulties which had prevented regular payments. Second, we must bring the amount of deficiency judgments back into the realm of *fair* compensation for the dealer. In England, the courts will not uphold outrageous deficiency judgments. In refusing to enforce a 75 percent deficiency judgment in 1953, a judge declared that the amount was not a valid estimate of the damage caused to the seller by the buyer's breach of contract. Such a deficiency judgment, he insisted, was rather a penalty, "an extravagant and extortionate sum held *in terrorem* over the head of the [purchaser]," to force him to carry out the contract rather than to justly compensate the seller. The courts traditionally refuse to uphold penalty clauses in contracts. The maximum that the British law will allow to be collected on repossessed merchandise is *one-half* of the total price, including credit charges.

We should consider similar legislation, setting a maximum on the amount that could be extracted for repossessed merchandise. Additionally, one should not be made to pay for finance charges and insurance charges which he has not used. If a car, for example, is repossessed within six months, the buyer should not have to pay three years' worth of finance charges as may be called for in the original contract. Such charges should be prorated for the six months in a manner giving just compensation to the dealer. Furthermore, the creditor should not be permitted to buy back the merchandise himself, and his failure to give sufficient notice to the purchaser of his right to redeem the merchandise should be cause for a cancellation of the debt.

HOLDER IN DUE COURSE

The single factor most responsible for consumer injustices is the holder in due course doctrine. A New Jersey judge called it "the mask behind which fraud hides." Finance companies can work hand in hand with fraudulent operators, and unless it can be proved that the finance company is a knowing party, it cannot be held responsible, and the consumer must pay the fraudulent debt regardless. As we have seen, many moneylenders do not even investigate the companies from whom they buy consumer paper. Some buy at such high discounts that it would seem apparent that something is amiss. All banks and finance companies have the option of buying such consumer contracts and notes with defenses or without. "With defenses" the lender can in turn sue the seller if the contract was induced through misrepresentations or fraud, but many lenders buy "without defenses" (no right to sue) because the paper is cheaper and because they know they are invulnerable under the law, making them an innocent third party.

Our financing institutions should no longer be allowed to evade completely all responsibility for consumer deception.

At the very least, the holder in due course doctrine should be altered so that the purchaser is allowed (and is told so explicitly in the contract) fifteen days in which to notify the bank or finance company of any deception, fraud or other irregularities or complaints regarding his credit purchase. By notifying the lender of his dissatisfaction within the time period, the consumer would then be entitled to assert in court the same defenses—that is, fraud, misrepresentation—against the bank or finance company as he could against the seller. The consumer, within the limits of the provision, would not have to pay off fraudulent debts as he does now; he could go to court and obtain a cancellation of the contract.

Recognizing, however, that some cases of fraud would not be discovered within the fifteen-day period and that many consumers, through ignorance, would not assert their rights during the time limit, we should also give serious consideration to eliminating holder in due course altogether in consumer credit transactions, thus holding the financing institutions as equally reponsible as the sellers for their involvement in consumer deception.

Some lenders complain that they could not do business without the protection of holder in due course. This is nonsense. Four states—California, Maryland, Massachusetts and Vermont—have eliminated holder in due course protection on consumer sales, and finance companies are still extending credit. Outlawing holder in due course would shift the risks and responsibilities of doing business back to moneylending institutions, help obliterate the finance companies that cater almost exclusively to known fraudulent firms and make it more difficult for fraudulent dealers to obtain the needed financing to carry on business.

All of these debt-collection reforms would bring debtor laws up to date by reestablishing a legal basis for fair bargaining and at long last free consumers from their bondage to practices that force them to pay unjust debts and subject them to exploitation. Such reforms, by allowing the consumer to escape entrapment, will also make the practice of deception much less lucrative and attractive.

There is no single solution to our consumer ills, just as there is no single cause. Realistic laws, vigorous enforcement, consumer education, especially among the poor, and an increased responsibility in the ethical business community are all vital to combating consumer deception. Curtailing the activities of the unscrupulous and rectifying wrongs if deception does occur demand an organized resistance against the exploiters, based on the humane, common-sense philosophy that in a society like ours there is no place for the trickery and deceit by which deceptive merchants can drain the economy, drive people into debt, steal their homes, force them onto welfare and lay waste to their lives under the guise of "doing business."

The ghost of "caveat emptor," which pits buyer against seller in a malevolent relationship, should finally be laid to rest. It is no longer appropriate, is seriously damaging to society and surely is not conducive to engendering the trust and confidence necessary in today's complex marketplace.

PART TWO

CHAPTER FIVE

200,000,000 GUINEA PIGS

In May 1967, N.B.C.'s nationally known television news correspondent Peter Hackes came to testify before the Senate Commerce Committee of which I am the chairman. The previous year, Mr. Hackes's daughter Carole, then eleven, dropped a match onto a cotton blouse she was wearing. As Mr. Hackes described it: "It ignited immediately. At first it smoldered and when she beat at it it appeared to go out. Momentarily, however, there came a lick of flame—which again looked to be out each time she beat it. But within seconds it had flared up. Carole panicked and ran . . . my wife ran after her. The running only served to fan the flames, which produced a sort of shock reaction and screams of pain. Finally my wife caught up with the child and managed to wrap her up in a large towel. But even the big towel didn't seem to smother the flames, which were doused only when my wife stood the screaming girl in a tub and turned on the water of a cold shower. I was spared the original horror of the accident because I was away from home at the time [covering a Gemini space flight] but flew back immediately upon receiving an emergency telephone call. The events of May 15, 1966, are seared into the minds of . . . my family— and especially into Carole's—like the details of a nightmare."

Carole was burned over 15 percent of her body, from a point just above the navel to high on the front of her neck just under the chin. She was hospitalized for nine weeks, and often during that time while the Hackeses stood outside her room, they could hear her screams as the doctor administered the painful burn treatments. Carole received skin grafts and plastic surgery in attempts to lessen long, tendon-like welts of angry red on her neck. She is still undergoing plastic surgery and must wear high-necked clothes to hide the scars, which are a painful embarrassment to a little girl just entering her teens. Carole is also under a psychiatrist's care to help remove the emotional scars resulting from her disfigurement.

Mr. Hackes was convinced that Carole must have been wearing a highly flammable material, forbidden by law. "I assumed," he said, "that under law I was protected against any harmful item, be it an explosive toy, a poisoned food, a hazardous electrical fixture." He had the remains of Carole's burned blouse tested and was told it was just ordinary cotton, and perfectly "safe" under the Federal Government's Flammable Fabrics Act. "Nothing, in other words, can be done under existing law to prevent another Carole from having to undergo the same torture from a severe burn caused by the same or a similar fabric," said Mr. Hackes.

Why are there few public complaints about such hazardous items? "The simple reason," said Mr. Hackes, "is that consumers like me *think* we're buying *safe* products."

Undoubtedly, Mr. Hackes has expressed the belief of the vast majority of Americans: they think they are buying only safe products—the safest products technology knows how to produce—and that they are protected from hazardous products by the law. Regrettably, both of these suppositions are too often wrong. Many products are made with utmost safety in mind; but others are poorly designed with little attention to safety or are, despite a safe design, made hazardous through a manufacturing defect.

Although we have passed some legislation to keep hazardous products off the market, these laws are spotty, sometimes inadequate, and leave many products free of safety restrictions. There is, for example, no all-inclusive law—federal, state or municipal—which requires that *all* products be even reasonably safe, although we do have laws that prohibit the sale of specific hazardous products. Nor do our laws set even the barest safety standards on thousands of potentially dangerous products that are widely used, such as power lawn mowers. On some products we have regulated, such as flammable fabrics, the standards are so low as to be extremely ineffective, as Mr. Hackes's experience shows.

In view of the fact that accidents constitute a major health problem, it seems to me a tragic oversight that we have neglected such an elementary preventive measure as imposing reasonable safety standards on all products capable of causing death and injury.

According to National Safety Council figures, 60,000 persons this year will be killed in nonvehicular accidents, and about nine million, other than motorists, will suffer disabling accidental injuries—some serious and disfiguring. For persons aged one through thirty-six, accidents are the number-one cause of death. It is impossible to predict how many of these accidents will be fully or partially caused by a hazardous product; the National Safety Council only recently began to collect figures on product involvement.

We can, however, make a number of estimates from past experience. One hundred thousand persons will be mangled or killed while operating power mowers, countless others by tools in the workshop. About 100,000 persons will be cut, disfigured or fatally injured while walking through glass doors. Twelve thousand persons will die, and 150,000 will suffer excruciating pain and often lifelong scars from fires, resulting from a match or lighted cigarette dropped on flammable clothing or upholstery. At least 1,000 will be electrocuted and many more burned and injured by faulty electrical equipment. Babies will strangle in ill-designed cribs; women will be poisoned by the noxious fumes of cleaning fluids; whole families will be asphyxiated by carbon monoxide from faulty heaters; youngsters will be cut, blinded and killed by dangerously designed toys. The list could go on almost endlessly.

The obvious question at this point is to what extent do

these accidents result from human negligence and to what extent from the product itself. How one answers that question depends to a great degree on philosophy. For years, accident prevention efforts have focused on the individual's responsibility for an accident, and only rarely on the culpability of the product he was using. If a man is electrocuted by a defective power drill, he is at fault for not grounding it. (Says Morris Kaplan, technical director of Consumers Union: "We warn a man not to use a drill while standing in a puddle, although conceivably we could design one he could use safely while sitting in a bathtub.") If a child with a frilly dress backs into a space heater and is engulfed in flame, few stop to consider that the dress fabric may have been needlessly flammable; we blame the mother for failing to watch her. If a youngster gets his hand caught in the wringer of a washing machine, again it is not the machine's faulty design that is to blame; it is his parents' negligence.

We have, persistently, stubbornly, and I think the accident figures show, foolishly, pinned all our hopes for reducing the accident toll on the "educational" method alone: warning people to use a product safely while almost totally ignoring the greater potential for preventing misery—building safety into the product itself. No one could deny that there is a critical need for more educational efforts in accident prevention. But when the main thrust of our efforts is to save humans from injury and death, we cannot close our eyes to an obvious solution that will accomplish our declared purpose, probably with undreamed-of speed. To allow human suffering to continue when we *know* how to relieve it would be unaccountably irresponsible. A tiny miscalculation in judgment, a bit of ignorance, should not condemn a man to accidental death if humanity and technology can conceivably prevent it.

Products *should* be made as safely as we know how, within the bounds of practicality. And I am convinced that the American people share that point of view. We naturally assume that when American ingenuity invents a "better mousetrap," it is automatically adopted. It was evident during the automobile safety controversy in 1966, which resulted in safety devices for cars, that a great number of Americans were surprised to discover that auto safety devices patented as long ago as the 1930's had not been incorporated into automobiles.

Periodically, Congress has taken action in response to public demand for protection. In 1953, after the country had been shocked by deaths and burns from sweaters that went up like torches, we passed a Flammable Fabrics Act, outlawing such outrageously combustible materials. In 1956, Congress reacted to the pathetic problem of youngsters suffocating inside refrigerators by requiring that refrigerator doors be made so they can be opened from the inside. In 1960, we passed a Hazardous Substances Labeling Act, requiring stringent warnings on all hazardous household substances. In 1966 came the passage of the Automobile Safety Act mandating a number of safety devices on automobiles, after the public outcry, resulting from Congressional hearings and the revelations of safety critics, including Ralph Nader, author of the best-selling book *Unsafe At Any Speed.* That same year, after a number of people were burned by an explosive waterproofing substance, called X-33, and several youngsters were injured by flammable dolls and poisonous beads, we passed the Child Protection Act, prohibiting the sale of all substances and toys too hazardous for common usage.

Essential as these measures are, they still provide only an ineffective patchwork of safety. They still leave Americans totally unprotected from vast numbers of potentially injurious and deadly products. Moreover, such measures are born of indignation and tragedy. Predictably, unless we take a reasoned look at the whole spectrum of hazardous products, there will be more tragedies and more indignation, as the horror of another accident "epidemic" is uncovered. Is this really the most sensible way to handle such a life and death problem? Why can we not ferret out and correct the hazards in products *before* they cause injuries and death? After-the-fact protection is of little consolation to the millions who have already suffered. As I recently observed in the Senate: "If there is ever a situation in which hindsight outshines foresight it is in the field of accident prevention." It is time that we reverse the direction of our vision.

Unquestionably, there are unsafe products on the market.

In 1967, Consumers Union met with representatives of our Commerce Committee and prepared a ten-year summary of hazardous products. During that period CU found radios and television sets so poorly constructed that they leaked current sufficient to deal a powerful shock; kitchen ranges, broilers, clothes dryers, portable heaters and a dehumidifier with dangerously exposed electrical terminals; power tool attachments without safety guards; power saws which could be inadvertently started; food waste disposers which spewed out objects at high speeds; garden sprayers which could explode; travel irons without fire-preventing thermostats, and children's toys with metal edges sharp enough to cut. In all, 376 products were rated by CU as Not Acceptable for ordinary household use. These products were not confined to fly-by-night firms; some came from the most reputable manufacturers in the country.

Underwriters' Laboratories, an independent testing laboratory in Chicago, reports that it rejects 50 percent of all new products it tests as being too hazardous to meet UL standards. How many of these hazardous products are marketed anyway without the UL approval is unknown. Undoubtedly, it is a substantial number. Of course, some manufacturers do not even submit their products to UL tests, for they *know* their product is not safe enough to qualify.

If we need dramatic proof that hazardous products are being taken into homes, we need only look at the recent colossal error in color television sets. In May 1967, the General Electric Company announced a search for 90,000 large-screen color television models that had been on the market for six months, from September 1966 through February 1967. It was discovered that the sets, during a redesign of the chassis, had been equipped with a small shunt voltage-regulator tube that gave off excessive X-rays through the bottom of the set. Some of the tubes were found to emit 50,000 millirocntgens an hour, or 100,000 times as much radiation as the maximum safe allowance of 0.5 milliroentgens per hour, recommended by the National Council on Radiation Protection. NCRP officials agreed that "anyone immediately in front of an offending set could be exposed" to excessive doses of radiation. There is no evidence that anyone was in fact harmed, and some authorities doubt that individuals were sufficiently exposed as to cause bodily damage. But radiation damage can be cumulative, causing cataracts, leukemia, congenital defects in offspring and sterility which may not be evident for years. Radiation from medical or dental X-rays cannot be avoided entirely, but that from TV sets can be. There is no excuse for a set that emits *any* measurable radiation.

When, in the summer of 1967, Congressional committees in both houses held hearings to probe the GE incident, more alarming facts came to light, showing the inadequacy of control over this awesome hazard. Hanson Blatz, director of the Office of Radiation Control of the New York Department of Health, told us on the Senate Commerce Committee that there were dozens of other devices that emitted radiation above desirable levels, including wrist and pocket watches with luminous faces; a variety of novelties given a luminous coating of radium to make them glow; voltage rectifier tubes; imported radioactive blankets, bandages and electric heating pads which contain radium and are sold as quick cures to arthritis victims.

Unlike other states, New York has a law enabling it to seize such dangerous items. A few years ago, Blatz's office learned that pocket watches with luminous faces giving off excessive radiation were being sold in New York, especially to children. Often the youngsters carried the watches right next to their abdomens, face-in, just a few inches from the reproductive organs. When studies showed that the exposure to the organs was considerably higher than permissible limits,

New York officials banned the watches from the market. The manufacturers immediately started shipping their merchandise to other states without such regulations. Although Blatz believes that manufacture of the watches has been discontinued, no one can be sure; and there is nothing to stop other manufacturers from knowingly or unknowingly producing equally harmful items to irradiate unsuspecting children.

Another disturbing thought raised by the GE incident is: how many other dangerous assembly-line mistakes or design errors go completely undetected or are never called to public attention? Prior to legislation in 1966 setting federal safety standards on automobiles, it was steadfastly maintained that mechanical defects caused only an infinitesimal number of accidents. Data collected by the National Safety Council revealed mechanical failure as the cause of only 2 to 3 percent of the motor vehicle accidents. A new study in California, released in 1967, in which accident wreckage was meticulously examined, showed that 18 to 20 percent of the accidents investigated were related to mechanical failure.

Between August 1966, when we passed the auto safety legislation, and December 1967, automobile manufacturers recalled *five million cars* for possible mechanical defects. Are we to believe that these potentially deadly mistakes are unique to the automobile industry? It would be incredible if production errors were concentrated solely in Detroit. It is more believable that if faults are appearing with such frequency on the assembly lines of auto manufacturers, they are also occurring with equal magnitude in the plants manufacturing other products, although we never hear of them. Beneath a chilling episode like that of the color television sets may lie a massive iceberg of dangerous mistakes that go forever unexposed.

Hardly a day passes when I and my staff do not hear of a new hazardous product.

A minister in New Orleans wrote, telling how his infant son was killed in a poorly designed crib. The crib was nylon mesh, with a hinged top which could be snapped shut. The baby wedged his head between the hinged top and the side of the crib. He was caught by the neck and strangled.

In Rochester, New York, recently, a three-year-old boy climbed into a clothes dryer and pulled the door shut after him. The dryer started automatically, tumbling him round and round in the intolerable heat. He died later from the burns and bruises. As the National Safety Council pointed out, "This accident could not have happened if all dryer manufacturers followed the example of the few whose machines turn off when the door is opened, and don't restart until a button is pushed on the control panel."

In Iowa, a newly born infant suffocated from smoke when the plastic top of a nearby vaporizer melted and started a fire.

It was discovered in January 1967 that 1,000 lamps capable of producing serious shock and starting fires had been sold in Kansas City stores. The lamps were designed to be rendered safe by a transformer; but the transformer had been left off.

During 1967, "sonic boom" toys were being sold that should never have been allowed on the market in the first place. After testing a Sonic Blaster resembling a bazooka, Consumers Union reported that the toy fired compressed air with a "deafening" blast, and could permanently impair the hearing of a youngster using it or that of a person standing in front of the muzzle. Advised *Consumer Reports:* "If your child has one, the only sensible course is to throw it out. But destroy it first so that it will not fall into the hands of some other child."

Recently, my own wife purchased a bottle of carbon tetrachloride cleaning fluid in a District of Columbia drugstore. Before it was opened, we discovered that breathing the vapors given off by carbon tetrachloride is so hazardous that it has been banned from the premises of virtually all industrial plants and commercial dry-cleaning plants.

Carbon tet, as it is called, is so poisonous that the evaporation of only three thimblefuls of the chemical in a ten-foot-square room can make the air dangerous to breathe. Inhalation of carbon tetrachloride vapors has in countless instances caused dizziness, nausea, liver damage and complete kidney collapse, leading to death. In New York City, a seven-year-old girl who sat on a chair that had recently been cleaned with carbon tetrachloride became violently ill within hours. When rushed to the hospital, she was near death because her kidneys had stopped functioning. She recovered after six weeks in the hospital.

For a medical reason, not fully understood, carbon tetrachloride is especially dangerous to persons who have been drinking alcohol. One woman who used the chemical as a spot remover on a suit which she subsequently wore that night to a cocktail party experienced kidney failure after having but one drink. A Coast Guard officer, who had consumed several drinks the night before, died after he inhaled carbon tetrachloride which his wife had used in the room where he slept.

Most of industry gave up using carbon tetrachloride as a solvent in the 1940's because too many employees using it developed cirrhosis of the liver and kidney and brain damage. Many doctors warn that no one, and particularly those with kidney and liver ailments, should ever use carbon tetrachloride in the house, especially since the danger is so needless. There are many comparatively nontoxic cleaning fluids on the market, of the type used by commercial dry-cleaning firms. Yet, in August 1967, a spot check in the Washington, D. C., area showed that thirteen out of fifteen drugstores carried carbon tetrachloride for home use.

Some products—such as carbon tetrachloride, in my opinion—are simply too hazardous for common use. (And in the special instance of carbon tetrachloride, under the Child Protection Act governing all hazardous *substances,* the Secretary of Health, Education and Welfare could remove the chemical from the market if he, after a hearing, determined that it was too toxic for ordinary safe usage.) Other products, like the GE television sets, may be unsafe because of a production defect. The majority of injury-producing products, however, are not ones we think of as being so extraordinarily hazardous that we would desire to live without them; they are, on the contrary, acceptable everyday products which are potentially hazardous and could be designed more safely.

Even a cursory examination of a few products reveals that simple design changes could eliminate a number of accidents. In some instances the design improvement is so simple and inexpensive that it is tragic it was not required years ago. A classic case of neglect is the wringer washing machine.

Contrary to what most of us may think, the wringer washer is still very much a part of the American scene. Millions of them are still in use, mainly in lower economic areas, and 500,000 new ones were sold in 1966. Every year, about 100,000 children and an equal number of adults undergo the horror of seeing their hands, fingers, arms and clothing being caught and fed through the turning rollers. Many injuries are minor—bruises and lacerations. Many others—one in six, estimates one doctor—are "crushing injuries to the soft tissues and muscle, erosion of the superficial and deep structures of the skin, fractures of the bones and occasional fatalities." Many injuries result in massive swelling and lifelong scars; and the emotional trauma to child-victims is immeasurable, say doctors.

Yet, since the late 1940's, the manufacturers of wringer washing machines have had available to them a simple "instinctive" safety release which would virtually eliminate these cruel injuries. A youngster rarely is tall enough, strong enough or has the presence of mind to operate the old-fashioned bar or lever on the sides of the wringer, which require a considerable blow before the rollers separate. With the instinctive release, a tug of a mere twelve pounds, as the child "instinctively" tries to withdraw his hand, causes the rollers to stop and come apart. The cost to the manufacturer for such a safety device is two dollars. Considering the small cost of the device and the magnitude of the problem, it is appalling then to discover that in 1966, about 60 percent of all new wringer washing machines put on the market did *not* possess this release.

At the urging of doctors, both Underwriters' Laboratories and the new United States of America Standards Institute (USASI, formerly the American Standards Association) plan to adopt a new standard, calling for an instinctive release on wringer washing machines. Reportedly, all manufacturers are preparing to meet this standard voluntarily by October 1968 when it becomes effective, although they are not required to do so by law. Surely, this action is welcome; however, about two million children would have been saved from injury had this device been incorporated when it first appeared.

Another case in point is the glass in patio doors, storm doors and shower doors. It is hardly a modern discovery that glass cuts viciously when a person breaks through it. For thirty years the windshields of our automobiles have been made of laminated safety glass, a sandwich of two sheets of glass with a middle layer of tough plastic. If broken, the laminated glass, instead of exploding into sharp pieces, tends to stick together. The side windows of automobiles contain tempered safety glass, which is three to five times stronger than ordinary or laminated glass and, when broken, crumbles into virtually harmless granules. Our knowledge in the auto field, however, did not carry over when we brought large expanses of glass into homes.

Much of the glass installed in sliding glass doors is only three-sixteenths of an inch thick, about twice the thickness of an ordinary windowpane. Every year, according to U. S. Public Health Service biostatisticians, about 100,000 persons are injured, some fatally, from walking or running into these doors, which appear to be open. The glass shatters viciously and sometimes loosens from the frame at the top and "comes crashing down on the victim like a guillotine." One little girl in Ohio was so badly cut after walking against a sliding glass door that her face required one hundred stitches. A man in Florida lost an eye after it was punctured by a flying splinter of glass from a shattering door. A teenage girl in Washington State dashed from the front porch to the living room to answer the phone and crashed through a glass panel; an artery in her leg was severed and she bled to death.

As early as 1961, safety officials pointed out that such injuries were needless, that they could be prevented by the use of safety glass in the doors. The extra cost to the consumer for tempered glass in a typical six-foot sliding glass door is but $10 to $13, in a storm door, $5 to $7. Only Washington and Los Angeles have passed laws requiring that all sliding glass doors in new and remodeled homes be safety glazed. In 1967, more than a million sliding glass doors were put into new construction and remodeled buildings. Despite vigorous campaigns for safety glass by the Architectural Aluminum Manufacturers Association and by public health and safety officials, many contractors are reportedly still installing highly dangerous glass doors.

Similarly, it seems apparent that all shower doors, where a person is particularly vulnerable to slipping, should be made of safety glass or plastic. Yet, a woman in Chicago wrote me in June 1967 that when she ordered a safety-glass shower enclosure for a remodeled home, it was a special order and took ten weeks to arrive.

No single household product holds such potential for human destruction as the power lawn mower, notably the rotary mower with its whirling blade that can amputate fingers, toes, hands and feet; and hurl wire, rocks, glass, nails and all manner of debris at speeds approaching that of a bullet. So fantastic is the force that bits of wire have been driven completely through the skull and fragments of glass have penetrated the heart.

Our defenses against this machine are severely limited. We are told to "get people, especially children, out of the way when mowing." Some objects, however, are hurled long distances, through windows and into neighbors' yards. One little boy was struck unconscious by a rock that was hurled fifty-five feet by a mower. In another instance a stick thrown by a mower went through the open window of a passing car, puncturing the eye of a passenger.

Eliminating such injuries by "properly cleaning the lawn before mowing," as we are instructed to do, is not entirely practicable. A quick tour of the lawn to check for debris might be a reasonable precaution; but it seems to me if one has to go over an entire lawn to remove every small stone and two-inch piece of wire that might be embedded in the grass, one might as well cut the lawn with scissors.

The caveat "always wear shoes when using a power mower" seems sensible enough, but is of little value when the high-horsepower engines rotate the blades at speeds great enough to slice through leather. One man had all the toes of his right foot amputated when he pulled a mower over his heavy engineering boot; the blade neatly sliced through the boot at mid-foot, severing a leather sole an inch thick.

For years we have been warned to turn off the motor when adjusting the blade or leaving the mower. Yet, thousands of children are maimed by getting caught in mowers left unattended, and thousands of adults have their fingers amputated when trying to remove grass and other debris from the housing while the blades are whirling.

Obviously then, with 80,000 Americans being hideously injured by these mowers every year, our futile efforts at education are no substitute for drastically needed safety improvements in the mower itself. In 1965, the University of Iowa's Institute of Agricultural Medicine noted in its study of power mower accidents: "The power mower that can perform with ease, power and optimum safety has yet to be put on the market. . . . Today's machine is potentially as dangerous as the first model."

It seems incredible that in all these years (the rotary mower came into popular use soon after World War II), American ingenuity has not been able to devise some method to confine dangerous objects within the mower's housing. L. W. Knapp, Jr., director of the University of Iowa's power mower study, says tests confirm that the lower the housing, the less the threat of expelled objects, and that "closing the housing clearance at the rear of the mower [perhaps by some sort of dragging apron] would stop the expulsion of objects to the rear altogether." The discharge chute on some mowers is angled toward the rear, making the operator a direct target for expelled objects. Some discharge chutes are aimed at an undesirably high angle, shooting projectiles out in high arcs, when a lower angle would tend to send them skittering harmlessly across the ground. Riding mowers are notoriously unstable; many have toppled over, trapping their occupants underneath. Moreover, few riding mowers have leakproof gasoline caps (which cost about two cents extra); thus, in case of tippage, gas could drop down onto the hot manifold and ignite. Additionally, controls on the mowers are not uniform; on one mower the brake may be on the left, on another, on the right.

Blades can undoubtedly be made safer. Said the Iowa report: "The blade should be designed to stop automatically any time the operator releases the handle or leaves the seat," just as an automatic clothes dryer stops when the door is opened. Investigators also noted that the high speeds of the blade are unnecessary. Tests show that the blade cuts grass just as well at 11,000 rpm as at the commonly used 21,000 rpm. A reduction in the blade speed would reduce the force with which objects are hurled and lessen the blade's ability to cut through protective clothing and tissue.

Recently, power mower manufacturers have become increasingly aware of the need to improve the safety of their mowers. The Outdoor Power Equipment Institute, Inc., a trade association which includes those companies manufacturing 86 percent of the power mowers in the country, has made commendable efforts to upgrade the design of mowers by sponsoring research, setting higher safety standards for members to follow and granting a "safety seal" to be used on all mowers meeting the standards. The results of their efforts, unfortunately, were somewhat marred when it was discovered that some OPEI members were irresponsibly affixing the new safety seal to mowers that did *not* meet the prescribed standards. Being a voluntary organization, OPEI has no means of policing its members, although inspection procedures to prevent such future misuse have been initiated.

Preventing electrical shock also has not been approached from the most practical point of view. Traditionally, we are told to avoid shock by "grounding the tool and not using electrical equipment around water." Grounding portable tools is undependable on two-wire systems and most homes do not have three-hole outlets to accommodate the third grounding wire on new tools. A better solution is double insulation, in which the manufacturer encloses the shock-producing interior of the product in two layers of insulation instead of the usual one. If the regular insulation breaks down, there is a second line of defense to prevent current leakage. Portable drills, hedge clippers, lawn mowers, sanders, saws, floor scrubbers, can be made with double insulation.

A surprising number of household appliances, as illustrated by the Consumers Union analysis of product testing, leak excessive current, enough to give a significant jolt. Morris Kaplan of CU points out that the threat of shock on some appliances could be eliminated by repositioning a component or by inserting an insulating washer between the component and the metal parts that extend to the outside casing. In old-fashioned ceiling lights, operated by a pull chain, one wooden insulating link was inserted midway in the metal chain to prevent a wayward current from coursing the full length of the chain. The same principle could be applied to appliances, such as radios. The cost of the insulating washers: about one-fourth of a cent apiece.

Recently, a New York attorney told me of some tragic cases of electrical accidents, caused not by products inside the house, but by overhead wires outside the house. He branded power lines as a far greater threat than is generally appreciated. On the heels of his remark, like a tragic punctuation mark, came a horrible accident on June 2, 1967, in North Springfield, Virginia. Six soldiers from nearby Ft. Belvoir were electrocuted en masse in a "blue-white flash" when the tip of a forty-foot flagpole they were erecting in an athletic field fell against a roadside power line which carried 7,200 volts of electricity. It was a scene of horror, as described by a newspaper account: "There was this big flash and then the GI's were just lying there in the mud with their clothes on fire." Reportedly, "one of the men held onto the pole after he fell. The hands of the others remained outstretched and cupped, as though frozen in the positions they held when the lethal charge coursed down the pole." All six were electrocuted instantaneously.

The power line was a standard aluminum cable of nineteen strands with a diameter of three-quarters of an inch, commonly known as a "distribution" line, of the type that leads from power poles into homes. The line was not insulated, a precaution that would have prevented the fatal contact; it was not legally required to be insulated, and thousands of miles of such potentially deadly lines are not. Few municipalities demand the wires be wrapped in shock-preventing insulation; and the National Electrical Code does not even *recommend* that distribution lines be insulated. "Because of this," says William Meese of the National Bureau of Standards, "and because the insulation requires extra cost—about one and one-half times as much as uninsulated wires initially and unknown replacement costs when the insulation wears off—*fewer and fewer distribution lines are being insulated.*"

An alternative to insulation which would guarantee public safety is burying the lines. This is usually not done unless communities' codes require it, and they sometimes do so, primarily for aesthetic reasons. Yet, the cost of putting distribution lines safely under ground decreased in the last decade from being ten times as costly as putting them overhead to one and one-half times as costly. (Distribution lines, those strung between telephone poles and from poles into houses, are distinguished from high-power transmission lines which carry high voltages of power across great distances. It is difficult to insulate and bury the latter lines, for the power is so great the insulation burns off.)

Unfortunately, a statistical breakdown of precisely how

many injuries or deaths are caused by high-power lines is unavailable. A clue to the magnitude of the hazard, however, is revealed by a survey done by Underwriters' Laboratories during the first eleven months of 1966. Of 138 electrocutions reported in newspaper clippings received by UL, 65, or 47 percent, were caused by overhead power lines. Thus, if the UL sample can be accurately projected, approximately *one-half* of all electrocutions in this country involve high-power lines. And that figure does not include injuries, which are often severe burns. One New York boy who came in contact with a dangling high-power line received such severe burns that one of his legs and an arm had to be amputated.

Although many who are injured or killed by power lines are utility company employees, a significant number are the general public: youngsters flying model planes, do-it-yourselfers erecting TV antennas which fall across the house wires. A sampling from UL's 1966 survey shows:

January: "Two men electrocuted—TV antenna being erected comes in contact with high-power line."

February: "Youth electrocuted while flying model airplane which nose-dived into 7,200 volt power line."

April: "Boy, six, electrocuted; touches 4,800 volt line while climbing tree."

October: "Five-year-old boy electrocuted—touches dangling power line" and "Boy electrocuted—makes contact with power lines downed in auto accident."

November: "Man electrocuted—climbs utility pole and touches wire."

There is no clear-cut answer to the dimensions of this hazard, but it is surely significant enough to deserve further investigation. We should determine why fewer of these power lines are being insulated or buried, despite decreasing costs, and why the utility companies are not exercising due caution for the lives of their employees and the general public.

On a moment's reflection, one could suggest dozens of design improvements to prevent accidents. One would be safety enclosures on medicine bottles, particularly children's flavored aspirin, which is the number-one poison hazard, accounting for 120,000 cases of accidental ingestion every year. (The so-called safety cap now on babies' aspirin bottles is easily removed; youngsters simply pry it off with their teeth.) A special committee for the Food and Drug Administration is considering a number of safety closure designs for recommendation to manufacturers. Other design improvements include:

The elimination of sharp edges on children's toys and the routine use of painted or felt eyes on stuffed toys instead of the old-fashioned "harpoon" eyes, which are simply stuck in the toy with a long pin or sharp piece of metal.

Narrower spaces between the slats in babies' playpens and cribs so it is impossible for the baby to wedge his head through the openings.

Outside air vents on all heaters intended for use indoors; some heaters come without vents on them and have caused carbon monoxide poisoning.

The removal of the hard, brittle plastic steering wheels from children's car seats, or their replacement by soft plastic. In accidents, the hard plastic often shatters and cuts a child's face.

Curl-up cords on electric coffee pots, instead of the long dangling ones that youngsters can grab, tipping the scalding liquid onto themselves.

Eyeglasses with lenses of shatterproof glass and nonflammable frames. Some frames made of cellulose nitrate literally explode in flames. One man, as he lit a cigar, suffered facial burns when the frame of his glasses "went up like a rag soaked in gasoline."

The possibilities are many. But nowhere is the need for upgrading safety standards more critical than in the flammability of fabrics.

About one million persons, according to the U.S. Public Health Service, suffer burn injuries every year, and estimates indicate that flammable clothing is implicated in about 150,000 of these burns. In addition, of the 6,000 persons who die every year in home fires—2,000 of them children—an inestimable number are victims of poisonous smoke produced by combustible interior furnishings that "feed the fire."

Few people appreciate how flammable ordinary clothing fabrics are. It is not an exotic cloth that is most often implicated in clothing-fire burns, but most often plain ordinary cotton. An analysis by the Academy of Pediatrics and the National Fire Protection Association in 1964 revealed that of 84 clothing-fire burns, fully 75 percent were due to the ignition of cotton and rayon. Partly accountable for this fact is that cotton is our most widely used fabric. However, through tests, the study also confirmed what is generally unappreciated among the public: that cotton is also the *fastest-burning* fabric in common use. Samples of the clothing causing the burns were collected by the academy and ignited. Cotton went up the fastest: one swatch ignited in one second, as compared with seven seconds required to light a sample from a wool sweater. (Wool, in fact, is our slowest burning natural fiber.) Synthetics, such as dacron and nylon, were also harder to ignite and slower to burn than cotton. In summary, the academy reported:

"Although most persons believe new synthetics are more flammable than cotton, the opposite is generally true. Rayon is not any more flammable than cotton, while all other synthetics are less flammable and some will hardly burn at all."

This does not mean, however, that synthetics are incapable of producing burns. Some nylons often melt and stick to the skin like molten lava, giving deep penetrating burns long after the flame has been extinguished.

Most of us have an abiding faith in the miracles of modern medicine: the belief that if the burns are not prevented, at least they can be healed. Thus, it is sobering indeed to hear the grim prognostications by many doctors about clothing-fire injuries. Burns are considered our most difficult injury to treat. During the hearings to amend the Flammable Fabrics Act, Dr. Abraham B. Bergman, director of the Outpatient

Services at the Children's Orthopedic Hospital and Medical Center in Seattle, told of the medical profession's helplessness in treating burn victims:

"The treatment of burns remains completely unsatisfactory despite advances in other fields of medicine. We haven't materially improved the survival rate in over thirty years, nor have we done much to alter morbidity. The best plastic surgery still leaves terrible scars. Our modern treatment of shock has merely meant that patients die three weeks after their burn rather than three days. Perhaps we can save an occasional life by some treatment methods that have recently come on the scene—but there is little hope on the horizon that medical science will materially alter this grim picture."

Dr. Bergman told of a recent tragedy: "Three weeks ago in Richmond, Washington, a little 2½-year-old girl, Suzanne, was playing in the living room with an older sister. The sister rushed into her parents' bedroom crying, 'Suzy's on fire!' Indeed she was! When her mother reached Suzy, she was a human torch. It was the all-too-familiar story. She was wearing a flannel nightgown, and there was a space heater in the room. She sustained full thickness burns (third degree) over 85 percent of her body. The only areas spared were her lower legs and feet. I have pictures of Suzy here with me, but have elected not to show them to you—there is no point. I didn't even have the heart to take my medical students into the room last week, because she looked so horrible.

"It was apparent from the moment we saw Suzy that she must inevitably die—the question was only how long it would take. In cases such as this I earnestly pray that the end comes sooner, rather than later. I spoke with the parents every day, attempting to comfort them and prepare them for the outcome. Understandably [the father], a patrolman in a small town, and his wife had a difficult time accepting this. What finally seemed to help was their eventual realization that were a miracle to ensue, her life, after surviving such a severe burn, would be worse than death.

"In all honesty I must say that I do not consider it a triumph when the life of a severely burned child is saved. A lifetime of operations, pain, disfigurement, scarring, and rejection by society and self lie ahead. Death may be more merciful."

Over and over, doctors see these hopeless cases: Margot, four and a half, whose nightgown sleeve caught fire while she played with a cigarette lighter, had her entire right arm and right side of her face permanently scarred; Ronnie, three, who stretched his arm over a stove burner, igniting his flannel pajamas, suffered burns of 70 percent of his body; Lynda, a beautiful teenage girl, who will never be beautiful again, had the edge of her frilly nightgown caught by a space heater and she ran, fanning the flames; a woman, eighty-three, attempting to cook for herself, brushed the sleeve of her cotton dress over a burner and was fatally burned; a man in his seventies, confined to a wheelchair, accidentally ignited his shirt while smoking and was helpless to rescue himself. An estimated 55 percent of all clothing-fires happen to youngsters under nine and to those over seventy-five.

Dr. Bergman tells of a boy now eighteen, who has been in the hospital thirteen separate times for a total of 130 days since he was burned at age fourteen months when his clothing brushed against a stove, burning him over 60 percent of his body. The boy quit school at age twelve because of his appearance and for the last four years has been a ward of the juvenile court. Another boy, sixteen, was severely burned at age four, failed in school and is under psychiatric care after being arrested for indecent exposure.

Not only are the human costs intolerable, but the costs of attempting to treat burn patients are astronomical. The cost for treating an acute burn patient runs about $100 a day, and the victim usually must remain hospitalized for months, with periodic returns. It is not unusual for a bill for the treatment of one burned youngster to reach $30,000. The cost of many victims' treatment must be absorbed by public funds.

Is not this problem of clothing burns another dramatic example of our backward approach to accident prevention?

We cry for more doctors to treat burned patients, more hospital facilities, more public funds, more medical research—all to alleviate this mountain of human suffering and waste, when right now we could take positive steps to *prevent* it by insisting on the use of fabric that does not turn youngsters' clothing into fiery torches.

Safety messages on the dangers of clothing-fires must sound hollow indeed to parents whose children have been killed or disfigured by burning clothing. As Dr. Bergman said: "I believe accidents will always be with us, and it doesn't do much good to be morally indignant about how they occur, particularly when they involve children. . . . Surely we must increase our efforts in safety education, but not use calls for safety education, which cost little and hurt no one, as a rapier to fend off action which will be more effective in achieving the end result. . . . What is needed to prevent serious burn injuries is clothing which does not readily support combustion."

The outcry against flammable fabrics is hardly new. In 1861, after the wife of Henry Wadsworth Longfellow was burned to death when her muslin dress caught fire, *Scientific American* magazine urged "the preparation of ladies' dresses with nonflammable material." More than one hundred years later, however, clothing of noncombustible fabrics is still not generally available to the public, although many such fabrics are technologically possible. Certain types of cotton materials can be successfully treated with chemicals to make them noncombustible. A number of synthetic fabrics have been created which because of their chemical composition are nearly impossible to ignite: for example, Dynel, developed by Union Carbide Corp.; Verel, from Eastman Chemical Products, Inc.; Nomex, by DuPont; fiberglass, made by several companies.

A demonstration before our consumer subcommittee by William V. White of the Accident Prevention Division of the U. S. Public Health Service, dramatically showed the life-saving properties of these fabrics. Mr. White produced two swatches of white cotton, one treated and one untreated. He touched a match flame to the ordinary cotton; it caught fire instantly and was quickly consumed in flame. (I am convinced that the average person would be not a little enlightened to see how readily and brightly cotton shoots up in flame.) Mr. White then applied a flame to the cotton swatch which had been commercially impregnated with a fire-retardant chemical called THPC. Although he held the flame to a corner of the cotton for several seconds, it would not ignite; the only sign of flame damage was a slight charring.

The chemical THPC treatment was developed fifteen years ago, in 1953, at the U. S. Department of Agriculture's Southern Regional Research Laboratory in New Orleans. It is true that this chemical additive is not the final answer for rendering *all* cottons flame-retardant. For, although there is no question of the treated cotton's durability (it will withstand 75 to 100 washings without losing its flame-retardancy), the treatment does result in a slight harshness and stiffness and added weight to the fabric, making it unsuitable for use in garments where softness and light weight are desired. The treatment also causes white cotton when bleached to turn slightly yellow.

In an attempt to overcome these objections, the USDA's Laboratory has developed a variation of the treatment, called THPOH. In September 1967, USDA researchers announced that with the THPOH formula, light-weight cotton fabrics can be treated without "an appreciable difference in hand." ("We have treated cotton fabrics as light weight as that in an Indian sari without a significant change in hand," says George Drake, head of USDA's special finishes investigation.) However, some weight is added by the new treatment—about 16 percent on gingham and 13 percent on sateen. There is no yellowing of the treated fabric during bleaching.

Additionally, the American Viscose Division of FMC Corporation has developed a fire-retardant treatment in which a phosphate chemical is injected into rayon fiber at the time it is manufactured. Since this results in a chemical displacement instead of a chemical add-on, the treatment causes no change in weight or hand of the material and thus could be used in all garments, even the most frilly. The Ciba Chemical and Dye Company, too, among other companies, is working on a new chemical treatment for nonflammable cotton which reportedly is extremely successful.

It is apparent that more research in the laboratories and testing in the mills are needed before the process of flame-retardancy for cotton is perfected, and all cotton garments can be made noncombustible on a wide commercial scale. Nevertheless THPC-treated cloth right now is suitable for heavy and medium weight cotton items. Army fliers in Vietnam are wearing suits of fire-retardant cotton. So are workers in steel mills, where molten metal could ignite clothing. Sears Roebuck and Co. offers sweat shirts made fire-safe with THPC. A number of articles of clothing—dresses, pajamas, robes—have been made up for children, as experimental models in this country. And in England, now, children are wearing cotton sleepwear—robes, pajamas, gowns—treated with Proban, a THPC process. Since October 1964, Great Britain has required by law that all sleeping garments designed to be sold to youngsters under age thirteen be fire-retardant. In addition, THPC flame-retardant draperies and cubicle curtains are being used in hospitals and nursing homes here and abroad. That we are not able to buy more items made from these lifesaving materials is regrettable. The extra retail cost of treated cotton items is about 20 percent and would be lower under mass production.

In his demonstration, Mr. White also proved with the match test that a number of the new synthetic fabrics will not readily support combustion, or even char.

Racing car drivers and the U. S. Forestry Department's smoke-jumpers who parachute into forest fires are wearing suits of flameproof Nomex. Verel is found in coats, slippers, carpets and rugs. After the tragic deaths of the three astronauts in the space capsule fire, suits for astronauts are now being made from fireproof fiberglass.

Mr. White in his demonstration again revealed that the lifesaving fruits of our technology can be purchased overseas —in England—but not in this country. Mr. White displayed a child's red robe, made of Verel. This robe will not burn or even char; it is virtually impossible to ignite with a match flame. Yet, this robe, made of material shipped from Eastman Chemical Products in Tennessee, is being worn by British children to save them from burns; it cannot be purchased anywhere in this country to protect our own children.

Too little attention has been given to the role of flammable fabrics in spreading fire and causing death from smoke inhalation. We know that a fire in a home must have something to feed on or it would go out; normally, that fuel is flammable draperies, carpeting, chair coverings, beddings and especially mattresses. The absence of combustible interior furnishings would prevent many fires. In addition, countless lives would be saved by the use of nonflammable fabrics for upholstery and bedding.

It is not generally known that the real killer in a home fire is not the flames, but poisonous smoke, produced by the burning combustibles. Actually, many of the dead are carried out of a fire without a burn on their bodies; according to some indications as many as 80 percent of all persons who die in fires are asphyxiated by poisonous smoke. Tests have shown that burning interior furnishings can give off at least a dozen poisonous gases, including carbon monoxide, hydrocyanic acid, hydrogen sulfide, ammonia and phosgene.

The number-one home fire hazard is smoking, causing an estimated 200,000 fires annually and the loss of 1,200 lives. A dropped cigarette burns through upholstery or a mattress and smolders in the stuffing, sometimes for hours, producing streams of odorless, invisible poisonous gases, before bursting into flame. Tests conducted by the Los Angeles Fire Department revealed that a smoldering chair will fill a room with a knockout concentration of carbon monoxide within an hour, without raising the temperature above a comfortable 70 degrees.

In such fires, the victims die quietly, often in their sleep. Not long ago in Michigan, firemen found a man and his wife and two children in their upstairs bedrooms, lying peacefully in their beds. All four had been asphyxiated by a fire that had started downstairs in the den and never spread from that room. A smoldering couch, ignited by a cigarette, had given off lethal gases which had risen silently, flooding the top floors of the house.

This tragedy would not have occurred if the couch had been covered with a fire-retardant fabric to prevent the cigarette from burning through into the stuffing.

Fireproof draperies, pillows, bedspreads, upholstery, carpeting—of fiberglass or other nonburn synthetics and of all patterns and prices (draperies from $4.98 to custom-made $400)—are now available in some stores. Dealers, however, have been reluctant to advertise this lifesaving property, under the old theory that "safety doesn't sell," and shoppers have a difficult time even finding a label indicating an item is "fireproof." Dealers and manufacturers would do a public service by pointing up these safety features, and, indeed, Owens Corning Fiberglas Corporation has recently initiated a multimillion-dollar advertising campaign to publicize the fire-retardant qualities of their products.

Unquestionably, certain fire-retardant fabrics are available which can and should be used to stop these tragic accidents from fires—if not at the initiative of industry, then at the insistence of government. We now have the legislation, in the Flammable Fabrics Act as amended in 1967, to enable us to set higher minimum standards of flammability for all fabrics. The original Flammable Fabrics Act, which was passed in 1953 in response to a number of tragedies from "torch" sweaters, was inadequate and, in some ways, gave the public a false sense of security.

Under this law, we were able to outlaw only the most outrageously flammable fabrics in wearing apparel, such as the brushed rayon "torch" sweaters which were completely consumed by flame in twenty to forty seconds. Such articles of clothing as hats, gloves and babies' receiving blankets were not included under the law. Nor did the definition of the term "fabric" under the law extend to upholstery materials, draperies, carpeting, sheets and blankets. Thus, while we were able to outlaw "torch" sweaters, we were helpless to protect the public from the estimated four million "torch" blankets, made from the identical brushed rayon, which are sold yearly to cover people while they sleep. In 1967, the Chicago Fire Commissioner ran a series of tests on these blankets, made of 88 percent rayon and 12 percent acrylic and widely sold in Chicago retail stores. A split second after a flame was touched to the blanket's edge, it became a mass of flames and was completely consumed in four seconds.

It was Congress's intent that the standards established by the 1953 Flammable Fabrics Act would be gradually stiffened in subsequent years. Yet, when our consumer subcommittee of the Senate Commerce Committee held hearings on updating the act in May 1967, I discovered that the committee to draw up tougher standards *had not met for ten years.*

The 1953 Flammable Fabrics Act, which was imperative at the time and was a piece of legislation I firmly supported, on reflection proved to be an inflexible, narrow approach to accident prevention, which appears to have actually stifled progress and frozen standards at a low level. The act illustrates the inadvisability of passing legislation to deal with a specific emergency in after-the-fact fashion. Our whole philosophy of safety legislation, instead, should be anticipatory and comprehensive. We should not wait until tragedy is upon us. We should study the potential hazards in a reasoned atmosphere and take precautionary measures *before* an epidemic of accidents occurs.

Toward that objective of prevention instead of panic-action, Congress in 1967 accepted my suggestions for amending the Flammable Fabrics Act. The amendments provide a flexible, continuing program for detecting hazards in flammable fabric hazards and for taking action to reduce them before they cause more deaths and injuries and become a subject of national outrage. Under the amendments, the Secretary of Commerce is authorized to conduct research into flammable fabrics; the Secretary of Health, Education and Welfare is directed to investigate continually deaths and injuries from accidental burns; and the Secretary of Commerce, drawing on his own and HEW's investigations and all other available information, is authorized to set flammability standards for fabrics when he discovers that such action is needed to protect the public from harm. Furthermore, the law is extended to cover not only clothing fabrics, but *all* fabrics, including those used in interior furnishings, such as bedding, draperies, carpets, upholstery, and any other conceivable product that could be created in the future.

How high these standards should be set is yet to be determined. But decidedly, it seems to me, no fabrics should be allowed in interior furnishings that do not meet even the minimal standards set by the 1953 Flammable Fabrics Act. "Torch" blankets should be no more legal than "torch" sweaters. Some of these blankets, after all, are used as receiving blankets for babies. Additionally, the hazards of smoldering overstuffed chairs and most certainly mattresses are well-documented. On such items, the extra cost of making coverings fire-resistant, to prevent cigarettes from burning through to the stuffing, would be insignificant or nonexistent. Flameproof synthetics are no more expensive and often are cheaper than flammable fabrics. Such upholstery for overstuffed furniture—and most assuredly mattress ticking—should be routinely fireproofed. The United Bedding Corporation in Los Angeles produces a flame-retardant mattress with ticking of treated cotton at no extra retail cost.

Eventually, technology should be able to make virtually all clothing flameproof. In the meantime, our youngsters should at least be protected as well as those in Great Britain. I suggest that under the new amendments, we mandate that fire-retardant fabrics be used in all children's sleeping garments now and eventually in all children's clothing.

For far too long we have abdicated our responsibility for

preserving life in the nebulous hope that safe products will emerge full-blown from conscience or competition within the business community. This is unrealistic. Such are competitive pressures that instead of promoting safety, our present quality of competition often militates against it. Safety is often not seen as a profitable commodity when pitted against styling, ease of operation and cost. When asked why they had not incorporated the $2 instinctive release on their wringer washing machine, one company admitted that even such a small expenditure that would require some alterations in production would require a higher price, giving competitors an edge in a low-income market, where every dollar-off counts. Competition did not bring us the livesaving devices on automobiles, such as the collapsible steering wheel, recessed instrument panels, disc brakes. Recently, an automotive engineer told me that many in the auto industry were secretly glad that a law was passed, mandating the use of the safety features by all companies, for competition had long prevented their adoption by one company alone.

The threat of lawsuits, ending in large personal injury settlements, reputedly spurs industry to develop safer products, and undoubtedly this is true to some extent. But Arnold Elkind, noted personal injury attorney in New York City, predicts that as the judgments become more common, some companies, instead of improving their product, will increase their insurance coverage and pass the extra cost for the premiums on to the consumer. Moreover, sacrificing humans in the hope that eventually their suffering will have some meaning for the rest of society seems to me, at the very least, a primitive approach to product improvement.

Industry, also, through a number of scientific and technical committees, trade associations and the United States of America Standards Institute (USASI), formulates uniform safety standards for products. Although such industry standards serve a useful purpose, they cannot be depended upon to guarantee us the safest products possible. The standards subscribed to by industry do not represent the greatest safety achievement possible; on the contrary, the standards are adopted by consensus and thus represent the lowest common denominator, the level at which nearly all the membership is willing to comply. Although the new USASI claims to be reconstituted to consider consumer opinion, the consumer ordinarily has little real voice in determining the standards. Consumers Union, a member of USASI, reports that its suggestions have consistently been voted down, overwhelmed by the "consensus" of industry.

Coming to the "consensus" is a slow, tedious process and is often of little immediate benefit to the consumer. In response to the outcry over glass door accidents, a USASI committee worked for nearly four years to develop an acceptable standard for the performance of safety glass and how to test it. The standard, however, does not specify that safety glass must be used—only that if it is used, it meet certain criteria. It is then up to the individual companies and trade associations of the industry affected to decide whether they wish to comply with the standard. In this instance, the Architectural Aluminum Manufacturers Association, a trade association for the makers of sliding glass doors, has required that its member companies use safety glass in all sliding doors as of June 30, 1968.

Not all companies, of course, subscribe to the agreed-on standards, and as we know, the companies that most need to improve their products are the least likely to belong to such groups. Nor, even within the membership of the standard-setting group, can the use of the standards be enforced, as was strikingly illustrated by the OPEI members who used the USASI safety seal on substandard mowers.

Once a standard is adopted by industry, it also seems to freeze and take on elevated importance, ascending from the position of "consensus" to the epitome of the possible. Compliance with industry standards, for example, is used in lawsuits as evidence that a product was not negligently designed because the design was agreed-on industry-wide. Government standards, too, that are set too low, actually militate against product improvement. Many lawyers have been defeated in attempting to prove an article of clothing excessively flammable because the manufacturer can show that it met government requirements and therefore must be safe.

Clearly, the consumer now is afforded only hit-and-miss protection against hazardous products, dependent upon an incoherent patchwork of voluntary industry standards, the possible threat to manufacturers of large personal injury settlements and a scattering of laws pertaining to specific products.

It is evident that the automobile is not an isolated cause for life-and-death concern. Just as we insist that automobiles be made as safe as technology and practicality permit, we should now apply that rule to other products, which are no less capable of killing and maiming.

In 1967, Congress supported our consumer subcommittee in its request that a Commission on Hazardous Household Products be established to make an intensive study of the problem, including the nature and scope of the hazards, the effectiveness of present legislation and industry standards and the impact of personal liability suits on safer design. The commission within two years after its appointment will issue a report of its findings and recommendations for action.

It is not possible to predict what the commission's recommendations will be, but if the commission in its broad study discovers the same facts and overall dismaying situation as I have found in my personal investigations, it is my strong hope that it will conclude, as I have, that Congress should now extend the philosophy in the 1967 Flammable Fabrics Act amendments to cover *all* products. This could be accomplished under an Omnibus Products Safety Act which would authorize the Secretary of Health, Education and Welfare to continually monitor hazardous and potentially hazardous products and when necessary to remove them from the market or require them to be designed and made more safe. Under the law, manufacturers should also be required to report immediately (General Electric delayed for six months before calling the public's attention to the television sets that were emitting excessive radiation) and recall any dangerously designed or defective product on the market.

By taking such action, we would be, as author Ralph Nader recently phrased it, "pioneering a sense of social values which does not think it necessary to wait upon disaster, recorded piles of corpses, or injured people before rational action is taken to foresee and forestall dangers. Prevention by legislative policy is preferable to belated legislative response in a nation that values human life and limb."

CHAPTER SIX

THE NEW QUACKERY

Although the old-time patent medicine man with his spiels for snake oil and other such nostrums has all but vanished from the American scene, medical quackery is far from a dwindling problem. It is, on the contrary, growing and becoming more dangerous. As FDA Commissioner James Goddard told participants at the American Medical Association's Conference on Quackery in 1966: "Today's fraud is more sophisticated. He runs a special 'clinic' outfitted with all the wonderful gadgetry of a space-conscious nation. . . . Here is the old-fashioned quack in a new disguise and a far more dangerous one." Moreover, said Goddard, Americans are more vulnerable than ever to medical hoaxes, for we are more health-conscious, more often exposed to health articles and advertisements, and more likely to accept miracle cures because we have witnessed scientific conquests once thought impossible for man to achieve.

Today's quack has discarded the sinister black cutaway for the symbol of medical professionalism—the sterile white coat. He speaks knowledgeably of magnetism, vibrations, ionic effects, atoms, rays, cosmic radiation, trace minerals, organic foods, and often uses proper medical language. He bedecks his walls with framed diplomas, sometimes from legitimate schools, often from one of the country's two hundred diploma mills. Some quackery has become so sophisticated that it is supported by research studies and gargantuan advertising budgets. On the basis of "research" many reputable doctors

and hospitals have bought and used diagnostic and therapeutic machines that were later proved worthless.

For this new quackery, Americans are paying at least one
billion dollars a year, and according to one estimate by John
Miner, deputy district attorney of Los Angeles, two billion.
That is more than we spend yearly for research on all disease
and is enough to pay the Medicare tab for one year.

If the monetary costs of quackery are astronomical, the
human costs are tragic and immeasurable. Millions of people,
many sick and dying, trustingly place themselves in the hands
of "doctors" who make a mockery of medicine and human
dignity.

After Mrs. Lorraine Allen, a young New Jersey housewife
stricken with rheumatoid arthritis, grew discouraged with
her progress, she resorted to quack cures and was finally
lured by an advertisement to one of the country's arthritis
"clinics" for six weeks of treatment at $900. There she was
taken off medically respected cortisone and subjected to
chiropractic spinal manipulations, colonic irrigations, radio-
wave and ultrasonic treatments, massages and baths. Instead
of improving, as the slick brochures had promised, Mrs. Allen
grew worse day by day. "I had managed to walk into the
clinic," she said, "but at the end of six weeks I was so sick and
in such pain I could not leave. They told me I must stay for
two more weeks, but even then they had to carry me out on
a stretcher." Mrs. Allen was hospitalized, and after operations
and physical therapy, her condition improved. Nevertheless,
her fingers are drawn up in tight fists, and she is still in much
pain. The two and a half years Mrs. Allen wasted on quackery have left her needlessly and permanently crippled.

In Spokane, Washington, a few years ago, Doris Hull,
weighing only 108 pounds, was taken by her husband to a
"sanipractor" named Otis C. Carroll. Carroll claimed to be
able to diagnose diseases by taking a drop of blood from a
patient's ear and then placing the blood sample in a "radi-
onics" machine. According to Carroll, Mrs. Hull's disease was
minor. He prescribed hot and cold compresses and a ten-day

fast, permitting her to take only water. Mrs. Hull's weight dwindled. Finally, weighing only 60 pounds, she died of starvation and tuberculosis, leaving both her husband and her child infected with tuberculosis.

Perhaps most heartbreaking of all is the case of eight-year-old Linda Epping, a beautiful blonde child who developed a small bump on her left eye which was diagnosed by doctors at UCLA Medical Center as cancer. Her parents were told the eye would have to be removed. While Linda was in the hospital awaiting operation, her parents learned of a chiropractor named Marvin Phillips, who claimed he could cure Linda without loss of the eye. They withdrew the child, and put her under Phillips's care at an initial fee of $500 and payments of $200 to $300 a month for medicine. Daily, the little girl was given vitamins, food supplements, laxatives, extract of beef eye (a daily dosage of 124 pills) and an iodine solution (11 glassfuls a day). During 23 days of this treatment, plus daily sessions of chiropractic manipulations, while Linda's parents watched, her eye grew steadily to the size of a tennis ball. Then Linda died. Said her grief-stricken mother who thought Phillips was a legitimate physician, "He had a nice shiny office, framed things on the wall, a lot of machines. How were we to suspect he was lying to us?"

Pondered deputy district attorney John Miner, who had seen Linda nine days before she died: "Except for the public executioner, only the medical quack is permitted to earn his living by killing people. . . . Whenever a quack guarantees a cure to a person who must have proper medical care to prolong or save life, he endangers that life. If his false representations keep the victim from the needed treatment until it is too late, he takes that life." To Miner, Linda's death was a case of murder. Indeed, Phillips was brought to trial in 1962, and despite a defense by the brilliant attorney, Melvin Belli, was convicted of murder. It was the first time in history a man had been condemned as a murderer for the practice of quackery, causing death. The verdict was appealed, and Phillips, on a legal technicality, was granted a new trial. In

November 1967, he was convicted again of second degree murder.

The amount of human destruction due to quackery is impossible to ascertain. But Miner declares: "Quackery kills more people than those who die from all crimes of violence put together. It is public crime number one. I personally know of thirty instances in which the victims died as a result of relying on the fraudulent promises of quacks."

Three doctors at Duke University have reported that of sixty-four cancer patients referred to a hospital after being treated by quacks, twenty-seven died who might have lived if they had received proper treatment earlier. Ten of the patients who did survive were mutilated for life; some were left with bulging eyes and monstrous-size sores because the cancer had been allowed to grow unchecked. Others had their noses and mouths eaten away by the quacks' applications of strong caustics, which destroyed far more of the healthy tissue than would have been necessary in an operation. Only twenty-seven patients were fortunate enough to have forsaken the worthless remedies in time to avoid death or irreparable damage.

People turn to quacks out of desperation, seeking "miracle cures" and hope, often when none exists—which makes their situation all the more tragic. Not long ago a well-educated man walked into an office of the Arthritis and Rheumatism Foundation wearing a cheap copper bracelet on his arm. "It's ridiculous, I know," he explained, "but I'm so desperate I'll try anything." Jerry Walsh, educational consultant for the foundation, who was stricken with rheumatoid arthritis at age eighteen, admits that during the first seven and a half years of his illness, he spent $3,000 on quack cures, for everything from radium gadgets to "magic" buckeyes.

Of the nation's thirteen million arthritics, it is estimated that about six million now spend 300 million dollars yearly for some form of quackery. Even when they are brought under professional medical care, 60 percent of the arthritic patients, according to studies, continue to try such nostrums as alfalfa seed, liniments, cod-liver oil, sea brine and iodine baths. Understanding this desperation, the quacks never give up. After one arthritic's name was mentioned recently in a *Saturday Evening Post* article, exposing the "Hucksters of Pain," he was deluged with letters from people offering to sell him quack cures to relieve his pain and crippling.

The American Cancer Society believes that testimonials, especially from friends and neighbors, or people who seem like friends and neighbors, are the most influential factor in convincing people to try quack cures. Some charlatans scribble off their own fictional testimonials. Others pay outright for signed letters of "Before I began taking Dr. X's miracle cure, I was a hopeless cancer victim." Recently, it was discovered that the glowing "return to health" testimonials widely distributed by one of the nation's arthritis "clinics" were written by college students, who earned part of their tuition by producing such harmful fiction.

Many testimonials, however, are voluntary and sincere. Dr. William Evans, deputy director of the Bureau of Medicine's Medical Review for the FDA, points out: "Quacks are always most 'successful' in treating diseases which have remissions and exacerbations—which come and go, periodically." Cancer has regressions. Arthritis flares up for inexplicable reasons, then may subside and leave the victim pain-free for months, even years. It has been reported that about one-fourth of all rheumatoid arthritics experience a "remission" after their first visit to a doctor or after taking their first nostrum. If a remission occurs at the same time as their adventure with quackery, they are convinced they have been cured. Undeniably, the placebo effect, as all doctors know, is also very strong. "Wave a wand over some patients, and they get well," says one FDA official.

Sometimes patients are misled into believing they are cured of a disease because of a false diagnosis. Some quacks call every mole, scar or blemish "cancer"; then when it disappears or fails to grow worse, they claim to have cured it. Reputable physicians, too, can make a wrong diagnosis, opening the way for a quack to take credit for curing a disease that never existed.

Although authorities believe that most quacks are knowing scoundrels, testimonials can convince even them of their own healing powers. Says Irene Bartlett, quackery authority for the American Cancer Society: "It's understandable how some quacks begin to believe in the value of their own methods when they are constantly subjected to gratitude from people insisting they owe their lives to the 'doctor.'"

Like everything else in quackery, the testimonial has been revamped to fit modern medicine and technology. No longer does the testimonial travel from the medicine man's platform to a small crowd of fifty people. Through mass media it can reach millions. When *Look* magazine in May 1962 ran an article on a "New Arthritis Controversy," discussing a hormone drug called Liefcort, it caused a mass exodus of arthritics to Canada where the drug was available. Although the magazine pointed out that the drug was controversial, that "patients say they get well with a secret medicine [but] medical authorities doubt it," victims of arthritis were more ready to believe the words and pictures of arthritics who said they were helped by the drug than the warnings of doctors. Unfortunately, Liefcort, developed by a Dr. Robert Liefman, proved to have toxic effects on some patients, and several died. A 71-year-old woman who flew to Canada for the drug, later developed severe internal bleeding. During an operation to stop the bleeding, she developed pneumonia and died. The FDA has warned Americans not to use Liefcort and has banned it from this country.

Harry M. Hoxsey, first of the big-time charlatans in cancer cures, had a daily half-hour radio broadcast in the 1940's during which he presented the prize patients he had "cured" with his "secret combination of potassium iodide, licorice, red clover, burdock root, stillingia root, berberis root, poke root, cascara, Aromatic USP 14, prickly ash bark, buckthorn bark." Hoxsey, although he had only completed eighth grade, permitted himself the title of "Doctor" and established a nationally advertised cancer sanitarium in Dallas, Texas, where patients could receive the Hoxsey treatment for $400 plus $60 for X-rays and examination. Reportedly his income in 1951 was about $200,000.

A particularly attractive "cured" patient whom Hoxsey once paraded before a press conference was a little girl named Kathy Allison of South Bend, Indiana. A year later, at age six, Kathy died. Hoxsey attributed her death to pneumonia. It was true that a doctor, after a hasty diagnosis, had suggested the child might have pneumonia. But when the facts were explored further the truth was revealed. Clearly noted on Kathy's death certificate was "carcinoma" as cause of death. Several people who had forsaken operations for the Hoxsey method subsequently died. In at least one instance Hoxsey himself performed an operation. Using a razor blade, he cut open the breast of a woman and then packed the incision with an arsenic compound. The woman died ten days later of metals poisoning. In 1953, the FDA banned Hoxsey's "cure" from interstate commerce and in 1960 finally obtained a permanent injunction, closing his Texas clinic. The FDA found that not only was the Hoxsey remedy worthless, it could actually stimulate the growth of cancer. Nevertheless, the ubiquitous testimonials that keep Hoxsey's quack-remedy alive still appear in health magazines today.

The power of the testimonials and the mass media in selling quackery has perhaps never been more cynically displayed than in the case of Regimen reducing drugs.

Early in 1957, through national advertising, including commercials on Dave Garroway's "Today Show," Americans were alerted to the Regimen wonder drug, which promised immediate weight loss with no dieting whatever. Trumpeted the ads: "It's true! If you're normally healthy, you can lose as much as 70 lbs. without cruel diet, without giving up all your favorite foods." As living proof, overweight "housewives," supposedly taking Regimen, weighed in weekly on the "Today Show," cheerily vowing that all week long they had eaten potatoes, bread, rich desserts, and yet the pounds were falling away all because of Regimen. Some were losing as much as a pound a day right before the eyes of millions of viewers. It was convincing proof; sales shot up and by 1963, Americans had spent 16 million dollars for four million bottles of the colorful Regimen pills.

Extensive investigation by the FDA, the U. S. attorney's office in Brooklyn and the U. S. Post Office revealed that the lovelies, sweetly praising Regimen before the cameras, were, when offstage, in teeth-gritting agony. They were not ordinary housewives; they were professional actresses. And they were on near-starvation diets of 500 calories daily; they were paid a fee for every commercial and a bonus for every pound they lost.

Regimen, as it turned out, was made up of three drugs, including ammonium chloride, a diuretic, and phenylpropanolamine, an appetite depressant. The former was in such weak dosage as to be inefficient, and the latter was totally ineffective. In other words, Regimen was a complete hoax. Yet, another amazing part of the Regimen story is that the efficacy of the drug was supported by four research studies, prepared by legitimate, and in two cases outstanding, researchers in medicine. In the new quackery, "substantiating product research" is a necessity; such research is the medicine man's wild claims clothed in the respectability of "science."

Through painstaking investigation, government officials dissected and then discarded the studies. Two were deceptively designed: in one, Regimen had been given to diabetics; and in another, to cardiac patients. The other two studies were good—too good. In truth, they were "graphite" studies; they had been written out without patients, without Regimen, without tests. Two well-respected researchers, holding thousands of dollars in research grants, supplied these falsified results in return for payments of $1,000 and $4,000 from the New Drug Institute, which was testing Regimen. One brilliant physiologist broke down and admitted that one evening she and a nurse had dashed off a study with fictional patients and fictional weight-loss.

In May 1965, the fraudulent merchants of Regimen were

convicted in a federal district court in New York on twenty-five counts of criminal fraud. The Drug Research Corporation, the makers of Regimen, was fined $53,000; its president, John Andreadis, was fined $50,000 and sentenced to eighteen months in prison; and the New York advertising agency, Kastor, Hilton, Chesley, Clifford and Atherton, which prepared the phony TV commercials, was fined $50,000. It was the first time in history an advertising agency had been held criminally responsible for its participation in fraudulent huckstering. The decision was appealed.

Every trick of modern merchandising is used to exploit the hopes of the seekers-after-health. Busy canvassing the country are "doorbell doctors" who sometimes work a neighborhood in teams of two. One knocks on doors, hoping to find a person suffering from a serious disease. Since about 45 percent of all Americans have a chronic disease, his chances are not bad. Under the guise of conducting a "health survey" (Is anyone ill? Is he under a doctor's care?), he elicits the desired information. Later, his colleague, working another street, comes to the house offering quack cures. "I understand you have a diabetic living here," or an arthritic, and so on. Thirty days or so after a sale, the salesman often checks back, asking how the medicine is working. If the victim says he is feeling better or the same, the salesman attempts to sell him other quack remedies to "cure you faster." Moreover, such hucksters exchange lists of customers; once a person buys, he is on the continuing quackery circuit, to receive not only salesmen, but dozens of publications and mailing pieces advertising health foods, wonder-clinics and a variety of nostrums and devices.

High-pressure tactics are noticeably being used by some unscrupulous salesmen to sell shoddy hearing aids to the elderly. Numerous people are paying $350 and up for hearing aids that are not suited to their particular hearing loss. One man in California was sold an expensive hearing aid, which was completely useless: he had nerve damage. Others have been duped into paying $30 for useless rubber plugs, containing a small tuning fork, under the misapprehension that it would enable them to hear. The device costs thirty cents to make.

A man in Indiana recently wrote me:

"I am writing this to you to tell you how two old 86- and 81-year-old couples here were taken for $370 on a phony hearing aid deal by a ruthless hard-boiled high-pressure hearing aid salesman. . . . This is how he works. He knocks on the door. . . . I am Mr. ——, sent to give you a free hearing test. . . . I am not going to sell you anything. . . . Then he took this machine into the kitchen, put it on the table, so he could test my hearing range. Then he turned some switches and knobs and put a hearing aid on my ear. He talked into the machine. The machine has a loudspeaker on it, but I didn't know it. Then he said I will give you a demonstration on how good our hearing aids are. He went into the next room. He was talking through the loudspeaker in the machine into my hearing aid. But I thought it was just his own voice. On the strength of this fake hearing aid demonstration I signed on the line, and was taken for $370." When the hearing aid came, the writer became suspicious and had his wife stand ten, then twenty, then fifty feet away and talk. "I couldn't hear her at all. Then I knew that the demonstration was a fake."

In the vicious world of big-business quackery, some entrepreneurs, as in other fields, have fashioned their practices to ensnare the poor. One of the most amazing commercializations in modern quackery is at this writing still in operation in New York City, although its mastermind, Bernarr Zovluck, a chiropractor, has been indicted for mail fraud. The operation is a "clinic," directed by full-bearded "Dr." Zovluck, whose talents reportedly earn him an income of more than half a million dollars a year. Dr. Zovluck, whose talents also got him convicted for impersonating a physician in 1962, heads a staff of four chiropractors, one medical doctor, several white-uniformed nurses and about thirty telephone operators, who occupy a whole floor in midtown Manhattan at

Forty-second Street. On busy days, it is said that the clerks don white coats and conduct physical examinations.

One room in the clinic is a-chatter with the voices of the thirty telephone solicitors scouring the city, mainly Harlem and the Puerto Rican district, for its poor and ill. Invitations are made for a "free medical examination at our clinic." Believing the clinic to be government-operated (some have been led to believe it is a part of Medicare), people swarm in, many feeble, some frighteningly ill and in need of professional care. Regardless of their ailments, they are routinely told they need an X-ray (for which they pay a fee) and are put on Dr. Zovluck's multiple-treatment plan, costing $300 or $400, for which the patient-victim *signs an installment contract.* If the patient does not find Dr. Zovluck's therapeutic plan beneficial (chiropractic manipulations and dietary restrictions) and refuses to return or pay, the doctor whom "God has chosen to help you get well" simply collects on the contract by having the patient's wages garnisheed. He also sends out intimidating dunning letters, headed "U. S. Credit Rating and Reporting Agency," reinforcing the notion that the clinic is government-run, and that if the patients don't pay, the government will force them to.

The horror is that many people seeking help are genuinely ill. Stephen Press, director of Massive Economic Neighborhood Development in Harlem, reports that he knows of four persons who have died and twenty who have become seriously ill after being treated by Dr. Zovluck. In one case, an elderly man under Dr. Zovluck's care became progressively weaker over a period of four months. Alarmed, the man's daughter accompanied him to the clinic where she told Zovluck of her father's deteriorating condition. But the doctor, she says, insisted that the enfeebled man was fine, and was progressing nicely on a diet of fruit and liquid. Outside the building, the man collapsed and was rushed to Bellevue Hospital. Two weeks after entering the hospital, the man died.

Quackery, in both drugs and medical devices, is becoming

more worrisome and difficult to control. Not only do old dangerous remedies and devices persist on the underground market, but new ones appear regularly. In the fast-moving world of medical discoveries where not even the experts agree, it is increasingly difficult to predict whether a "new miracle cure" will live up to its name or go down in history as another remnant of black magic.

Nowhere is the dilemma of the new quackery more evident than in drugs, especially those purporting to cure cancer. In keeping with the more sophisticated tenor of quackery, the American Cancer Society renamed its Quackery Committee the Committee on New and Unproved Methods of Cancer Treatment. Its confidential list of "unproved methods" for treating cancer, many now being used throughout the country, contains nearly five hundred dubious remedies; among them are bamboo grass; mistletoe therapy; "Greendrink" (liquified herbs); the "Grape Cure"; the Hoxsey method; the Macrobiotic (or Zen) diet of rice cream, lotus roots, buckwheat bread and tea; Diamond Carbon Compound; Laetrile; Koch antitoxins; Krebiozen; and the Rand Coupled Fortified Antigen.

Newest of these is the Rand vaccine, which in August 1966 was widely heralded as a possible new cancer cure. Based on the theory that cancer is caused by a virus, the anticancer vaccine was developed by the Rand Corporation, a private research organization in Cleveland, Ohio. It is claimed the vaccine builds up antibodies in the patient's blood which attack cancerous cells only. The antibodies are guided to their target by a hapten (a protein) which exists on the cell walls of tumors, but not on healthy cells. The antibody goes after this hapten, according to a Rand Corporation spokesman, shatters the cell wall and destroys the tumor.

According to early testing on sixteen dying cancer patients, twelve reportedly were saved by the vaccine. As this news found its way into the press, it caused a sensation. Hope-filled patients and families begged doctors for the vaccine.

In the fall of 1966, Rand's "broadscale investigation" of the reputed cancer cure involved 75 doctors in 35 Ohio hospitals and 200 patients. By December, according to a trade newspaper, about 1,000 persons were receiving the vaccine.

Legally, the new vaccine could be tested only within the borders of Ohio. The Rand Corporation, under the 1962 Kefauver-Harris amendments, applied to the FDA for permission to test it in all fifty states as a new investigational drug. Under the law's provisions a company must show that the drug can be tested in humans with reasonable safety and effectiveness before it can be shipped across state lines. The Rand Corporation was unable to demonstrate that the vaccine was either reasonably safe or effective. They could not show that it met reasonable standards of quality or purity. Researchers had no adequate data to show that it was free of toxic side effects. They also failed to disclose that in one study of laboratory animals the vaccine had actually enhanced the growth of cancer. Thus, the FDA was forced to reject Rand's application for interstate distribution on the basis of insufficient data.

Nevertheless, Rand, without authorization, secretly shipped the vaccine to New York, Miami and the West Coast. When vials of the vaccine were seized by the FDA, it was discovered that the vaccine had been manufactured under such substandard conditions of sanitation that it was contaminated with live bacteria. Because of the health risk as well as violation of the law, a federal court injunction was issued in March 1967 against the manufacture and distribution of the Rand vaccine in either Ohio or any other state until such time as the company is willing to do the preliminary research necessary to show that the vaccine has scientific validity and does not cause unreasonable risk to patients. Such an incident is truly regrettable, for it serves to darken rather than enlighten the way to a cancer cure. We must not, in any way, stifle legitimate cancer research; on the other hand, we cannot allow the nation's ill to be used as guinea pigs. It is not too much to expect that any company, and especially one with the resources of the Rand Corporation, be able to meet reasonable standards of sanitation, scientific research and safety before releasing an alleged livesaving product to the nation's cancer sufferers.

Similarly, the controversial drug Krebiozen, which inflamed people's hopes for several years, was discredited, although its chief proponent was Dr. Andrew Ivy, a scientist of some reputation and a former vice-president of the University of Illinois. After investigation, the FDA branded Krebiozen "a cruel hoax," warning that "each day a person with treatable cancer relies upon Krebiozen is a day that brings him closer to death." In 1964, Dr. Ivy and three other doctors using the drug, Dr. Stevan Durovic, Marko Durovic and Dr. William Phillips, were tried in Chicago for mail fraud, violation of the Food, Drug and Cosmetic Act, and conspiracy. All were found not guilty. Nevertheless, Krebiozen, identified by the FDA as nothing more than creatine, a simple amino acid available in meat, cannot legally be sold across state lines.

Dr. Ivy, now a man of seventy-five, tirelessly continues to experiment with Krebiozen (although he now calls it carcalon) in a small top-floor laboratory at Chicago's Roosevelt University. The university has granted him a staff of one; in former days, he had "thirty or forty" assistants at his disposal. Despite the government's disapproval of the drug, many cancer victims are still receiving Krebiozen via underground sources.

As the experience with Krebiozen illustrates, once a remedy receives wide acclaim and attracts a number of supporters who believe they have been cured by it, suppressing its use is nearly impossible. Such "cures" persist for years. Laetrile, derived from the kernel of an apricot, has been around since the 1920's and has been branded "worthless." Yet its popularity comes and goes, and it is today one of the more popular among the underground cancer-cures.

For sheer tenacity, the Hoxsey "cure" cannot be matched. Now forty years old and completely denounced (one FDA official calls it "an outright fraud"), it is still being used on an alarming scale. Between 1957 and 1966, under its cancer anti-quackery law, California issued eighteen cease and desist orders against practitioners using fake cancer-cure drugs. Of these, five were ordered to stop using the Hoxsey remedy.

Especially disturbing in the marketplace of the new quackery is the illegitimate sale of potent drugs which, when properly used, do have legitimate purposes. Even the mail-order quack—the most small-time operator of all—has turned to peddling commercial drugs. When postal authorities investigated a recent scheme to treat epileptics by mail, they discovered the remedy was hardly a homemade honey and herb mixture; it was phenobarbital, cleverly promoted as a secret new drug. (Phenobarbital, besides being dangerous in large doses, is not accepted as a universal treatment for epilepsy.) Similarly, when California authorities looked into a direct mail piece promising rejuvenation, they did not find bottled water from Ponce de León's mythical fountain of youth. The liquid sold to "prolong mental and physical activities, as well as retard the symptoms of aging" was an injectible, called paraminobenzoic acid, a drug treatment from Rumania.

A most irresponsible dispensing of drugs is witnessed in the new "obesity clinics," plush salons, operated by osteopaths, chiropractors and even some physicians, where pounds are taken off for exorbitant fees, as high as $50 per visit. The patients are given "rainbow pills," five drugs plus a laxative put up in different colored tablets. They contain thyroid to speed up metabolism, digitalis to stimulate the heart, thiazide diuretics to cause loss of body water, amphetamines to depress the appetite and barbiturates to counteract the jittery feeling produced by the amphetamines. In other words, drugs are given on top of drugs—one to counteract the possible effects of the others.

Such medical conduct was criticized at the American Medical Association's 1966 Congress on Medical Quackery as "shameful to the medical profession." It may also be dangerous. If the truth were known, an official at FDA told me, the obesity clinics would be "as great a scandal as thalidomide."

The combination of the five drugs, in commonly used high dosages, can cause a dangerous chemical imbalance in the body. For example, digitalis in an overdose will cause the heart to stop, and a loss of potassium in the body, caused by the diuretic, makes the heart extraordinarily sensitive to digitalis.

In the September 11, 1967, issue of the *Journal of the American Medical Association,* Dr. Russell C. Henry, Oregon's state medical examiner, reported that at least six women had died, apparently from the "rainbow pill" treatment. He regards insufficient potassium levels in the body as a contributing factor in their deaths. This theory is partly confirmed by the fact that one woman, about to be put into an iron lung, recovered quickly after being given a dose of potassium. Unfortunately, as long as the "rainbow" drugs are properly branded, the FDA has no jurisdiction over how they are used.

Also of grave concern to medical authorities are the so-called medical "devices" sold to detect and cure a dictionary of diseases such as bursitis, rheumatism, cancer, diabetes, heart disease, Bright's disease, tuberculosis, gout, insomnia, neuralgia, liver ailments, asthma, hepatitis, ear infections, skin diseases, brain tumors. A few are crude and relatively inexpensive: copper bracelets with "lifegiving properties," "magic crushed-rock amulets from Africa," health sandals, radium belts. But the majority are so well constructed and elaborate that they would not look out of place in a doctor's office. Most are expensive and bear pseudoscientific names, such as "microtabulometer," "Ionic charger," "Quot-Electronic Instrument," "Endocardiograph." In fiscal 1967, the Food and Drug Administration initiated more than eighty court cases involving such devices.

In some instances the cure-all devices are sold directly to the sufferer. A network of more than one hundred agents in twelve states recently peddled small generators that produced ozone (pure oxygen) which they billed as "tri-atomic oxygen—a concentrated and superactive form of oxygen."

According to the promoters, ozone will cure almost anything and was recommended for forty-seven diseases, including cancer, heart disease, high blood pressure, sinus infections, tumors, diabetes and ulcers. In truth, these small ozone boxes would cure nothing and were potentially harmful. Ozone is about 1,000 times more poisonous than carbon monoxide. In laboratory tests, the ozone-generators killed mice in a matter of hours, and could, according to experts, cause severe lung damage to humans. Before the scheme was stopped, more than 3,000 generators had been sold in California alone at $154 each. The nationwide take was 1.5 million dollars.

One of the most ingenious machine frauds was the Film-O-Sonic, an ordinary tape recorder from which the speaker had been removed. Wired to the machine were pads which the victim was to moisten and place against his body. The special vibrations from the silently playing tape were supposed to flow through the wires to the body, and in the case of cancer, seek it out and cause the tumor to disintegrate. When the tapes were played on a recorder with sound, the cancer "cure" was a rendition of "Smoke Gets in Your Eyes." The arteriosclerosis "cure" was "Holiday for Strings."

Although devices for home use account for millions of dollars' worth of misery, far bigger business are the pseudo-scientific contraptions that are used in the charlatan's "clinic" or "salon." Some of these cost thousands of dollars, but are a lucrative investment. One man in distress paid $28,000 to a quack for sessions with a machine that claimed to psychoanalyze him. For forty years, until her death in 1965 at the age of seventy-four, Ruth Drown, a chiropractor in Los Angeles, was the queen of modern machine quackery. Mrs. Drown was a disciple of Dr. Albert Abrams, an eminent cardiologist, who, early in the 1900's, with the advent of radio, became convinced that radio waves could both diagnose and cure all diseases. His theory was that every disease gives off radiations at a specified frequency, which can be measured on a "radionics" machine from a drop of a person's blood on a blotter. Once diagnosed, the disease is "cured" by broadcasting back into the sick patient at the same frequency emitted by the disease, thus destroying it by canceling it out. Dr. Abrams charged patients $100 to $200 for a series of treatments on his numerous machines. He died in 1924, leaving an estate of 2 million dollars, a legacy of machine quackery and a number of disciples, including Ruth Drown.

Mrs. Drown, a pert, grey-haired little lady, who dressed in professional white in her clinic, treated more than 35,000 persons in Los Angeles County alone, bilking them of at least half a million dollars. Her bungalow was given over to a clinic, full of about 125 machines. When Tyrone Power and his wife were injured in a plane crash in Italy, Mrs. Drown claimed that she treated them by broadcasting her radionic vibrations for six thousand miles. So big was Mrs. Drown's business that handling it required, in addition to herself and her daughter, a staff of four nurses and a bookkeeper.

Finally, in 1963, Mrs. Drown and her daughter, Cynthia Chatfield, were indicted for grand theft. An undercover agent for the district attorney's office had sent Mrs. Drown a blood sample purporting to be that of a little girl. Mrs. Drown claimed the child had mumps and chicken pox. Actually, the blood sample came from a perfectly healthy turkey. Mrs. Drown died during the trial. Her daughter was convicted.

Some worthless machines are even finding their way into hospitals and physicians' offices. During a medical convention in 1958, physicians noted a marked similarity between the machines in an FDA quackery exhibit and a new machine called "Diapulse," being demonstrated in a nearby booth and offered for sale. After a lengthy investigation, the FDA, for the first time, took action against a so-called legitimate medical device being sold to reputable medical practitioners.

From 2,000 to 3,000 Diapulse machines were bought by medical practitioners and hospitals throughout the country for $2,300 each. The device was based on an unproved medical theory of "pulsed diathermy," advanced in the 1930's and discredited in Europe at that time. Theoretically, Diapulse's pulsating current penetrated deep into the body to the diseased organs, stimulating the body's production of antibodies and other defense mechanisms. According to the Diapulse Manufacturing Corp., its product accelerated healing in at least fifty ailments, including diabetic ulcer, arthritis ("effective where other treatment fails"), fractures, acute bacterial infections, upper respiratory infections, the common cold, acute tonsilitis, low blood pressure, migraine headaches, liver disease and inflammation of the gums.

During a 1967 trial, expert witnesses testified that according to the best available evidence, the machine was worthless. The jury agreed, and declared Diapulse misbranded. The company is appealing the verdict.

After the jury's landmark decision on Diapulse, the FDA moved against other medical devices, not commonly considered quackery. The most troublesome are the muscle stimulators, such as the nationally advertised Relax-A-Cizor, which, their makers claim, by causing muscles to relax and contract, take off pounds, destroy wrinkles, restore vitality. Critics of these stimulators maintain that the machines simply administer a slight shock of no therapeutic value. The FDA has asked for an injunction against Relax-A-Cizor and has made 15 seizures of various misbranded muscle stimulators.

As the line between outright quack devices and those mistakenly used by men of some reputation draws ever finer, government officials are confronted with another unanticipated serious problem. Many devices are now implanted in the body—for example, artificial heart valves, synthetic arteries, metal leg plates, hip pins, joint prostheses. As medical science spurts ahead at fantastic speeds toward the "artificial man," we can expect to see humans equipped with even more vital artificialities: transistorized hearts, mechanical kidneys and perhaps one day even artificial lungs and livers.

Such wonder devices could hardly be called quackery, for they have a legitimate health purpose and are implanted exclusively by licensed M.D.'s. Nevertheless, some of the prosthetic devices now being used skirt uncomfortably close to being termed quack in the sense that they are misrepresented, unreliable, a danger to health and, as the American Cancer Society would term it, "new and unproved" for their intended purpose.

Many prosthetic devices are subjected to scrupulous testing before marketing to be sure they are safe. But others are so irresponsibly made that they rust, break inside the patient and trigger biological reactions that cause infections and destroy tissue. In one instance, an elderly woman's broken hip was repaired with a nylon ball and metal pin. Within four months the woman's hip joint was completely destroyed. The nylon had reacted with the tissue, releasing a toxic material causing an abscess. Dr. Joseph Davis, chief of medical devices of the FDA's Bureau of Medicine, has twenty-four different types of metal and plastic artificial eyes that were removed from patients because of defects in the material or poor design that caused severe tissue reaction and serious infection. In most cases, the tissue damage to the sockets was so extensive that the person could not be fitted with another artificial eye.

Breakage of metal hip pins and plates within a patient is extraordinarily common. Recently an engineer set up manufacturing in a California garage, turning out large metal nails designed to join the two parts of a broken hip. Within six months, there were three reported cases in a thirty-mile radius of the nails snapping in two after being imbedded in patients. Ironically this therapeutic hardware was advertised as being the strongest available. Said one ad: "Keeps Fracture Patient Up—Never Lets Him Down."

Metal screws, bone plates and hip nails also corrode inside the patient. One surgical device, inserted as a hip pin, turned out to be an ordinary hardware store nail. Unless the metal is of a special type, biologically inert, it will create an electrolysis reaction, causing infection and pain, and will have to be removed.

FDA has a file drawer filled with reports of nylon arteries rotting away inside patients, heart-pacemakers failing, aortic valves malfunctioning. Doctors at a prominent university recently found that of ninety-five patients who underwent operations for insertion of a graphite-coated heart valve, thirty-seven died. Two of the deaths were definitely traced to defective heart valves, and it was suspected, although not confirmed by autopsy, that other deaths were due to the heart valve. Several patients died of cerebral strokes. A question that went unanswered: Did bits of the graphite come off, creating an embolus that went to the brain, causing a fatal clot? In another study of seventeen cases, three patients died after the vital ball in their heart valve was expelled, and four others died because of valve leakage.

Unfortunately, under present laws, neither surgeons nor patients have protection from these defective, dangerously designed implants, which cause demonstrable harm and death. Anyone can make them and sell them. During Senate hearings before the Subcommittee on Frauds and Misrepresentations Affecting the Elderly in 1964, my colleague, Senator Ralph W. Yarborough of Texas questioned Dr. Martin Dobelle, at that time a medical officer for FDA.

Senator Yarborough: Now what protection does the surgeon have in introducing these pins into the human body? What protection has the surgeon got to know that the metals in these pins are the kind that have been made biologically inert and that they will not be hostile to human tissue?

Dr. Dobelle: Actually he has no protection whatsoever. Unfortunately, we have a gaining tide of malpractice suits, but counsel and attorneys in general now are aware of the fact that the defective device, even though the physician is a prime target, actually is the fault and the responsibility of the manufacturer.

Senator Yarborough: You mean . . . a competent surgeon

introduces one of these pins into the body, to pin a broken hip, it is hostile, and the surgeon gets a suit for malpractice. There is no law or rule or regulation about the manufacture of these devices, these pins, these bolts, these metal braces that are put in the human body. There is no protection for the surgeon there except his judgment of the manufacturer; is that right?

Dr. Dobelle: That is correct, sir.

Surely all of these facts point to one disturbing conclusion: *that the public is not being adequately protected*—from either failure or misrepresentation of legitimate medical devices—and most decidedly, is not safeguarded from the purveyors of falsity who intentionally or unintentionally peddle suffering and death in the name of healing. Perhaps because we continue to think of the quack as a quaint crackpot in a top hat, we have been slow to recognize and to move against the horrors of modern quackery.

Most states actually license some quacks, legally entitling them to use the title "Doctor" or other titles of seemingly medical respectability: naturopath, naprapath, sanipractor, electrotherapist, scientologist, physiotherapist. If the quack does tangle with the law, he is often acquitted, or the sentence is suspended and the fine light—so light that many quacks laughingly refer to them as "license fees." When the redoubtable Mrs. Drown was convicted in federal court in 1951, after a woman had died from relying on one of her machines, she was fined $1,000, given a one-year suspended sentence and five years' probation. She continued her business without interruption, and in 1963 when arrested bragged: "The advertising will be good for me. When I get back to my office, I'll have more patients than ever."

A distributor of a quack radon generator, selling for $300, was fined $25. A "Doctor" who had treated nearly 1,000 patients on his "Electrometabograph" machine at fees as high as $1,500 was fined $750. After an elderly lady suffering from advanced tuberculosis was discovered in a third-rate hotel sitting on a radium pad to cure her "arthritis," the several vendors were apprehended and fined. Seldom did the fine exceed the profit from *one sale.*

Most quacks enjoy a lifetime of comfort, free from the law. But, if their businesses are shut down, they move easily from state to state. Before coming to New York City to prey on Harlem's sick, Dr. Zovluck ran a clinic in Baton Rouge, Louisiana, with a staff of two hundred. Roy Wright De-Welles, a long-time quack, operated a clinic in Los Angeles until 1961. He used a pressurized enema device called a "Detoxacolon," which he claimed flushed out the colon, removing toxins which caused all ailments, including cancer, asthma, arthritis, colitis, epilepsy. Such an instrument can perforate colon walls, remove vital body salts and spread infections. An investigation by the California State Department of Health revealed that more than 13 percent of De-Welles's patients died after his treatments. The state closed down the clinic; DeWelles was brought to trial but acquitted. Within the following year he had organized one of his infamous "traveling clinics" in Indiana, using the same dangerous Detoxacolon. This time, however, an Indianapolis judge, deploring the light sentences that allow quacks to continue to operate, sentenced DeWelles, then age sixty-one, to ten years in prison. It was one of the stiffest sentences ever given to a medical con man.

Nevertheless, during his long, lucrative career, DeWelles had sold at least two hundred Detoxacolon devices to other practitioners for $2,500 each. The FDA managed to find and destroy only a few of these potentially deadly machines. Nearly all of the original two hundred still are in use today— and perhaps will be until subsequent deaths bring the machines to the attention of law officials.

Definitely we need a renewed public awakening—among patient-victims, legislators and even the medical profession itself—to the dangers and scope of today's quackery problem. This does not mean that all has been silence. The American

Medical Association's three quackery conferences, in 1961, 1963 and 1966, presented critical and constructive forums which drew nationwide attention. The AMA, along with other groups, such as the American Cancer Society and the Arthritis and Rheumatism Foundation, carry on a relentless battle against quackery. The latter two organizations are now engaged in a reemphasis in their campaign against health hucksters.

Realizing that people resort to quackery out of ignorance, desperation and a fear that the medical profession can do nothing, both ACS and the Arthritis Foundation are increasingly stressing not only the dangers of quackery, but how much *legitimate* medicine *can* do. Although these are facts that rarely make the headlines, about one million and a half cured cancer victims are alive in this country today—people who have not suffered a recurrence of malignancy in the last five years. And, in 70 percent of the cases, crippling from arthritis can be prevented by early treatment.

The FDA, the FTC and the Post Office constantly publicize and take action against misleading and fraudulent health claims. The Post Office reports that the vast majority of its work in fraud concerns false health claims, although once again, the Post Office is hampered by having to prove intent to defraud. Nowhere is proving intent more difficult than among the phony health-hucksters. Many defendants—after offering phony mail-order remedies for baldness, devices to aid male potency, salve to erase varicose veins, all manner of machines and pills—appear before a hearing office for the Post Office and insist they thought the product was legitimate. Often they bring letters from doctors supporting their claims; sometimes a doctor testifies in their behalf. It has been held by one postal hearing officer that such testimony from one doctor is *prima facie* evidence that the seller did not intentionally deceive. In such circumstances, though the product be medical hokum, the Post Office cannot take any action to stop the swindle. This illustrates again the need for removing from the Post Office's civil statute the need to prove intent.

Perhaps no single effort to draw attention to quackery has been more intensive or successful than the hearings of the Subcommittee on Frauds and Misrepresentations Affecting the Elderly (now called Consumer Subcommittee) of the Senate's Special Committee on Aging. This subcommittee, under the chairmanship of Senator Harrison A. Williams, Jr., of New Jersey, recorded page after page of scandal in the health field, and in 1965 issued a report recommending certain reforms. Yet, despite the subcommittee's excellent work and recommendations, these reforms have not yet been put into effect.

What needs to be done?

1. Of urgent importance is federal legislation to prevent unsafe and worthless medical devices from being marketed, and Senator Williams has introduced such a bill. It is sad and wasteful that year after year we stand by helplessly while dangerous and ineffective medical devices are sold, and then make futile, costly attempts to remove them from the market *after they have caused harm.* It is shameful that the public, through taxes, bears the financial burden of simply halting *further* marketing of the devices—by means of FDA seizures, FDA administrative and FDA-requested court proceedings. Prosecution of the Diapulse case alone cost an estimated $150,000.

Moreover, FDA's after-the-fact action does not rid the country of devices already sold. As in the case of the dangerous Detoxacolon, the devices continue to be used long after their makers are forced out of business. The FDA seizures, except in extreme cases of health-danger, are not designed, as many believe, to remove *all* phony devices from the market. Often only one seizure of a misbranded medical device is made, as a prerequisite for legal action. Only one Diapulse machine was seized, for example. The other 2,999 or so, as far as anyone knows, are still in use.

We do not allow drugs to be tested on humans to determine if they are safe and efficacious. Nor should we allow this kind of inhuman experimentation and exploitation by medical devices. The makers of medical devices, like those of drugs, should be required to supply sound scientific evidence that their product is safe and effective for its intended uses *before* the government allows it to be marketed.

The Kefauver-Harris Amendments of 1962, requiring the drug premarketing clearance, originally included the same provisions for medical devices, but this aspect of the bill was lost in the battle over drugs. Similar medical device legislation was introduced in 1966 and 1967, but did not create much of a stir, despite Presidential endorsement. Obviously, with each passing year, need for the law becomes more pressing. We must prevent any new saturation of the country with such patently fraudulent diagnostic and therapeutic devices as the Drown machines, the ozone generators, the Sonic Tape Recorders. (Some would exclude from the law diagnostic devices, but it seems to me some of these are the most dangerous of all and should not be granted immunity.)

Perhaps more important for the future—and this is the main thrust of the legislation—it would for the first time set uniform standards for the manufacture of legitimate medical devices, such as the heart valves, hip pins and mechanical miracles to come. Both patients and surgeons deserve the assurance that these human implants are as safe as they can be made.

2. An Anti-Quackery Bureau should be established in the Department of Health, Education and Welfare. Throughout the country, on federal, state and local levels, hundreds are working tirelessly to curtail quackery, but as John Miner, the Los Angeles prosecutor, observes, "The right hand rarely knows what the left hand does." There is no national clearing house for information on quackery. Quacks can skip all over the country before the FDA or the postal officials hear of their existence. An FDA study of five hundred medical devices showed that FDA officials did not even learn of the violations in most cases until months, sometimes years, had

passed. One wrist device to "cure" arthritis was on the market in 1892, but was not removed by FDA until 1958.

A national anti-quackery bureau would provide a center for information, to be exchanged among federal agencies, local officials, private health organizations and the public. By coordinating both enforcement and educational activities nationwide through the bureau, we could for the first time present a formidable united front against the evils of quackery.

3. States should pass anti-quackery legislation and enforce it vigorously. Although a sizable percentage of the nation's quackery takes place within state borders, few states have adequate laws to handle it. Twenty states do not even have a basic, comprehensive food, drug and cosmetic act, which would empower them to take the same action locally as the FDA can take nationally. The Council of State Governments has drawn up model food and drug legislation and urges all states to adopt it. Such legislation provides an essential groundwork for fighting quackery.

Few states that do have comprehensive laws have updated them to require the premarket testing of drugs to parallel the 1962 federal drug amendments. And, only California, in a law passed in 1962, has raced ahead of the Federal Government to require that new medical devices be determined safe and worthwhile before they can be sold.

California, plagued with an overpopulation of quacks, and sometimes called the "Mecca of Quackery," can also be called the "Land of Anti-Quackery." That state is and should be emulated for its progressive anti-quackery laws and vigorous pursuit of quacks. In 1959, California was the first to pass a special cancer control law, under which the state can issue regulations banning cancer remedies found by a fifteen-member council of experts to be unproved. The law enables authorities to move swiftly to remove old, persistent quack cures, such as the Hoxsey remedy, without having to bring lengthy court proceedings. Anyone found selling one of the outlawed cancer remedies can be immediately forbidden to do so, under a cease and desist order, and if necessary, with a court injunction. Six other states also now have cancer anti-quackery laws, based on California's. They are Colorado, Kentucky, Maryland, Nevada, North Dakota and Pennsylvania. The American Cancer Society urges all states to pass such legislation and has drawn up a model law to facilitate passage and uniformity.

In 1967, California, in an unprecedented hard crackdown on quacks, raised the crime of practicing medicine without a license from a mere misdemeanor, subject to a maximum $500 fine and six months in jail, to a felony, which carries a possible prison sentence of ten years.

In addition to considering these laws, it seems to me states should reexamine their medical licensing procedures and be quicker to revoke the licenses of quacks, and perhaps refuse to grant licenses to pseudomedical practitioners at all. South Carolina, for example, recently outlawed naturopaths, after the State Medical Society brought pressure and the brother of a state legislator had tragically died at the hands of a naturopath. The FTC has also urged states to follow Oregon's lead in licensing hearing-aid dealers and salesmen. Sellers would be required to pass an examination for competency, and in the case of misbehavior, their licenses could be revoked.

State medical boards, as well as local and national medical groups, might also take a more stringent approach to censuring and revoking the licenses of their members who indulge in quackery. Although it is a serious move to jeopardize a man's livelihood, it is even more serious to allow him to jeopardize the lives of others. If I, as a practicing lawyer, consistently refused to follow the established rules of the court, I would expect to be quickly disbarred. A continued faith in the medical profession is essential to defeating quackery.

However, no matter how much people respect and trust their own doctors, those who hold out false hopes of miracle cures—of an easier, faster, better way to relieve pain, cure illnesses and prolong life—will always find a pathetically eager market. We must marshal every force, including strong, stringently enforced laws, to stop modern-day quacks from such cynical exploitation of the gullible, the frightened and the desperate.

CHAPTER SEVEN

TOWARD A SAFER CIGARETTE?

In 1954, the year that the American Cancer Society first delivered its deadly verdict against cigarette smoking, 39 million Americans smoked. In 1967, 49 million Americans were smoking. Although about one million health-conscious adults give up cigarettes yearly, a million and a half youngsters take up cigarette smoking every year.

For the last several years, especially since the Surgeon General's Smoking and Health Report of 1964, we have referred to the danger of cigarettes as the "smoking controversy." Millions of Americans have refused to face the grim fact that they may be smoking themselves into an early grave. And the tobacco industry has steadfastly questioned the evidence that links cigarettes with disease and death, clinging to every last hope and maverick voice in the research wilderness that might release their product from blame.

In scientific truth, there is no longer any "controversy." Since the surgeon general's definitive report, hundreds of other studies have confirmed that cigarette smoking is linked to a number of diseases. In the laboratories cigarette tar painted on the backs of mice has induced cancer. Dogs and rabbits, taught to smoke through machines, have developed precancerous lung changes and emphysema. The clinical evidence is even more indisputable. A recent autopsy study of the cross sections of human lung tissue revealed that 93.2 percent of the smokers had abnormal lung cells as compared with only 1.2 percent of the nonsmokers. In a 1966 study of one million men and women, Dr. E. C. Hammond of the American Cancer Society found that male smokers between the ages of forty-five and sixty-four had a death rate from all causes that was twice as high as that of nonsmokers.

Perhaps the most dramatic single piece of evidence of the causal relationship between smoking and lung cancer is the experience of British physicians. In 1951 the percentage of male English doctors smoking cigarettes was 56 percent. Alarmed by the demonstrated health hazards, many doctors gave up cigarettes. By 1958 only 40 percent of the British doctors smoked cigarettes. As the lung cancer rate among the general public in Great Britain rose by 22 percent between 1951 and 1961, the lung cancer rate among doctors dropped by 7 percent.

Although we don't have all the answers about why and how smoking causes damage, it is increasingly evident that tar, the brownish black residue which is left after the smoke is demoisturized or "condensed," is a significant factor. Studies on both animals and humans reveal that the higher the dose of tar and nicotine (which is a particular substance in tar), the greater the danger to health. For example, mice subjected to twice as much tar developed twice as many tumors. Smokers who turn to cigarettes with a lower tar-nicotine content show significantly less coughing and shortness of breath than those who stay with higher tar-nicotine brands. A study in 1967 by Saxon Graham, at the State University of New York in Buffalo, demonstrated that smokers develop individual techniques of smoking, and that those who smoke in such a way as to extract the greatest amounts of tar from their cigarettes appear to have the highest incidence of lung cancer. (Taking the same number of puffs over a longer period of time, allowing the cigarette to burn down reducing filtration length and puffing more at the end of the cigarette rather than at the beginning yielded the largest amounts of tar.)

The harmful effects of nicotine are also documented. According to Dr. Hammond: "Milligram for milligram, nicotine is one of the most powerful and fastest acting of all known poisons. However, when an amount which would produce rapid death if administered in a single dose is split into many small doses and administered during the course of the day, the effects are very different. Under these conditions, nicotine produces marked, acute effects upon the heart, the peripheral arteries and the nervous system; and it has an effect upon the functioning of certain glands." Furthermore, there is some evidence from English researchers that nicotine is partially converted by the body into a chemical called cotinine, which has proved to be carcinogenic when given to rats in drinking water. (The amount of nicotine found in a cigarette is almost always in direct proportion to the amount of tar.)

The magnitude of the health problem from smoking is enormous. According to the estimate of one authority, 300,000 persons will die prematurely this year because of smoking. As Surgeon General William H. Stewart has pointed out, fifty years ago lung cancer was a rare disease; today it is increasing at epidemic proportions. In 1930, deaths from lung cancer in the United States totaled 2,500. This year about 50,000 American men and women will die of the disease, 40,000 primarily as a result of cigarette smoking. (Smokers are ten times more likely than nonsmokers to die of lung cancer.) By 1976, unless the epidemic is checked, twice that number, or 80,000 yearly, will die of the disease.

Emphysema, too, is a relatively new major medical phenomenon. In 1955, 4,000 persons died of emphysema, a slow suffocating death. By 1966, the number of deaths from emphysema and bronchitis had risen to 20,000. And within ten years, the death toll from these two diseases, which doubles every five years, could be well over 80,000. Although we do not know the exact cause of emphysema, it is thirteen times more likely to strike smokers than nonsmokers. Cigarette smoking is also implicated in circulatory diseases, cancer of the bladder, peptic ulcer, even influenza.

"Cigarette smoking is, without question, the greatest single public health problem this nation has ever faced," says Dr.

Charles A. Ross, chief of thoracic surgery at Roswell Park Memorial Institute, a leading cancer research institution. Surgeon General Stewart in September 1967 opened the World Conference on Smoking and Health by stating: "I am convinced that, in one important dimension, our controversy is no longer controversial. The proposition that cigarette smoking is hazardous to human health long ago passed the realm of possibility. It has now gone beyond the probable, to the point of demonstrable fact. . . . The sentence with which all of us are familiar—'Caution: Cigarette smoking may be hazardous to your health'—is inadequate as a description of the present state of our knowledge. Cigarette smoking *is* hazardous to health. . . . This is no longer a matter of opinion nor an evangelical slogan. It is a flat scientific fact."

Confronted with such scientific data, what can we do and what are we doing to curb the toll from cigarettes?

In persuading Americans to stop smoking we have failed abysmally. Since 1910 and most especially since 1935, cigarette production has risen dramatically. With publication of the surgeon general's report, cigarette production dipped, for the first time in sixty years, but by the following year, it was on a relentless upswing and in 1966 reached an all-time high. That year, 8.2 billion dollars' worth of cigarettes—539 billion —were produced and consumed in the United States.

After the initial impact of the surgeon general's report, per capita consumption of cigarettes dropped in 1964 but then climbed again and leveled off. In 1966, Americans over eighteen were smoking at a per capita rate of 4,300 cigarettes a year—215 packs a year for *every* adult American.

At present about 51 percent of the men in the country are smokers and 34 percent of the women. It is true that an inestimable number of Americans have stopped smoking for health reasons. The best indication of the medical respect paid to the evidence of the hazard is revealed by the fact that more than half of the nation's physicians who were smokers have given up cigarettes. In the early 1950's more than 60 percent of the country's doctors smoked; today less than 30 percent are smokers. Nevertheless, so deeply ingrained is the habit that millions of smokers have been unable or unwilling to stop smoking. More alarming, for every adult who does quit, there is an eager young teenager, unimpressed with the medical evidence, uncaring of what fifty years will bring, who takes his place. Studies, according to the American Cancer Society, show that 1.5 million youngsters between the ages of twelve and sixteen took up cigarette smoking during 1966.

Clearly, although the percentage of Americans smoking has declined slightly, presumably because of health warnings, the number of Americans smoking cigarettes has risen. We are plainly not succeeding in erasing or even making a significant impact on this, our most widespread public health problem. In view of the enormity of the danger, our remedies have been pathetically ineffective.

Our most significant measure to date has been the warning on the cigarette label. In 1965, we in Congress succeeded in requiring the now-familiar "Caution: Cigarette smoking may be hazardous to your health" on every package of cigarettes. As Dr. Stewart pointed out, this warning is now outdated and inadequate. The warning was a symbolic gesture of government disapproval (Cancer Society posters warned: "Congress has acted. The next step is up to you"), but it is doubtful that the message has made many converts to the ranks of the nonsmoking.

Our one-sentence warning on cigarette packages and our scattered spot commercials against smoking, as required by the Federal Communications Commission, are small efforts when pitted against the industry's countervailing monumental expenditures for cigarette advertising. While the government was warning us not to smoke, the tobacco companies in 1966 spent 297 million dollars, two-thirds of it on television commercials, which convey the impression that smoking is satisfying, pleasurable and socially desirable and not harmful to our health.

A Federal Trade Commission analysis of television cigarette advertising, released in June 1967, revealed that Madison Avenue still plays up sensual gratification as an important theme. We are told that Chesterfield Kings have "true" flavor, the taste of L & M and Tareyton filters is "rich" and that Viceroy filters have "the taste that's right," that Kool is "fresher" and Lucky Strike Green "cooler tasting" with a "forest fresh taste." The appeal to status and success is also strong. Discriminating: "Particular about taste . . . I'm particular" (Pall Mall Kings), and "The smokers who know" (Camel filters); success: "tastes rich, good, rewarding (Viceroy filters), and "This man was born rich" (Camel filters); independence: "Break away from the crowd . . . the cigarette for independent people" (Old Gold filters); associate with important people: "Chairmen are never bored with them" (Benson and Hedges filters).

But an undercurrent of much cigarette advertising is the implicit health theme—the subtle insinuations, undermining our national effort to create a contrary impression, that smoking is an activity enjoyed by the robust, the fit and the healthy. (Cigarette advertisers, perhaps instinctively sensing the fears about health among their audience, first introduced the health issue by disclaiming ill effects through such slogans as "More doctors smoke Camels than any other brand" and "Not a cough in a carload." As the hypocrisy of such implied health claims was exposed by scientific evidence, advertisers retreated but did not give up. Assuaging the anxiety of its audience was more necessary than ever.)

As the FTC report points out, cigarette advertising attempts to counteract the prevailing medical evidence against smoking in a number of subtle ways. There is the escape from reality in which, says the report: "Some cigarette advertising transcends mere image association and projects its own separate and unique world. Examples include 'Salem Country,' a land in which romantic couples romp and preen through shifting, sylvan settings; the 'Night People,' whose post evening encounters can lead to smoking Parliament filters; and 'Marlboro Country,' where there daily unfolds the simple male heroic virtues of the 'Old West.' Worry over health has been banished from these Shangri-las."

Equally disturbing in television commercials is the connection between outdoor athletic activities and smoking in which youthful, fit, personable models are placed against an appealing outdoor backdrop. Sailboating (Tareyton, Pall Mall, Parliament and Viceroy filters); fishing (Viceroy filters and Camel menthols); golf and outdoor cooking (Viceroy filters); bowling and "sand-bathing" (Winston filters). As the FTC report states, "This activity suggests that the smoking depicted in the foreground, if not conducive to rousingly good health, is certainly not incompatible with it." Television viewers agree. In a recent USPHS survey, 58 percent of the public felt that current cigarette advertising leaves the impression that smoking is a healthy thing to do.

Most insidious of all the advertising techniques is exploitation of the public's belief that filters remove some of the hazardous substances in cigarette smoke, decreasing the risk. In some instances this is true, and I am convinced that effective filters are one of the most promising solutions to our problem. Some responsible cigarette manufacturers have worked to create and promote less hazardous cigarettes with filters that do trap a significant amount of the tar-nicotine particles. But other companies have taken unconscionable advantage of the public's widespread belief that "filter" means "less hazard." They have produced cigarettes with filters which are, in fact, more dangerous than other brands without filters and even more dangerous than the *same brand without the filter*. Then the manufacturers have through advertising subtly led the unknowing viewer, who may be searching for a safer cigarette, to switch in the belief that the filtered brand presents a diminished health threat but possesses the same satisfying taste.

For example, Lucky Strike advertises that its filtered cigarettes have "a filter that's rolled tobacco and charcoal inside" to give you a new "soft taste." This claim in the past has been accompanied by pictorial dissections of filters, conveying the impression that they prevent the passage of dangerous tars and gases into the mouth. Anyone seeing these ads, especially with all the attention paid to the supposed value of charcoal filtering and the emphasis on words like "mild" and "soft" as euphemisms cloaking the dangers of smoking, would be certain that the filtered Lucky Strike was safer than the regular nonfilter Lucky Strike. This was not found to be true, according to researchers at Roswell Park Memorial Institute who analyzed the tar-nicotine yield of fifty-six brands of cigarettes. Their study, published in March 1967, revealed the following: The regular Lucky Strike contained 27.1 milligrams of tar on the average. The filtered Lucky Strike contained 27.3 milligrams of tar. Similarly, a regular nonfiltered Chesterfield contained 27.0 milligrams of the hazardous tar and 1.18 milligrams of nicotine, as compared with the filtered counterpart which contained 27.6 milligrams of tar and 1.72 milligrams of nicotine. A regular Camel, too, produced less tar than the filtered variety. Without the filter, the cigarette yielded 31.3 milligrams of tar and 1.69 milligrams of nicotine. With the filter, the Camel yielded 32.4 milligrams of tar per cigarette and 1.77 milligrams of nicotine.

No brand revealed a greater gap between the tar yields of its filtered and nonfiltered cigarettes than Pall Mall, which was the first to promote the new super-size 100 millimeter cigarette. The commercials, of course, without stating so directly, left the impression that the filter was added for health protection. What else could it be for? "You get Pall Mall's famous extra length of fine tobaccos . . . and a filter tip. Result? A new longer length, a full 100 millimeters long and a new milder taste." "Milder" again inevitably translates in the viewer's mind as "less harmful, innocuous." However, whereas the nonfiltered Pall Mall in the red package gave off 33.0 milligrams of tar and 1.75 milligrams of nicotine; the new 100 millimeter filtered cigarette in the rich-looking gold Pall Mall pack delivered 41.6 milligrams of tar and 2.20 milligrams of nicotine—more than any other cigarette on the market except the king-size nonfiltered Raleigh.

It is true that the tobacco industry in 1965—primarily as a move to stave off governmental action—adopted a "Cigarette Advertising Code," administered by Robert Meyner, former governor of New Jersey. The code, although it has been somewhat successful in eliminating the most blatant abuses of cigarette advertising, has in general proved to be feeble and irrelevant. It does not accomplish its original purpose of reducing the advertising messages to youngsters. And instead of encouraging the development and advertising of low tar-nicotine cigarettes, as it well could and should, the code, as it is administered at present, actually discourages manufacturers from making and advertising a less hazardous cigarette.

The self-imposed code requires that female models in ads be over age twenty-five; that celebrities may not endorse cigarettes (ordinary attractive unknown actors can); that cigarettes cannot be advertised in college football programs, although cigarette companies can sponsor football games so long as it is clear that the commercial originates from the studio and not in the stadium. The code also prohibits the cigarette sponsorship of programs "primarily" designed for children. "Primarily," according to Mr. Meyner's interpretation, means an audience with more than 45 percent children (those under twenty-one), which of course, especially in popular shows, can mean millions of children. Paradoxically, a program with an audience of ten million, half of whom were children, could not bring a cigarette sponsor's message, but a "family show" with an audience of fifty million could attract twenty million children and still qualify for a cigarette sponsor.

There is no doubt that regardless of the advertising code, youngsters are getting the message. According to the FTC, youngsters are subjected to an average of twelve cigarette commercials every day. In fact, a spot check of television programs sponsored by cigarette companies during the week of January 9, 1967, revealed that youngsters are probably getting a larger dose of cigarette advertising than adults. Of the sixty network shows sponsored in whole or part by cigarette companies, youngsters aged thirteen through seventeen on the average watched 7.8 of the programs; persons of all ages watched only an average of 5.9 programs during a week. Concluded the FTC: "Intentional or fortuitous [for the cigarette companies], teenagers appear to be a prime target for televised cigarette advertising."

The most unenlightened part of the industry's advertising code is its provision that low tar and nicotine claims for a certain cigarette can be advertised only if: (1) the administrator determines that such claims are scientifically significant to health or (2) in the absence of such a determination, the advertising of tar content carries a disclaimer as to its health significance.

At one time the code's administrator was justified in refusing to permit the listing of tar-nicotine content on packages or in ads which failed to carry the disclaimer, "No health claim is intended or implied." For the FTC, in 1959, faced with wildly conflicting tar and nicotine claims in advertising, obtained a voluntary ban on all mention of tar and nicotine content in advertising.

However, in the spring of 1966, as the evidence implicating tar-nicotine in smoking disease and death by smoking became overwhelming, the FTC reversed its earlier position and acknowledged that the advertising of tar-nicotine levels was in the public interest. Soon after the FTC ban was lifted, American Tobacco attempted to promote actively the reduced tar and nicotine qualities of its Carlton brand. And the P. Lorillard Company—which a decade earlier had pioneered the marketing of an effective filter cigarette in its Kent brand—brought out the sharply reduced tar and nicotine cigarette "True" and sought to advertise its low tar-nicotine without the health disclaimer required by the industry code. In both instances the companies were prevented from informing the public of the reduced health danger of their products by Mr. Meyner's interpretation of the advertising code. Consequently, both American Tobacco and Lorillard withdrew from the code. At this writing the code's restrictive and unreasonable policy on tar-nicotine advertising is still in effect.

Equally frustrating was the experience of Stephano Bros., a small family-owned cigarette firm in Philadelphia, which also deliberately reduced the tar-nicotine in its two brands, Cascades and Marvels. Originally, these cigarettes were as high as many others in tar-nicotine content; but in 1966 the company's president, Constantine Stephano, came to see me, determined to embark on a drastic reduction of the tar-nicotine in his cigarettes. According to the recent Roswell Park study, Marvels and Cascades yielded the least tar and nicotine of any cigarettes in the country. Yet, when Mr. Stephano had a bold and truthful advertisement drawn up, calling attention to the significance of the reduced tar and nicotine, the ad was rejected by a major national news magazine.

The reluctance of the tobacco industry in general to publicize tar-nicotine content is not without self-serving motive and a certain measure of cynicism. The giant cigarette companies do not want to become engaged in a competition to make their cigarettes less hazardous by reducing tar and nicotine, although they could do it readily. They know that they command the market primarily because they continue, despite all health risks, deliberately to manufacture cigarettes relatively high in tar-nicotine. The very loyalty of their users depends to a great extent on the tar-nicotine strength of the cigarette. For the higher the tar content the greater the "flavor" (although artificial flavorings also help produce a satisfactory flavor); and the greater the amount of nicotine, the greater the "kick," and, in those cases where the smoker's habit approaches true addiction, the greater the satisfaction of his nicotine dependency. Thus, to disclose the actual tar content and risk a competitive race toward safer cigarettes is not to the advantage of the major cigarette companies. Lowering tar-nicotine would lessen their grip on their carefully cultivated users. Furthermore, manufacturers fear that letting tar-nicotine disclosures creep into advertising could serve as constant reminders of the basic harm of cigarettes and perhaps even induce a few smokers to quit.

If such a cynical approach, when people are dying, cannot be excused, it can at least be understood as a desire—common to us all—to maintain the status quo. Personally, I deplore such an attitude, and believe that the reluctance of the tobacco companies to reduce substantially the potency of their dangerous product is thoroughly disappointing. However, when certain companies, instead of engaging in vigorous competition to produce less hazardous cigarettes, actually enter competition which results in the production of deadlier ones, such conduct in my opinion can only be termed grossly irresponsible. I refer to what is one of the most mindless marketing developments in American commercial history: the extra-long 100 millimeter cigarette. It is almost incredible that at this stage of our awareness of cigarette smoking as a major health problem, the market could be flooded with cigarettes which, because of their greater length, contain up to twice as much tar-nicotine as the average cigarette now being sold.

Four years ago 100 millimeter cigarettes were unheard of; our longest king-size cigarettes were 85 millimeters in length. But American Tobacco Company, casting about for novel ideas to capture new buyers, developed the longer cigarette in 1964, packaged it in a gold-foil Pall Mall wrapper, added a nickel to the price and tested it in exclusive Manhattan restaurants. The following year Philip Morris brought out its Benson and Hedges 100's on the same higher-priced basis. In 1966, American dropped the premium price for its Pall Malls and began mass marketing. Reportedly sales tripled almost immediately. Benson and Hedges followed the reduction to popular prices and engaged the advertising skills of Mary Wells of the new advertising agency of Wells, Rich, Greene, who produced some marvelously imaginative, if cynically inspired, commercials poking fun at the consequences of smoking the new longer Benson and Hedges 100's. A smoker could not turn around to girl-watch without bumping his cigarette against a car window, or enter an elevator without having the end of the cigarette caught in the closing doors. The ad campaign resulted in spectacular sales. (A 1967 survey showed that the Benson and Hedges commercials were more appealing to teenagers than any other TV commercial on the air.)

After the sales figures for the new 100's were made public in 1966, other cigarette companies joined the 100 millimeter race. We now have the Winston Super King, Tareyton 100's, Lucky Strike Filter 100's, Colony Hundreds, Ambassador 100's, Kent 100's, Newport 100's, Century Great Length, L & M Golden 100's, Lark 100's, Kool 100's, Viceroy 100's. And Chesterfields have even accentuated the trend toward bigness, going everyone else better by adding an extra millimeter to their 100's, calling them the Chesterfield 101 ("A silly millimeter longer," as the ads say). The first nine months of 1967 saw twenty-seven new 100 millimeter brand cigarettes introduced. Almost all of the best-selling brands are now available in the new super-size—in menthol and regular, in soft pack and box.

The tragedy of this merchandising development is that consumers who switch to the 100 millimeter cigarette may expose themselves to heightened danger without realizing it. By virtue of their size, the longer cigarettes generally contain added dosages of tar and nicotine, although a cigarette of 100 millimeters or longer length is not more dangerous *per se*. (American Tobacco also came out with a Silva Thin filter cigarette, which is smaller in diameter than the other 100's, and hence has less tobacco content and a lower tar yield— only 17 milligrams.)

Researchers who conducted the recent study at Roswell Park Memorial Institute called the trend toward longer cigarettes "highly disturbing." They said: "A smoker who switches from one of the medium tar filter cigarettes to Pall Mall filters or Benson and Hedges 100 immediately doubles his exposure to tar and nicotine, if, as is likely, he continues to smoke the same number of cigarettes and to smoke them to approximately the same butt length. The smoker may be unaware of his greatly increased health hazard since he may suppose that he is being protected by the filter."

Surgeon General Stewart, testifying before the Senate Commerce Committee in August 1967, confirmed that studies show those who switch to a longer cigarette continue to smoke just as many cigarettes and even more of each cigarette than before. Thus, the 100 millimeter cigarette could have a pronounced effect on raising the cigarette death and disease toll. Said Dr. Stewart: "It is unconscionable that the cigarette industry should introduce and heavily promote the 100 millimeter cigarette which cannot but help increase the hazard. . . . The 100 millimeter cigarettes hold close to 15 percent of the whole market, thereby effectively canceling the modest benefits to the public accruing from the introduction of the new low tar and nicotine brands."

Clearly, despite the accumulation of scientific knowledge, we have not come to grips with smoking as a national threat to health: when more people than ever are dying of cigarette-connected disease, when more youngsters than ever are adopting the habit, when some cigarette companies instead of marketing safer cigarettes are producing more hazardous ones and when information on tar content is being suppressed, we must face the fact that in the four years since the historic release of the surgeon general's report, the situation has not improved and in some ways has worsened. Faced with the evidence of industry irresponsibility and the public's resistance to giving up smoking, we must devise more realistic methods of coping with the problem. There are many possible courses of action.

It has been suggested that we abolish price supports for tobacco on the grounds that it is morally unjustifiable for a country to promote the cultivation of a product which its public health officials condemn as lethal. There is a certain grim logic to this proposition, but it does not seem to me to be a rational or a just solution. For we must avoid actions and attitudes that, although born of moral indignation, do not take us closer to our primary objective of saving lives. The price support program was designed to give those tobacco farmers who accept crop controls a fair price for their product. If we eliminate the controls, the farmer is freed of production restraints and indeed *must* produce as much tobacco as his land will bear to survive economically; the market price under such circumstances would hit rock bottom. As a consequence, we will have accomplished only two things: we will have punished and impoverished the tobacco farmers, the only truly innocent sector of our tobacco economy, and we will have given the cigarette manufacturer an abundant supply of dirt-cheap tobacco. Neither of these is consistent with our ultimate goal of saving lives.

Senator Robert Kennedy of New York has recently suggested that Congress ban all television advertising of cigarettes and apply a sliding scale of taxation on cigarettes in proportion to their tar-nicotine content—the higher the content, the greater the tax. Both of these reforms deserve serious consideration. Some Congressmen suggest that the airwaves are a public resource, licensed by the Federal Government, on the stipulation that they be operated in the public interest. That inducing people to smoke, especially youngsters, is contrary to the public interest is indisputable. The broadcasting industry by following its own code could, in fact, obviate the necessity for Congressional action by voluntarily refusing cigarette advertising, as they now refuse advertising for firearms and hard liquor. The broadcasters' code recognizes that "television and all who participate in it are jointly accountable to the American public for respect for the special needs of children, for community responsibility . . . and for propriety in advertising. . . ."

Although such television advertising may be objectionable, we again should not be overconfident that its abolition would cause a dramatic reduction in smoking. We simply do not know—nor is it possible to ascertain—how much television advertising contributes to a person's decision to take up smoking or to continue smoking. There is, however, a firm conviction among educators and public health officials who have worked with the teenage smoking problem that, even if advertising does not prompt a youngster to smoke, the constant barrage of commercials does reinforce youngsters' judgments that smoking is socially desirable and thus is a factor in their decision.

On August 1, 1965, Great Britain banned the television advertising of cigarettes, but one year later there was no noticeable reduction in smoking. A 1966 report from the British Tobacco Research Council, citing statistics on the number of smokers for that and previous years, was forced to conclude: "On the basis of the figures it would be difficult to claim that the first year free of cigarette advertisements on TV screens in Britain had produced any improvement." The percentage of male smokers remained about the same and the percentage of women smokers actually increased between 1965 and 1966.

Of course, the long-term effect of the British ban on commercials is yet to be seen. It is also possible that the results in Britain would not be as significant as those in the United States, for much popular television in Britain is government-sponsored through the B.B.C. and thus carries no commercials.

Senator Kennedy's proposal to penalize companies which produce cigarettes with high tar content by higher taxation is especially pertinent, for it brings us to what is rapidly becoming the central issue in the cigarette problem: the development of less hazardous cigarettes. Understandably, some of the men who pioneered the public disclosure of the cigarette hazard were uncompromising in their belief that the only answer was to bring a timely end to all cigarette smoking. Surely, stopping smoking is the most foolproof antidote to death and disease by smoking, for we know that the person who never smokes has zero risk and the person who stops smoking, even if he has been a heavy smoker, reduces the risk of cigarette damage considerably. Men between the ages of fifty-five and sixty-four, according to a recent study, who have not smoked for ten years, even though they once smoked more than a pack a day, have a 50 percent lower death rate than those who are still smoking. Much of our educational effort is and should be directed toward discouraging smoking, especially among youngsters.

It is time, however, that we realize that exhortations against cigarettes—moral as that attitude may be—are not effective as a public health measure, any more than Prohibition was in stopping the consumption of alcohol. In sixty years the cigarette habit has become deeply engrained, because cigarettes are cheap and accessible and offer personal and social gratification. Smoking can stimulate the body, providing pleasant sensations; it can satisfy the need to do something with the hands; it can help smokers cope with anxiety, stress, embarrassment; it can become a mechanical habit. As Daniel Horn, director of the National Clearinghouse for Smoking and Health of the USPHS, has said: "A smoker of a pack a day takes about 60,000 puffs a year. When you learn to smoke you learn it very well, by practicing over and over again. How can you help but be hooked?"

The hold exerted by the cigarette is hard to exaggerate. In World War I, General Pershing, in Europe with the American Expeditionary Forces, cabled dramatically home: "You ask me what we need to win this war." The answer: "Tobacco as much as bullets." President Johnson gave up smoking in 1956 on doctor's orders, following his heart attack. If you ask him whether he still misses his cigarettes, he answers "every minute of the day."

"We must face up to the fact that the cigarette caught hold because it fulfilled certain functions that needed to be fulfilled for a great many people," says Dr. Horn. "The cigarette offered an accessible inexpensive way to deal with a variety of problems. Perhaps not a very effective way, since the effect does not last; yet, if there were no harmful consequences it would have served mankind well. We have simply had the rotten luck to have discovered after all these years that the harmful effects are overwhelming."

Millions of smokers are unmoved by our public health warnings. They are unable to perceive the health danger, to translate it into personal terms, or to determine that the long-term deleterious effects outweigh the momentary satisfactions. Others, according to evidence, are so habituated to smoking that they will not give it up regardless of the health threat. Many Americans, however, indicate that they will, if given the opportunity, turn to a less hazardous cigarette.

This is a recourse that we have not adequately pursued. Especially in the beginning, many devoted doctors, officials, educators and reformed smokers adopted a Victorian-morality, temperance-movement stance. They felt that it was somehow improper to seek ways to enable people to continue smoking when the hazard was so self-evident. Fortunately, that attitude is changing, and we are beginning to realize that our ultimate objective is not to rid the world of cigarette smoking, but to rid the world of the death and disease caused by cigarette smoking. As Dr. Horn commented recently: "I wouldn't care if people smoked some four or five packs a day, if the cigarettes could be made safe." Remarked Dr. Hans L. Falk of the National Cancer Institute: "Now we're saying, 'Smoke as many cigarettes as you want but we will take out everything that's bad for you and leave in everything that's good for you.'"

We are not on the threshold of an absolutely safe cigarette, nor do we know if it is possible to produce a perfectly safe cigarette that anyone would care to smoke. For, as we have noted, it is often the harmful ingredients, tar and nicotine, which induce the pleasure and the desire. Millions of dollars, however, are going into research toward a safer cigarette in many places, including the laboratories at the U. S. Department of Agriculture; Sloan-Kettering Institute for Cancer Research in New York City; the Veteran's Administration Hospital in East Orange, New Jersey; Roswell Park Memorial Institute near Buffalo, New York; and even in the laboratories of the cigarette manufacturers themselves, although they are reluctant to admit it.

We do not know nearly enough about the actual biological causes of smoking-induced death: which of the many chemicals in tar produce the damage and how; whether toxic gases given off by smoke, such as carbon monoxide, cyanide and hydrogen sulfide, contribute to the harm. Thus, we must pursue all areas which will further our knowledge of the hazard. However, we do right now have compelling evidence that tar-nicotine causes harm in proportion to its content, and that by reducing the tar-nicotine, we can reduce the health danger. We need not wait longer for research in this area. We must immediately take measures to decrease the dose of tar per cigarette and to warn the public of the tar danger in particular brands.

There is a wide range in tar content. The Roswell Park study showed that the tar yielded by cigarettes ranged from 8.3 milligrams per cigarette (Marvels) to 43.4 milligrams (Raleigh king-size). It was also apparent that some filters were not filtering out the tar particles effectively. The range in tar recovery from filters was 8.3 milligrams per cigarette for Marvels to 41.6 milligrams per cigarette with Pall Mall's 100 millimeter filter. Generally, the amount of tar depended on two factors: (1) the length of the cigarette; the longer it was the greater total amount of tar, and (2) the weight of the filter; heavier, more dense filters (with a harder draw) trap more of the tar particles. For example, the Marvel filter weighs 20 milligrams and gives off .9 milligrams of tar per puff, whereas the high-tar Pall Mall filter weighed only 15 milligrams and yielded 3.1 milligrams per puff. Failure to produce low tar-nicotine cigarettes is not due to lack of technology. Concluded the researchers: "It seems clear that manufacturers are able to produce cigarettes with almost any yield of tar and nicotine from very low to very high."

At present, the general public does not know which cigarettes are more hazardous. Such vital information must be made available to guide smokers in choosing less hazardous brands and to prevent their switching to a more dangerous brand in the mistaken belief it is safer. The tar-nicotine yield should be clearly marked on each package of cigarettes and noted in every advertisement. In May 1967, I was joined by Senator Frank E. Moss of Utah and Senator Robert Kennedy of New York in introducing legislation in Congress that would compel manufacturers to meet such a requirement. Additionally, the FTC at my request has established a cigarette testing laboratory and will periodically supply tar-nicotine test results for wide circulation in the form of a "consumer report," which we are working to have distributed by national retail chains and local volunteers for display at cigarette stands, supermarkets, drugstores and vending machines. (The FTC issued its first report in November 1967 on the tar-nicotine recovery from fifty-nine varieties of cigarettes. The complete results of the FTC tests by brand name can be found in the Appendix.)

Moreover, we are beginning to accumulate data on which brands actually are associated with the greatest incidence of cigarette-caused disease and death. Recently, a well-known cancer researcher told me that it was difficult to collect information on diseases among smokers over age fifty who smoke a certain well-known brand. "You just don't find many smokers of that brand alive after fifty," he said. Within the next year or so the Public Health Service should be in a position to publish death and disease rates by the brand smoked.

The dissemination of information on relative hazards by brand name should force cigarette companies to lower the tar-nicotine yield of their products as a matter of competitive survival. It is hardly likely that Americans will deliberately buy the highest tar-producing cigarettes when they are told the comparative dangers. The enormous swing to filters illustrates that American smokers are health conscious. Within the last fifteen years filters have captured 70 percent of the market. Since the spring of 1966, P. Lorillard Company's True has become a major brand, the first of the low tar-nicotine cigarettes to succeed. Sales are also up for the low tar-nicotine Carltons, Cascades and Marvels. Even American

Tobacco has introduced a new "Fifty-Fifty" (half tobacco–half filter) to meet the increasing demand for a safer cigarette. In general, cigarettes are very slowly becoming less hazardous; the cigarette of 1966 on the average contained about two-thirds as much tar and nicotine as the average cigarette in 1960.

Nevertheless, the hazard is of such magnitude that we cannot depend only on competition and the sporadic consciences of tobacco companies to reduce the tar-nicotine to the necessary levels for the protection of health, as manufacturers have proved by their excursion into the 100 millimeter field. Therefore, I have also formulated legislation which will gradually, over a period of years, substantially reduce the dangerous tar-nicotine of cigarettes. The Surgeon General of the Public Health Service would be empowered to set maximum permissible tar and nicotine yields for all cigarettes sold in the United States. We do not know, nor are we likely to know in the near future, what levels, if any, of tar and nicotine can be considered safe. But we can at least eliminate those cigarettes, including many of the 100 millimeters, which are unconscionably lethal in the tar-nicotine output in the light of present knowledge.

Realistically, we cannot suddenly effect by legislation a drastic across-the-board decrease in tar levels, for it is evident that many Americans are so addicted that the "withdrawal symptoms" might be intolerable, and a black market for high tar-nicotine cigarettes might spring up with an attendant criminality and a breakdown in law as it did during Prohibition. Rather, under the surgeon general's direction, manufacturers should be permitted to reduce the tar-nicotine levels of each of their brands gradually, until the low permissible level has been reached. Over several years, the tar-nicotine yields would be lowered to a relatively innocuous dosage without undue distress to smokers. (Dr. George E. Moore, director of Public Health Research, New York State Department of Health, believes that the output of tar should not exceed 15 milligrams. The Roswell Park study identified six brands that could meet that test: Marvels, Cascade, Carlton, King Sano, Duke and Life. Dr. Moore says: "If the industry would use filters that would reduce the delivery of tar to a level of 15 milligrams per cigarette or below, such cigarettes would be approximately one-half as dangerous as the average cigarette. In other words, a smoker might use one pack a day but would be exposed to the equivalent of one-half a pack.")

We must also remember that a lower tar-nicotine content will impose no hardship on youngsters who do decide to smoke; they will never have known the stronger brands. Of course all of our efforts would be canceled out if, in response, smokers simply began smoking more cigarettes to obtain a desired quota of tar. Studies show that this does not happen; those who switch to low tar and nicotine cigarettes generally smoke the same number as their old brand and often fewer. The switch to low tar-nicotine cigarettes also is not infrequently a first step toward quitting.

The design of the filter is the best, most obvious method of reducing the tar-nicotine output. Filters that effectively filter are immediately available and in use on some brands. Generally, these filters remove particles of tar on a nonselective basis—the tighter the filter, the more particles of tar it catches. Eventually, it might be possible to filter out only those substances of the tar which cause the harm, but at present we do not know which of the specific tar agents are dangerous. The filter can also be designed to prevent the smoking of the cigarette down to a small butt. The final puffs on a cigarette contain much more tar than the initial puffs because the tobacco-filtering length of the cigarette has been decreased steadily with each puff. The last one-third of a cigarette accounts for about 50 percent of the entire cigarette's tar yield. A longer filter or a longer paper overwrap would automatically cut off the burning and delivery of tar at a critical stage, preventing smokers from obtaining that last lethal dosage of tar. Tobacco companies could also select less lethal tobacco by choosing leaves from the lower part of the stalk which are known to contain less tar-nicotine than those at the top.

As long as cigarette sales continue to soar, the tobacco industry will regard health warnings as an annoyance—of little consequence. It is clear that for the protection of the health of American consumers, Congress must once again, as we must in the areas of hazardous products and quackery, take strong decisive action in stemming the flow of dangerous products into the marketplace by striking at the source—in this case, by modifying the cigarette itself.

APPENDIX

APPENDIX

FEDERAL TRADE COMMISSION REPORT OF TAR
AND NICOTINE CONTENT OF THE SMOKE OF 59
VARIETIES OF CIGARETTES (NOVEMBER 20, 1967)

Shown in increasing order of tar content

NAME	TYPE *		TAR	NICOTINE
Marvels	F, SP	70 mm	3.9	0.12
Marvels	F, SP	85 mm	6.4	0.22
Carlton	F, SP	85 mm	7.2	0.50
Cascade	F, M, SP	85 mm	7.8	0.27
Duke of Durham	F, SP	85 mm	10.4	0.38
True	F, M, SP	85 mm	12.7	0.68
True	F, SP	85 mm	12.8	0.65
King Sano	F, SP	85 mm	12.9	0.38
King Sano	F, M, SP	85 mm	13.8	0.42
Domino	F, M, SP	85 mm	15.0	0.71
Parliament	F, HP	80 mm	15.8	1.01
Parliament	F, SP	85 mm	16.1	1.05
Kent	F, SP	85 mm	17.4	1.09

* NF—nonfilter; F—filter; M—menthol; HP—hard pack; SP—soft pack;
HWP—hard wide pack; mm—millimeters.

NAME	TYPE *		TAR	NICOTINE
Tareyton	F, SP	85 mm	17.5	1.07
L & M	F, SP	70 mm	18.5	0.93
Philip Morris	F, SP	85 mm	18.9	1.29
Lucky Strike	F, M, SP	100 mm	19.4	1.03
L & M	F, HP	80 mm	19.4	1.06
Philip Morris	F, M, SP	85 mm	20.0	1.28
Kool	F, M, SP	85 mm	20.2	1.56
Tareyton	F, SP	100 mm	20.2	1.23
Marlboro	F, HP	80 mm	20.4	1.34
Winston	F, SP	85 mm	20.4	1.29
Sano	NF, SP	70 mm	20.5	0.61
Lucky Strike	F, SP	100 mm	20.6	1.28
Marlboro	F, SP	85 mm	20.7	1.41
Lucky Strike	F, M, SP	85 mm	20.7	1.22
Raleigh	F, SP	85 mm	20.8	1.53
Winston	F, HP	80 mm	20.8	1.22
Marlboro	F, SP	100 mm	20.9	1.38
Viceroy	F, SP	85 mm	21.0	1.43
Camel	F, SP	85 mm	21.0	1.26
Chesterfield	F, M, SP	85 mm	21.0	1.19
Salem	F, M, SP	85 mm	21.1	1.36
L & M	F, SP	85 mm	21.3	1.15
Viceroy	F, HP	80 mm	21.4	1.43
Lucky Strike	F, SP	85 mm	21.7	1.33
Marvels	NF, SP	85 mm	21.8	0.82
Pall Mall	F, M, SP	100 mm	22.3	1.47
Chesterfield	F, SP	85 mm	22.4	1.16
Chesterfield	NF, SP	70 mm	22.7	1.20
Philip Morris	NF, SP	70 mm	22.7	1.45
Pall Mall	F, SP	100 mm	23.1	1.56
Kent	F, SP	100 mm	23.4	1.46
Camel	NF, SP	70 mm	24.2	1.39
Marlboro	F, M, SP	85 mm	24.4	1.72
Winston	F, M, SP	100 mm	25.2	1.66
L & M	F, M, SP	100 mm	25.3	1.44
L & M	F, SP	100 mm	25.6	1.41

NAME	TYPE *		TAR	NICOTINE
Pall Mall	F, M, HWP	95 mm	25.9	1.45
Kool	NF, M, SP	70 mm	26.3	1.84
Lucky Strike	NF, SP	70 mm	26.4	1.55
Winston	F, SP	100 mm	26.7	1.74
Salem	F, M, SP	100 mm	27.0	1.74
Pall Mall	NF, SP	85 mm	27.1	1.60
Raleigh	NF, SP	85 mm	27.8	1.98
Philip Morris Commander	NF, SP	85 mm	28.1	1.79
Pall Mall	F, HWP	95 mm	28.1	1.58
Chesterfield	NF, SP	85 mm	28.6	1.54

BIBLIOGRAPHY

BIBLIOGRAPHY

Much of the source material for this book came from personal knowledge, communications and interviews. However, the reader who would like to explore the subject further has available a number of excellent sources. The authors found the following articles, books and other publications especially valuable in preparing this book.

PART ONE

Amount of Earnings Exempt from Garnishment under State Laws. U. S. Department of Labor, Bureau of Statistics, July 1967.

"Are Changes Coming in Those One-Sided Credit Laws?" *Consumer Reports,* XXXI (Mar. 1966), 108–12.

Armbrister, Trevor, "Land Frauds: The Ads Promise Wonders But Look Before You Buy." *Saturday Evening Post* (Apr. 27, 1963), 17–22.

Berton, Pierre, *The Big Sell.* New York: Alfred A. Knopf, 1963.

Bivens, Gordon E., *The Spender Syndrome: Case Studies of Sixty-Eight Families and Their Consumer Problems,* ed.

by Brenda Dervin. Milwaukee, Wisconsin: University of Wisconsin Center for Consumer Affairs, 1965.

Borrie, Gordon J., and Diamond, Aubrey L., *The Consumer, Society and the Law*, rev. ed. London: MacGibbon and Kee, Ltd., 1966.

Brunn, George, "Wage Garnishment in California: A Study and Recommendations," 53 *Calif. L. Rev.* 1214 (1965).

Caplovitz, David, "On the Value of Consumer Action Programs in the War on Poverty." Office of Economic Opportunity, Mar. 8, 1966.

————. *The Poor Pay More: Consumer Practices of Low-Income Families*. New York: Free Press, 1963.

The Challenge of Crime in a Free Society. Washington, D. C.: Report by the President's Commission on Law Enforcement and Administration of Justice, 1967.

Consumer Issues '66. Washington, D. C.: Report to the President from the Consumer Advisory Council, 1966.

Consumers Voice. Philadelphia: Consumers' Education and Protective Association monthly newspaper, 1966–67.

Curran, Barbara A., *Trends in Consumer Credit Legislation*. Illinois: University of Chicago Press, 1965.

"Developments in the Law—Deceptive Advertising," 80 *Harv. L. Rev.* 1005 (1967).

Fact Booklet Series. Boston: Better Business Bureau Educational Division.

First Annual Report on Justice and the Poor of Washington State. Seattle-King County: Legal Services Center, Feb. 1967.

"Fraud: Victims Frightened by Legal Threats." *The Evening Star*, Washington, D. C., Aug. 30, 1966.

Gentry, Curt, *The Vulnerable Americans*. Garden City, New York: Doubleday and Company, Inc., 1966.

Gotschall, Gale P., "Help! Help! or Why FTC Seeks Aid of the Attorneys General in Combatting Consumer Deception and Unfair Competition." Santa Fe, New Mexico: Remarks before the Western Conference, National Association of Attorneys General, Sept. 2, 1966.

————. "How the Federal Trade Commission Can Work with Businessmen and Prosecutors." Tampa, Florida: Remarks before the First Annual Seminar, Florida Council on Commercial Frauds, Feb. 18, 1967.

————. "Let's Join Hands to Prevent Consumer Deception." Remarks before the National District Attorneys Association, June 6, 1966.

Jones, Commissioner Mary Gardiner, "Deception in the Marketplace of the Poor: The Role of the Federal Trade Commission." Washington, D. C.: Remarks before the Zonta Club, June 22, 1966.

————. "Our Most Urgent Task: To Protect the Consumer Needs of Our Poverty-Stricken Families." Miami, Florida: Remarks before the Spring Community Forum "Women on the Move" of the Greater Miami Section, National Council of Jewish Women, Inc., Apr. 22, 1966.

Kiernan, Gladys, ed., *1966 Retailers Manual of Laws and Regulations.* Oct. 1966.

Lefkowitz, Louis J., *Report of Bureau of Consumer Frauds and Protection.* New York: Department of Law, State of New York, 1966.

McMaster, John B., *History of the People of the United States from the Revolution to the Civil War,* ed. by Louis Filler. New York: Farrar, Straus and Co., 1964.

Mindell, Stephen, "The New York Bureau of Consumer Frauds and Protection—A Review of its Consumer Protection Activities," 11 *New York Law Forum* 603 (1965).

1965 Law and Poverty. Washington, D. C.: Report of the National Conference on Law and Poverty, June 23–25, 1965.

O'Connell, John J., "The Art of Losing Money," Seattle, Washington: Remarks before the 34th Annual Convention, Washington Credit Union League, Apr. 14, 1967.

————. "Consumer Protection in the State of Washington." *State Government,* XXXIX (Autumn 1966), 230–39.

————. "Highlights of Consumer Protection Legislation Passed by the 40th Session Washington State Legislature." Report for the Washington State Labor Council AFL–CIO, Tenth Annual Convention, Aug. 28–31, 1967.

Ora Lee Williams v. Walker-Thomas Furniture Co., 350 F 2d 445.

People of Illinois, ex rel. William G. Clark v. Raymond E. Hackler and Richard Burkholder, d/b/a Burkholder and Hackler, and Raymond E. Hackler, Richard E. Burkholder and Theodore "Ted" Hatfield as individuals, Circuit Court of Cook County, Illinois, 63 C 4565.

Peterson, Mrs. Esther, "Equality in the Marketplace." Los Angeles, California: Remarks before the National Conference of the NAACP, July 7, 1966.

Proceedings: 57th Annual Meeting. National Association of Attorneys General, Dec. 1963.

Proceedings: 59th Annual Meeting. National Association of Attorneys General, Dec. 1965.

Public Hearings of the Subcommittee of the New York State Finance Committee. Mar. 9, 1967.

"The Regulation of Advertising," 56 *Colum. L. Rev.* 1018 (1956).

"A Salesman Says." *Home Furnishings Daily*, July 14–28, 1958.

Sand, Michael A. and Weisburg, Joel, "Translating Sympathy for Deceived Consumers into Effective Programs for Protection," 114 *Pennsylvania L. Rev.* 395 (1966).

Schur, Jerome, "A Study of Consumer Credit Legislation." Municipal Division of the Circuit Court of Cook County, Illinois, 1966.

Sherwood and Roberts-Yakima, Inc. v. Leach, 409 2d 160 (1965).

Smith, Ralph Lee, "Saga of the Little Green Pig." *Reporter* (Nov. 3, 1966), 39–42.

State by Lefkowitz v. ITM, Inc., 275 NYS 2d 303.

United States of America before the Federal Trade Commission: In the Matter of Allied Enterprises, Inc., a corporation, and William Marion, individually, and as an officer of said corporation. Docket No. 8722.

United States of America before the Federal Trade Commission: In the Matter of The Empeco Corporation, a corporation, d/b/a Empire Furniture and Appliance Co., and as Empire Home Improvement Co., and Allen C. Baverman, individually, and as an officer of said corporation. Docket No. 8702.

United States of America before the Federal Trade Commission: In the Matter of Holland Furnace Company. Docket No. 6203.

United States of America before the Federal Trade Commission: In the Matter of John A. Guziak, an individual trading as General Aluminum Company, a corporation, and as Superior Improvement Company, a corporation. Docket No. 8614.

U. S. Congress. House. Committee on Banking and Currency. *H. R. 11601, Consumer Credit Protection Act.* Hearings before the Subcommittee on Consumer Affairs, 90th Cong., 1st Sess. (Aug. 7, 8, 9, 10, 11, 14, 15, 16, 17, 18, 1967).

U. S. Congress. Senate. Committee on Banking and Currency. *S. 275, Interstate Land Sales Full Disclosure Act of 1967.* Hearings before the Subcommittee on Securities, 90th Cong. 1st Sess. (Feb. 28, Mar. 1, 1967).

U. S. Congress. House. Committee on Post Office and Civil Service. *H. R. 1411, to Amend Title 39, United States Code, with respect to Use of the Mails to Obtain Money or Property under False Misrepresentations.* Hearings before the Subcommittee on Postal Operations, 90th Cong., 1st Sess. (Apr. 12, 1967).

U. S. Congress. Senate. Committee on Post Office and Civil Service. *S. 274, to Amend Sec. 4005, Title 39, United States Code, Relating to Fraudulent, False or Misleading and Lottery Mail.* Hearings before the Subcommittee on Postal Affairs, 90th Cong., 1st Sess. (Aug. 15, 1967).

U. S. Congress. Senate. Special Committee on Aging. *Health Frauds and Quackery: Eye Care.* Hearings before the

Subcommittee on Frauds and Misrepresentations Affecting the Elderly, 88th Cong., 2nd Sess. (Apr. 6, 1964).

U. S. Congress. Senate. Special Committee on Aging. Subcommittee on Frauds and Misrepresentations Affecting the Elderly. *1964 Investigations, Findings, Recommendations: 1964 Report.* 1965 (89th Cong., 1st Sess. Committee Print.)

Weston, Glen E., "Deceptive Advertising and the Federal Trade Commission: Decline of Caveat Emptor," 24 *Federal Bar Journal* 548 (1964).

PART TWO

Accident Facts. National Safety Council. 1967.

Bylinsky, Gene, "The Search for a Safer Cigarette." *Fortune* (Nov. 1967), 146–49, 200, 202, 204, 206, 209.

Carper, Jean, "At Last—Clothing That Won't Burn." *Family Safety,* XXIV (Spring 1965), 10–13.

————. *Stay Alive!* Garden City, New York: Doubleday and Company, Inc., 1965.

Consumer Reports, 1963–1967.

"Crackdown on Quackery." *Life,* LV (Nov. 1963), 72B–83.

"Estimates of Injuries Associated with Products, Equipment and Appliances in the Home Environment." Injury Control Program, Public Health Service, Department of Health, Education and Welfare, Aug. 18, 1966.

"Facts on Glass Door Safety." Architectural Aluminum Manufacturers Association, Sept. 6, 1967.

Facts on Quacks—What You Should Know About Health Quackery. American Medical Association Department of Investigation, 1967.

FDA Report on Enforcement and Compliance, 1963–1966.

Graham, Saxon, Ph. D., "Lung Cancer as Related to Smoking Behavior Patterns." Paper presented at the American Public Health Association, Oct. 26, 1967.

Grant, Roald N., M. D., and Bartlett, Irene, *Unproven Methods of Cancer Treatment.* American Cancer Society, Inc., 1966.

"Health Characteristics by Geographic Region, Large Metropolitan Areas and Other Places of Residence." *Vital and Health Statistics,* National Center for Health Statistics, U. S. Dept. of Health, Education and Welfare, Ser. 10, No. 36 (July 1963–June 1965).

Hedrick, Dr. James L., "Facts on Smoking, Tobacco and Health." Draft prepared for National Clearinghouse for Smoking and Health, Public Health Service, Dept. of Health, Education and Welfare. Bethesda, Maryland: Resource Management Corporation, Sept. 1967.

Horn, Daniel, Ph. D., "How Did Society Get Into the Cigarette Mess? Why Is It So Hard to Find a Way Out?" New York: World Conference on Smoking and Health, Sept. 12, 1967.

Kaplan, Jack, "Doctor Abrams—Dean of Machine Quacks." *Today's Health* (Apr. 1966), 21, 70–73, 77–80.

Magnuson, Warren G., "Establishment of a National Commission on Product Safety." *Congressional Record* (Feb. 8, 1967), S. 1755–1758.

———. "Flammable Fabrics Act Amendments." *Congressional Record* (Feb. 16, 1967), S. 2037–2038.

———. "Introduction of Amendments to the Cigarette Labeling and Advertising Act." *Congressional Record* (May 17, 1967), S. 6975–6983.

———. "Power Lawn Mower Safety." *Congressional Record* (July 23, 1965), 17380–17382.

———. "Strengthening the Cigarette Labeling Act." *Congressional Record* (July 27, 1966), 16467–16474.

Manchester, Harland, "What You Should Know About Flammable Fabrics." *Reader's Digest,* XC (May 1967), 37–38, 40.

McConnell, William H. and Knapp, L. W., "Epidemiology of Rotary Power Lawn Mower Injuries." *Bulletin No. 9,*

Institute of Agricultural Medicine, Dept. of Preventive Medicine and Environmental Health, College of Medicine, University of Iowa, 1965.

Meserve, William G., "Cigarettes and Congress." California: Remarks before the California Conference on Cigarette Smoking and Health, Oct. 29, 1967.

Miner, John, "The Phillips Case—A New Dimension in Murder." *Journal of Forensic Sciences,* IX (Jan. 1964).

Moore, George E., M. D., Ph. D., Bros, Irwin, Ph. D., Shamberger, Raymond, Ph. D., and Bock, Fred G., Ph. D., *Tar and Nicotine Retrieval from Fifty-Six Brands of Cigarettes.* Buffalo, New York: Roswell Park Memorial Institute (New York State Department of Health), 1967.

Nader, Ralph, "The Engineer's Professional Role: Universities, Corporations, and Professional Societies." *Engineering Education* (Feb. 1967), 450–54.

Neuberger, Maurine B., *Smoke Screen: Tobacco and the Public Welfare.* Englewood Cliffs, New Jersey: Prentice-Hall, Inc., 1963.

"The 100 mm. Mess." *Tobacco Reporter,* XC (Oct. 1967), 20–24, 62.

Press, Edward, M. D., "Wringer Washer Machines Injuries." *American Journal of Public Health,* LIV (May 1964), 812–22.

"The Price of Faulty Design Gets Steeper Every Day." *Product Engineering* (Aug. 1, 1966), 34–43.

Proceedings: National Congress on Medical Quackery. Sponsored by the American Medical Association and the Food and Drug Administration, Oct. 6–7, 1961.

Proceedings: 2nd National Congress on Medical Quackery. Sponsored by the American Medical Association and the Food and Drug Administration, Oct. 25–26, 1963.

Proceedings: 3rd National Congress on Medical Quackery. Sponsored by the American Medical Association and the Food and Drug Administration, Oct. 7–8, 1966.

Report to Congress Pursuant to the Federal Cigarette Label-

ing and Advertising Act. Federal Trade Commission, June 30, 1967.

Stewart, William H., M. D., "Keynote Address: Influencing Smoking Behavior." New York: World Conference on Smoking and Health, Sept. 12, 1967.

Textile Flammability Conference. Boston, Massachusetts: National Fire Protection Association International, Oct. 2–3, 1962.

Underwriters' Laboratories Report of Electrical Accidents. Jan.–Nov., 1966.

USA v. Bernarr Zovluck, Alvin Eisenstein and Anne Friedman, U. S. Dist. Crt., Southern Dist. of N. Y., Indictment 73 CR 513.

U. S. Congress. Senate. Committee on Commerce. *S. 2507 and S. 2508, Overhead and Underground Transmission Lines.* Hearings before the Committee, 89th Cong., 2nd Sess. (May 4, 1966).

U. S. Congress. Senate. Committee on Commerce. *S. 3298, Child Protection Act of 1966.* Hearings before the Consumer Subcommittee, 89th Cong., 2nd Sess. (Aug. 24, 26, 1966).

U. S. Congress. Senate. Committee on Commerce. *S. J. Res. 33, to Establish a National Commission on Products Safety.* Hearings before the Consumer Subcommittee, 90th Cong., 1st Sess. (Mar. 1, 1967).

U. S. Congress. Senate. Committee on Commerce. *S. 1003, to Amend the Flammable Fabrics Act.* Hearings before the Consumer Subcommittee, 90th Cong., 1st Sess. (May 3, 4, 5, 1967).

U. S. Congress. Senate. Committee on Commerce. *Report on Flammable Fabrics Act Amendments of 1967.* 90th Cong., 1st Sess. (July 25, 1967).

U. S. Congress. Senate. Committee on Commerce. *S. 2067, Radiation Control for Health and Safety Act of 1967.* Hearings before the Committee, 90th Cong., 1st Sess. (Aug. 28, 29, 30, 1967).

U. S. Congress. Senate. Committee on Commerce. *To Review the Progress Toward the Development and Marketing of a Less Hazardous Cigarette.* Hearings before the Consumer Subcommittee, 90th Cong., 1st Sess. (Aug. 23, 24, 25, 1967).

U. S. Congress. Senate. Special Committee on Aging. *Frauds and Quackery Affecting the Older Citizen.* Hearings before the Committee, 88th Cong., 1st Sess. (Jan. 15, 1963).

U. S. Congress. Senate. Special Committee on Aging. *Health Frauds and Quackery.* Hearings before the Subcommittee on Frauds and Misrepresentations Affecting the Elderly, 88th Cong., 2nd Sess. (Jan. 13 and Mar. 9, 1964).

U. S. Congress. Senate. Special Committee on Aging. Subcommittee on Frauds and Misrepresentations Affecting the Elderly. *1964 Investigations, Findings, Recommendations: 1964 Report.* 89th Cong., 1st Sess. Committee Print. (1965).

U. S. Congress. Senate. Special Committee on Aging. *Consumer Interests of the Elderly.* Hearings before the Subcommittee on Consumer Interests of the Elderly, 90th Cong., 1st Sess. (Jan. 17, 18, 1967).

U. S. Congress. House. Committee on Post Office and Civil Service. *H. R. 6102 to Amend Sec. 4005, Title 39, United States Code, Relating to Fraudulent, False or Misleading and Lottery Mail.* Hearings before the Subcommittee on Postal Operations, 89th Cong., 2nd Sess. (June 7, 1966).

U. S. Public Health Service. *The Health Consequences of Smoking: A Public Health Service Review: 1967.* Washington, D. C.: U. S. Department of Health, Education and Welfare, 1967.

Walrad, Ruth, *The Misrepresentation of Arthritis Drugs and Devices in the United States.* New York: Arthritis and Rheumatism Foundation, 1960.

White, William V., *Accidental Injuries Associated with Rotary Lawn Mowers.* Outdoor Power Equipment Institute in cooperation with the National Safety Council, n.d.

———. *Preventing Burns from Clothing Fires: The Public Health Approach*. Public Health Service, U. S. Department of Health Education and Welfare, and the National Fire Protection Association, n.d.

INDEX

INDEX